THE ENGLISH CONNECTION

A Content-Based Grammar and Discussion Text

SECOND EDITION

Gail Fingado
Columbia University

Leslie J. Freeman
Columbia University

Mary Reinbold Jerome
Columbia University

Catherine Vaden Summers
Columbia University

Heinle & Heinle Publishers
A Division of Wadsworth, Inc.
Boston, Massachusetts 02116 U.S.A.

Director: Laurie E. Likoff
Full-Service Manager: Michael Weinstein
Production Coordinator: Cynthia Funkhouser
Text Design: Lucy Leziak Design
Cover Design: Caliber Design Planning
Text Illustrations: Susan Detrich
Photo Research: Jacquelyn Wong
Production: Spectrum Publisher Services
Compositor: Graphic Sciences
Printer and Binder: Malloy Lithographing

Photo Credits: p. 26, NASA; p. 47, Alaska Division of Tourism; p. 72, National Archives and Records Administration; p. 92, Brian J. Berman Photography, © 1990; p. 116, © Mark Altman, The Image Works; p. 132, UPI/Bettman; p. 156, Courtesy of Sears, Roebuck and Co.; p. 179, Courtesy of Clyde Beatty-Cole Brothers Circus; p. 246, New York State Department of Economic Development Photo Unit; p. 268, © Michael J. Okoniewski/The Image Works; p. 289, © Michael J. Okoniewski/The Image Works; p. 307, © Alan Carey/The Image Works; p. 328, © Rohn Engh/The Image Works; p. 345, Washington, D.C., Convention and Visitors Bureau; p. 360, Courtesy of UCLA; p. 382, Courtesy of Honda of America Manufacturing Inc.; p. 402, Valentine Museum, Richmond, Virginia; p. 436, American Institute of Physics Niels Bohr Library; p. 450, The Metropolitan Museum of Art, Rogers Fund, 1970.

The English Connection: A Content-Based Grammar and Discussion Text

Library of Congress Cataloging-in-Publication Data

The English connection : a content-based grammar and discussion text /
  Gail Fingado . . . [et al.]. — 2nd ed.
     p.   cm.
  Includes index.
  ISBN 0-8384-2909-2
  1. English language—Textbooks for foreign speakers. I. Fingado,
Gail.
PE1128.E543   1991
428.2'4—dc20

                               90-24017
                                   CIP

95 96 97 98 99 9 8 7 6 5

For
Kenny Brawner
Joel Brodkin
Eva Linnell Jerome
Jerry Leff

PREFACE TO THE SECOND EDITION

The new revised edition of *The English Connection* is designed to make this popular text more user-friendly for both the student and the instructor. It now has a clearer, easier-to-use format with new illustrations. The new layout is more attractive, allowing the student's eye to travel more easily over the page. The exercises (now referred to as activities) have been rearranged within each chapter in order to break up overly long and dense sections of grammar explanation and to allow the students to practice one point before moving on to the explanation of the next. Outdated information and topics have been replaced with more current ones such as the greenhouse effect, the use of steroids by athletes, or the budget deficit, the trade deficit, and the possibility of a change in the economic strength of the United States in the world community. Through the addition of several exercises, greater attention has been given to the accomplishments of some famous women in the United States. In order to provide a better balance with controlled activities such as fill-ins or dialogs, more open-ended or interactive activities have been added. To make the text easier for the instructor to use, comprehension questions now follow every dialog; an audiotape of the dialogs is now available for purchase, allowing the instructor to use the dialogs for listening comprehension. In addition, to allow the instructor to get more mileage out of fill-ins, listening comprehension questions have been added at the end of many of these exercises. Thus, the instructor can use the exercise to practice listening skills before the students are asked to focus exclusively on the grammar.

The authors are confident that instructors who have enjoyed working with this unique text in the past will find that the revised edition is much improved. Instructors trying *The English Connection* for the first time will be delighted to find how easy it is to plan the curriculum around the text.

To the Teacher

Intended for intermediate students of English as a Second Language, this grammar text uses topics of current interest to provide a context for the explanation and the illustration of the structures it presents. Although intermediate students have already had some exposure to many of the major structures of English, they need additional practice to attain mastery of these structures. At the same time, they need to be challenged by adult content. This book therefore focuses on social, economic, interpersonal, and political questions. It is expected that this material will not only be absorbing and informative but will also provoke stimulating discussions. Four characters are used throughout the text in the dialogs, examples, and activities. They meet, interact, develop, and to some extent provide a model for discussing the issues and ideas that are presented. Throughout the book, students are encouraged to draw on their own experience and to share their opinions and feelings with one another.

The text is divided into twenty-six primary chapters. Each has a specific grammatical and thematic focus, and each includes a wide range of exercises—some controlled, some free—providing practice of the structures taught in the chapter. Students can use this text independently at home or in a classroom situation. While the chapters are arranged in order of increasing complexity, there is no reason the students cannot study the structures in a different sequence. It is hoped that this grammar text will provide the student of English as a second language with fresh and exciting material as well as clear and concise explanations of the language.

This book can be used for both the introduction and review of English structures. It is assumed that the student has some familiarity with the basic patterns of English but needs additional work to master the structures presented here and to achieve fluency with them.

Format of Each Chapter

Each chapter opens with a dialog in which the target structures are illustrated. Within the limits set by the grammar focus, the language aims to be as close to natural spoken English as possible. A grammar explanation follows, along with examples in which the new structures are highlighted in a context thematically related to the whole chapter. Activities of varying levels of control provide an opportunity for practice, mastery, and testing of the grammar. Every chapter concludes with a series of questions that invite the students to use their personal perceptions and experiences in expressing ideas and opinions evoked by the material presented in the chapter. While each chapter builds to some degree on preceding chapters, there is no reason chapters cannot be used in a different sequence. Neither is there any reason the dialog must introduce the chapter; it is equally possible to use the dialog for an integration at the conclusion of the lesson.

How to Use Each Chapter

While this text lends itself to many different teaching approaches, here are some suggestions that you may find useful.

The Dialog

Each dialog involves two or more of the four characters who reappear throughout the book. You might begin by having the students read the dialog silently and notice the grammar structures in bold type as a preview to the chapter. Ask them to read it a second time and then to answer the comprehension questions that follow the dialog. If you wish to use the dialog as a listening comprehension exercise, there is a tape with all the dialogs available for purchase. You might start by describing the situation of the dialog and directing the students to preview the comprehension questions in the text, reminding them not to read the dialog. The class will probably need at least two chances to listen before they attempt to answer the questions. If you do not have the tape at hand, you can read the dialog out loud to your class, writing the names of the speakers on the board and shifting positions as you read their respective lines.

Next, to help the students focus on the grammar while they are listening, you might wish to xerox the dialog, white out the structures in boldface type, make copies for the students, and instruct them to fill in as they listen. Another way to use the dialog is to break the class up into small groups and direct them to read and practice the dialog as a preparation for role playing or improvisation. As they practice, the students should use the read-and-look-up technique to keep the pronunciation and intonation as natural as possible. The student reads a sentence (or part of a long, complex sentence) silently and then looks up from the text when he or she feels ready to say it. You can move around the room to help the students with the dialog and to correct pronunciation. The students can also be asked to use their imaginations to continue the conversation in the dialog in either written or spoken form. You can expand on the vocabulary and idiomatic expressions in the dialog by suggesting other ways to express similar emotions. If a dialog involves an argument, for example, you can provide other expressions used in arguments. After completing the work on the dialog, students often want to react to and comment on the issues raised in the dialog. You may want to look at the "Expressing Your Ideas," which appears at the end of each chapter and have several discussion questions in mind for some free conversation as a follow-up to the more controlled activities.

Grammar Explanations and Examples

The examples can be used as either short reading selections or listening comprehension passages. Students enjoy listening to the examples and then answering questions or asking questions of one another about the content. Grammar practice often flows naturally from the situations provided. If you do not wish to take class time reading the explanations and examples, you can ask the students to read through them at home so that you can focus on the dialog, discussion, and exercises in class.

Activities

The activities can be done by the students as homework and collected by you, or they can be corrected in class either in small groups or by calling on the students to read the correct answer. In some cases, you will have to use your judgment, as more than one answer may be correct. Many activities can be used as listening comprehension passages before students are asked to fill in answers. Often the directions indicate that listening comprehension questions are provided at the end of a fill-in activity, and the students are instructed to read them and to keep them in mind before listening to you read the passage. The answers would then be discussed in class before the students work on the fill-in activity. The longer and more complex fill-in activities can also be used as reading passages after the answers have been corrected. For some activities, reading comprehension questions are provided and students are directed to go back and read carefully as a follow-up activity for filling in the blanks. Again, we encourage you to have discussion questions in mind so that controlled activities, such as fill-ins and answering comprehension questions, can be balanced with free conversation. Often such questions are provided after activities. We hope that the teacher, in working with this book, will always strive for a balance between controlled grammar-focused activities and free conversation.

In this edition, multipart activities feature an open box (□) preceding the directions for each part of the activity.

Expressing Your Ideas

Each chapter concludes with a series of questions about the issues raised in the chapter. These questions help the students use the grammar and the vocabulary of the chapter in a freer context. They also allow the students to draw on their own experience and background and to make comparisons between their own countries and the United States.

To the Student

This book has been written to provide a review of the important structures of English, as well as information about the United States and the world that will capture your interest. Many people think grammar has to be boring. On the contrary, grammar can be fascinating if it is taught in a relevant context. For this reason, the topics we selected are frequently controversial. There are four main characters throughout the book in the dialogs and examples; they are shown in real-life situations. This book is addressed to you as adult learners, to whom issues of social, economic, and political significance are of interest. The authors hope that you will find it an interesting and challenging way to review and learn English structure.

Acknowledgments

We would like to express our appreciation to the following people who have assisted us with this book.

To our students and colleagues at the American Language Program of Columbia University, especially Lou Levi, Dick Faust, Henrietta Dunham, Frank Horowitz, Thad Ferguson, Linda Lane, and Arley Gray.

To Joel Brodkin, Sheila Fields, and the Students of the New York Institute of Technology.

To our families and friends, especially Kenny Brawner, Jim Jerome, Bill Jerome, Ann Raimes, and Teri Phillips.

BRIEF CONTENTS

CONTENTS

1 THE PRESENT CONTINUOUS TENSE

Hearts and Flowers

Computer Dating Service Questionnaire

Name _____

Address _____

Age _____ Height _____ Weight _____ Color of Eyes _____

Color of Hair _____ Present Job _____

Educational Background _____

Where have you lived in the United States? _____

Have you traveled abroad? Where? _____

Do you speak other languages? Which ones? _____

What do you like to do in your spare time? List your specific interests or hobbies.

_____

What kinds of books do you like to read? _____

What kinds of movies do you like to go to? _____

Are you athletic? What sports do you enjoy? _____

Do you want to get married? ____ Do you want to have children? ____

How many? ____

Where do you want to live—in a small town or in a large city? _____

What is your astrological sign? _____

Which of these qualities describe you best? Check the appropriate boxes.

☐ romantic   ☐ impulsive   ☐ warm
☐ jealous   ☐ cautious   ☐ dependent
☐ artistic   ☐ tense   ☐ independent
☐ shy   ☐ relaxed   ☐ distant
☐ outgoing   ☐ practical   ☐ hot-tempered
☐ competitive   ☐ spontaneous   ☐ affectionate

What qualities do you look for in a man or in a woman? Number the
following qualities in the order of importance to you, beginning with the
most important.

kindness   social status   good looks
intelligence   creativity   same age
openness   good taste in clothes good conversational
                                             ability

Dialog

(Arnold and Jack are sitting in a cafe and discussing their love life.)

JACK: Hey, Arnold. How **are** things **going** with you and Susan?

ARNOLD: Don't ask. Things **aren't working** out at all. We **aren't seeing**[1] each other much anymore.

JACK: That's too bad.

ARNOLD: Yeah. She**'s going** out with someone else now. I have rotten luck with women.

JACK: Well, I guess we're in the same boat[2] now. I**'m trying** to meet someone too.

ARNOLD: It's really tough to meet people.

JACK: What about a computer dating service? I**'m trying** one next week.

ARNOLD: **Are** you **kidding**? That's not going to work.

JACK: How do you know? It's worth a try.[3]

ARNOLD: Hey, Jack. Look at those two over there.

JACK: What two where?

ARNOLD: What do you mean what? I**'m talking** about those two women at the next table.

JACK: Arnold, you**'re staring** at them.

ARNOLD: That's okay. They**'re staring** at us.

JACK: Hey, the girl with the dark hair **is waving** to us.

ARNOLD: I think she**'s inviting** us to their table. (He gets up and starts walking toward the other table.)

JACK: Wait a minute. What **are you doing**? Where **are you going**?

ARNOLD: Come on. What **are** you **waiting** for? Let's go.

Listening Comprehension Questions

1. Are Arnold and Susan going out with each other often now?
2. Does Arnold think he has good luck with women?
3. Is Jack going out with anyone now?
4. Is Jack going to a computer dating service soon?
5. What are the two women at the next table doing?

[1]*See someone* (idiomatic) means "to date someone."
[2]*We're in the same boat* means "We have the same problem."
[3]*It's worth a try* means "There's a chance you will succeed."

THE PRESENT CONTINUOUS TENSE

The present continuous tense is used in three ways:

1. to talk about an action that is happening now
    They**'re staring** at us.

2. to talk about an action in the extended present
    We **aren't seeing** each other much.

3. to talk about an action in the future
    I**'m trying** a computer dating service next week.

Statements

> subject + $\left\{ \begin{array}{l} \textbf{am} \\ \textbf{is} \\ \textbf{are} \end{array} \right\}$ **(not)** + base form[4] + **-ing**
>
> *Someone is waving to Arnold.*

Questions

> (Question word) + $\left\{ \begin{array}{l} \textbf{am} \\ \textbf{is} \\ \textbf{are} \end{array} \right\}$ + subject + base form + **-ing?**
>
> **What**
> **Who(m)**
> **Where**   *What is Arnold doing?*
> **Why**
> **How**

Short Answers: **Yes**, subject + $\left\{ \begin{array}{l} \textbf{am.} \\ \textbf{is.} \\ \textbf{are.} \end{array} \right\}$

               No, subject + $\left\{ \begin{array}{l} \textbf{am + not.} \\ \textbf{isn't.} \\ \textbf{aren't.} \end{array} \right\}$

Note: We do not use contractions with affirmative short answers.

---

[4]The *base form* is the form of the verb without any marking for tense of person. This is the form of the verb you find in a dictionary.

Negative Questions

$$\text{(Question word)} \begin{cases} \mathbf{+\ aren't\ +} \begin{cases} \mathbf{I} \\ \mathbf{you} \\ \mathbf{we} \\ \mathbf{they} \end{cases} \\ \mathbf{+\ isn't\ +} \begin{cases} \mathbf{he} \\ \mathbf{she} \\ \mathbf{it} \end{cases} \end{cases} \mathbf{+\ base\ form\ +\ -ing?}$$

Why aren't you listening?

THE PRESENT MOMENT

Many languages use only one present tense. English has two. We use the present continuous tense to talk about an action that is happening now (at the present moment).

You **are reading** about the present continuous tense now.

THE EXTENDED PRESENT

We often use the present continuous tense to talk about an action that is happening in the extended present—"these days" or "nowadays." When we use the present continuous tense in this way, we are often talking about changes.

Dating customs are changing these days in the United States.

Examples

Extended Present

These days many single people **are complaining** that it is very difficult to meet people. More and more singles **are turning** to special services that help people meet each other.

Present Moment

A reporter for television station WKJB is doing a special report on computer dating services.

REPORTER: **I'm standing** in the office of Hearts and Flowers Computer Dating Service. As you can see, they **are doing** a good business in here today. By the way, if my wife **is watching** this show—Honey, **I'm not looking** for anyone new. **I'm just reporting**[5] on the singles scene[5] in this city.

These people **are filling** out questionnaires. They**'re answering** questions about their age, their interests, their hobbies, and the qualities they prefer in a man or a woman.

Here's the computer, Big Joe. Right now Joe **is processing** applications and **is matching** men and women with similar interests.

Here's a happy-looking man. Sir, what **are** you **doing** here?

MR. X: **I'm talking** to this very nice woman.

REPORTER: Oh, aren't you lucky! Did the computer match you two?

MR. X: No, we met right here in the office. Forget the computer. We're on our way to lunch together.

■ ACTIVITY 1A

Fill in the correct form of the present continuous tense. Use the verb below in parentheses.

REPORTER: Tonight I _'m reporting_ to you from a video dating
(report)

service. The owner, Mr. Peterson, _____ next to
(stand)

me. Mr. Peterson, this is a very unusual service. How

_____ your business _____?
(do)

MR. PETERSON: Business _____. New people _____ in
(boom) (come)

every day. Our list of customers _____ by leaps
(grow)

and bounds.[6]

REPORTER: Mr. Peterson, please tell our viewers about your unique

service.

---

[5]*Singles scene* means "the different places single people go to, to meet one another."
[6]*By leaps and bounds* means "rapidly."

MR. PETERSON: In this room, Miss Quinn _____ a videotape. The
(make)

gentleman next to her is one of my employees. He

_____ her.
(interview)

REPORTER: What about the people in this room? What _____

they _____?
(do)

MR. PETERSON: These customers _____ our library of videotapes
(view)

and _____ about which people they would like to
(think)

date.

REPORTER: Then what happens?

MR. PETERSON: Well, for example, if Miss Quinn chooses Mr. Dirkson's

tape, then Mr. Dirkson comes into the office to see Miss

Quinn's tape. If he likes her tape, then we arrange a date

for them.

REPORTER: Oh, here's Miss Quinn. _____ all this
(negative)

_____ you nervous?
(make)

MISS QUINN: Yes, _____. Look at my hands. They
(short answer)

_____. What _____ you _____
(shake)   (do)

here? _____ you _____ a videotape too?
(make)

REPORTER: No, _____. I'm with WKJB Television News.
(short answer, negative)

Millions of people _____ this program right now.
(watch)

MISS QUINN: Millions! Oh, no! that _____ me even more nervous.
(make)

REPORTER: Tell me something, Miss Quinn. _____ people
(negative)

_____ each other in traditional ways anymore?
(meet)

MISS QUINN: Sure, _____. People these days _____ still
(short answer)

_____ in churches and in schools and at parties.
(meet)

REPORTER: Why then _____ people _____ out services
(seek)

such as video dating?

MISS QUINN: Well, I think it's the isolation in big cities. Many people

_____ to church anymore, and they're out of
(negative, **go**)

school. So more and more people _____ for new
(look)

ways to make friends.

REPORTER: Thank you very much, Miss Quinn. We _____ now
(break)

for a commercial.

FUTURE MEANING

When we have a definite plan for the future, we can sometimes use the present continuous tense to talk about this plan.

Examples

REPORTER: **Are** you **leaving**, miss? Did you have much luck here?

MISS Y: Yes, this place is great. **I'm meeting** a new date *this weekend*, and **I'm bringing** my girl friend here *tomorrow*.

REPORTER: Well, that's all, folks. *Tomorrow* **I'm reporting** on video dating services. Tune in then.

■ ACTIVITY 1B

❑ Fill in the correct form of the present continuous tense to express a definite plan for the future. Use the verbs below in parentheses.

REPORTER: Today I am reporting to you from the offices of Club Meet.

Club Meet has resorts all over the world. Many of these

resorts are extremely popular with singles. Sir,

are you taking a Club Meet vacation?
(take)

MR. FRANK: Yes. I _____ to Martinique tomorrow.
(fly)

REPORTER: _____ you _____ alone?
(go)

MR. FRANK: Yes. I _____.
                       (short answer)

REPORTER: How long _____ you _____?
                                                (stay)

MR. FRANK: I _____ for a week.
                       (go)

REPORTER: I guess you _____ your heavy winter coat.
                                  (negative, **take**)

MR. FRANK: No. I _____. I _____ the whole day on the
                       (short answer)   (spend)

             beach tomorrow.

REPORTER: It sounds like a great vacation. Have a wonderful time.

QUESTIONS WITH *WHO* AND *WHAT* WHEN THEY ARE THE SUBJECT OF THE SENTENCE

When *Who* or *What* is the subject of the verb in a question, notice these things.

1. The verb is always in the singular, even when the answer is plural.

2. Begin the question with *Who* or *What* and follow the normal word order.

3. These rules are true for all tenses.

Who
What } + **is** + base form + **-ing**?

Short Answers: singular subject + **is**.
                          plural subject + **are**.

Look at these questions about the scene in the computer dating office.

Who's asking questions about the dating service?
  A reporter **is**.

Who's leaving to have lunch?
  Two clients **are**.

What television station **is** broadcasting this report.
  WKJB **is**.

Notice the difference between *Who/What* subject questions and *Who/What* object questions (the reporter is talking to Mr. Peterson, the owner of the computer dating service).

Who's talking to Mr. Peterson?
   The reporter is.

Who (**Whom**) is the reporter talking **to**?
   He's talking **to Mr. Peterson**.

Notice that the question word *Whom* as the object in the question is the correct form, but in conversational English we rarely use it. We usually say, "*Who.*"

SPELLING PROBLEMS FOR THE PRESENT CONTINUOUS TENSE

Double Consonants

When you see this pattern in one-syllable words, the final consonant almost always doubles.

consonant   vowel[7]   consonant

> sit → sitting
> cut → cutting
> rob → robbing
> swim → swimming
> shop → shopping

With words of more than one syllable, the rules are difficult to follow. Use your dictionary.

Final *e*

Drop the final *e* of the base form when you add *-ing*. Do not double the consonant.

> write → writing
> smoke → smoking
> take → taking
> change → changing

[7] *Vowels* are the letters *a, e, i, o,* and *u.*

Final *ie*

When the base form ends in *ie,* change the *ie* to *y* and add *-ing.*

```
die → dying
lie → lying
tie → tying
```

Final *y*

If the base form ends in *y,* keep the *y* and add *-ing.*

```
carry → carrying
hurry → hurrying
```

■ ACTIVITY 1C

❑ Write questions with *Who* about the subjects of these sentences. Look at the answer first. This is a continuation of the scene in the opening dialog.

1. Arnold is talking to Jack.

   Question: Who *is talking to Jack?* _____
   Answer: Arnold is.

2. Molly and Yolanda are looking at Arnold and Jack.

   Question: Who _____
   Answer: Molly and Yolanda are.

3. The waiter is taking Molly's order.

   Question: Who _____
   Answer: The waiter is.

4. Arnold and Jack are walking toward Molly and Yolanda's table.

   Question: Who _____
   Answer: Arnold and Jack are.

❑ Write questions with *Who(m)* about the objects of these sentences.

1. Arnold is talking to Jack.

   Question: Who *is Arnold talking to?* _____
   Answer: To Jack.

2. Molly and Yolanda are looking at Jack and Arnold.

   Question: Who _____
   Answer: At Jack and Arnold.

❑ Write questions with *Who* about the subjects or objects of these sentences. Look at each answer first to decide if the question is about the subject or the object.

1. Yolanda is introducing Molly to Jack and Arnold.

   Question: Who *is introducing Molly to Jack and Arnold?*
   Answer: Yolanda is.

2. Molly and Jack are shaking hands.

   Question: Who _____
   Answer: Molly and Jack are.

3. The waiter is pouring water for their table.

   Question: Who _____
   Answer: The waiter is.

4. The bill is wrong. Jack is complaining to the manager.

   Question: Who _____
   Answer: To the manager.

5. Jack is paying the cashier.

   Question: Who _____
   Answer: The cashier.

EXPRESSING YOUR IDEAS

1. Are matchmaking services such as computers, newspapers, and television shows becoming popular in your country? What is your opinion of these services?

2. Are dating customs changing in your country? If so, how?

3. Imagine you are in a nightclub watching what is going on around you. There are many different people in the nightclub. Write about what each person is doing.

> **Example**
>
> A tall dark man is playing a saxophone.

Yolanda

Yolanda is a reporter for a television station. She and Molly are best friends.

Arnold

Arnold is a rock musician. His best friend is Jack.

Jack

Jack is a graduate student. He's working on a doctorate in astronomy.

Molly

Molly is a college student majoring in history. She plans to be a high school teacher.

Dialog

(Tonight MOLLY and YOLANDA are going to go out with JACK and ARNOLD for the first time. YOLANDA and MOLLY are talking on the telephone.)

YOLANDA: Hello?

MOLLY: Hi, Yolanda. This is Molly.

YOLANDA: Hi, Molly, What's up?[1]

MOLLY: I'm really nervous about this date tonight. **I'm going to need** your help.

YOLANDA: What's the matter?

MOLLY: It's my first date with Jack. What **am I going to do**? What **am I going to say** to him?

YOLANDA: Wait a minute, Molly. Things **will work** out.

MOLLY: Okay. But I'm really nervous. I can't think straight.[2] **Are** you **going to offer** to pay for your ticket?

YOLANDA: Yes, I am. A lot of women are paying for themselves these days.

MOLLY: Yeah, that's true. What time **are** they **going to pick** us **up**?[3]

YOLANDA: They **aren't**. We**'re going to meet** them at eight o'clock sharp[4] in front of the theater. Be sure to be there on time.

MOLLY: What? **Aren't** they **going to pick** us **up**?

YOLANDA: No. They want to meet us at the movie.

MOLLY: I don't want to go alone.

YOLANDA: **I'll pick** you **up** on my way to the theater. **Will** you **meet** me downstairs?

MOLLY: All right. But don't forget to call me before you leave your house.

YOLANDA: All right. I **won't**.

MOLLY: Yolanda, there's another question on my mind. **Are** you **going to go** up to Arnold's apartment after the movie?

YOLANDA: Mmm . . . I don't know, Molly. It's only our first date. **I'm going to play** it by ear.[5]

---

[1]*What's up?* means "What's new? What's going on?"
[2]*Think straight* means "think clearly."
[3]*Pick someone up* means "meet someone at his or her home to go out on a date."
[4]*Sharp* means "precisely."
[5]*Play it by ear* means "leave plans indefinite and decide later."

MOLLY: I'm so nervous! I know I**'m going to do** something stupid and **put my foot in my mouth.**[6] This **isn't going to be** an easy evening for me. I can feel it.

Listening Comprehension Questions

1. How does Molly feel about her first date with Jack?
2. Are Molly and Yolanda going to a baseball game with Arnold and Jack tonight?
3. Will Yolanda offer to pay for her ticket tonight?
4. Where are they going to meet Jack and Arnold tonight?
5. Why isn't tonight going to be an easy evening for Molly? What's she afraid she's going to do?

GOING TO

When we talk about our plans or intentions for the future, we usually use the *going to* form for the future.

---

subject + **be (am, is, are)** + **going to** + base form

They are going to meet at 8:00.

Here are some time expressions that we frequently use to talk about the future.

tomorrow	next week	a few minutes from now
the day after tomorrow	next month	
tonight	next year	in a second
		in a minute
this weekend		in a week
this afternoon		in a little while
this evening		

in the future
in the near future
in the distant future

[6]*Put your foot in your mouth* means "to say something stupid or embarrassing."

Examples

(YOLANDA, ARNOLD, JACK, and MOLLY are standing in line in front of the movie theater.)

ARNOLD: Look at that line! It's a mile long. **I'm going to have** a cigarette. Who has a match?

YOLANDA: I have some, but **I'm not going to give** them to you. Cigarettes are really bad for you.

ARNOLD: Come on, Yolanda. Have a heart. Give me the matches.

YOLANDA: Well . . . , I don't know.

MOLLY: Wait, I have a match right here. (She opens her purse and drops it. Ten candy bars fall out.)

JACK: Molly! **What are you going to do** with all those candy bars? **Are you going to eat** them all yourself?

YOLANDA: (laughs) I'm so jumpy. First dates are really hard for everyone, aren't they? **I'm going to bite** my fingernails in the movie. Molly**'s** probably **going to eat** too much. And Arnold**'s** probably **going to smoke** too much. What's your nervous habit, Jack?

JACK: Who's nervous?

◼ ACTIVITY 2A

Read the following situations. Write questions about what you think is going to happen. Then write answers to your questions. Include at least one negative sentence.

1. Jack is sitting in front of a pile of books, holding his head. He is reaching for a bottle of aspirin. He says, "I have a terrible headache."

   a. What *is he going to do?*
      (do)
   b. *Is he going to study* _____ any more tonight?
   Story: **(study)**

   Jack is going to take a break. He isn't going to study any more tonight. He is going to take some aspirin, and then he's going to take a walk.

2. Arnold is looking down in surprise at a hundred-dollar bill on the sidewalk. A policeman is walking toward him.

   a. _____ ?
      (pick up)
   b. _____ to the policeman?
      (give)

c. How much _____ on a date with Yolanda?
        (spend)

d. What _____ with the money?
Story: (do)

3. Jack is sitting on a bench with a "Wet Paint" sign on it. Molly is covering her mouth in horror and pointing at the sign.

   a. What _____ ?
                (Molly, do)

   b. What _____ ?
                (Jack, do)

   c. _____ on the bench?
          (Molly, sit)

   d. What _____ with his pants?
   Story: (Jack, do)

4. Arnold and Yolanda are standing on a corner in formal clothes under an umbrella. There is an enormous puddle of water in front of them. A cabdriver is just about to drive into the puddle of water.

   a. What _____ ?
                (happen)

   b. Who _____ ?
               (get wet)

   c. How _____ ?
               (look)

   d. How _____ ?
               (feel)

   e. _____ the cleaning bill?
        (the cabdriver, pay)

   f. _____ their clothes?
   Story: (change)

WILL

Will of Promise

In general, *going to* is used in more situations than *will.* In some situations, you can use *will* or *going to* for the same meaning. However, there is one situation in which we almost always use *will*—when we make a promise or offer our help. We also use *will* in questions when we make a request for help or offer an invitation.

I
you
he, she, it } + **will** + base form
we
they

It will work out, Molly. I promise.

Contractions
I
you
he, she, it } + **'ll** + base form
we
they

I'll pick you up.

Examples

(ARNOLD, JACK, YOLANDA, and MOLLY are leaving the movie theater and are deciding what to do.)

YOLANDA: That was a great movie. What are we going to do now?

JACK: Let's go to my place. It's just two blocks from here. How about it, Molly and Yolanda? **Will** you **come**?

MOLLY: Sure.

YOLANDA: Sure.

ARNOLD: Do you have any coffee?

JACK: No.

ARNOLD: **I'll get** some. Oh, no! I don't have any more money.

YOLANDA: That's okay. You paid for the movie. Molly and I **will buy** the coffee.

> JACK: **I'll go** back and straighten up[7] my apartment. **Will** you **get** some sandwiches and cookies too?
>
> YOLANDA: Sure, we **will**.
>
> JACK: Here's some money.
>
> YOLANDA: No, it's okay. We**'ll get** some coffee, sandwiches, and cookies, and we**'ll see** you in a few minutes.

Negative of *Will—Won't*

Won't is the negative form of *will*. We use *won't* for three different situations:

1. when we promise not to do something

2. when we refuse to do something

3. when something is broken and isn't working

---

subject + **will** + **not** + base form
Contraction:

        won't + base form

Yolanda won't forget to pick Molly up.

Example

(In JACK'S apartment an hour later.)

YOLANDA: Jack, your place is really nice.

JACK: Thank you. Oh, no. There's a pair of my socks under the sofa!

YOLANDA: Who cares? We **won't look** under the sofa. We promise. And Jack, please don't look under the sofa in my place, or the chairs, or the bed.

JACK: Okay, I **won't**. Say, Arnold. What about that new guitar you saw? Are you going to buy it?

ARNOLD: No, my father **won't lend** me the money, and I don't have enough myself.

JACK: That's too bad.

YOLANDA: Jack, will you come here for a minute? Where is your bread knife? This old knife **won't cut** anything.

JACK: I'll be right there.

---

[7]*Straighten up* means "put things in order."

Will of Prediction

When we want to make a prediction about the future, we frequently use *will*.

> ### *Example*
> ARNOLD: I never have any money. I'm tired of being poor.
> YOLANDA: A musician's life is really hard sometimes. Be patient. You**'ll be** famous someday. Then you**'ll be** rich.
> ARNOLD: I hope you're right. But when **will** it **happen**?

■ **ACTIVITY 2B**

Your boyfriend or girlfriend is afraid of marriage. You are proposing. Make promises about how wonderful married life will be. You can role play this situation in class or do it for homework.

Affirmative Statements

1. We _____ very happy together.
   (be)

2. I _____ you forever.
   (love)

3. I _____ you everything you want.
   (give)

4. We _____ beautiful children.
   (have)

Now make more promises about your house, your children, a job, and your standard of living.

5. _____

6. _____

7. _____

8. _____

9. _____

10. _____

Now make promises about what will *not* happen.

11. I _____ anyone but you.
    (love)

12. We _____ about anything.
    (argue)

13. I _____ you until the day I die.
        (leave)

■ ACTIVITY 2C

Read the following situations. Then write negative statements to mean "refuse to". Use *won't*.

1. A politician and a reporter are talking. The reporter says, "Is it true that United Oil Company gave you a million dollars for your campaign?" The politician answers, "No comment."

    The politician *won't answer* the reporter's question.
                    (answer)

2. Molly and Jack are in a room. Molly is struggling to remove the lid from a jar of mustard. Jack is struggling to open a window.

    Molly is trying to open the mustard jar, but the lid _____
                                                          (come off)

    _____ .

    Jack is trying to open the window, but it's stuck. It _____
                                                          (open)

    _____ .

3. Yolanda and her landlord are in Yolanda's apartment. Yolanda looks very angry. Yolanda says, "Will you please paint this place, fix the ceiling, and give me a new refrigerator?" The landlord answers, "No!"

    The landlord _____ her apartment.
                  (paint)

    The landlord _____ the ceiling.
                  (fix)

    The landlord _____ a new refrigerator for her.
                  (buy)

■ ACTIVITY 2D

The world is changing very fast nowadays. Nobody knows what changes the future will bring or how fast they will happen. Write predictions about the year 2030 using *will*. You can write about transportation, family life, communication, food, or space travel.

> *Example*
>
> *Everyone will have a computer in his or her home.*

■ ACTIVITY 2E

Fill in the blanks with *going to* or *will*. Remember, we usually use *going to* to state an intention or to plan and *will* to make a promise or to offer help. (Either *going to* or *will* is correct in some examples. However, a native speaker usually follows the rules we gave in this chapter.)

1. (JACK and MOLLY are in a restaurant.)

   MOLLY: What's the matter, Jack?

   JACK: There's a fly in my soup! I can't believe it. I *'m going*
   (complain)

   to complain to the manager.

   MOLLY: I _____ the waiter for you.
   (call)

   JACK: I _____ sick.
   (be)

   WAITER: Oh, I'm sorry, sir. I _____ another bowl of soup
   (bring)
   for you. Please sit right there. Don't leave.

   JACK: Okay, I _____ .
   (negative)

   WAITER: Here's your soup, sir. We _____ you anything.
   (negative, **charge**)

2. (JACK is at ARNOLD'S apartment.)

   ARNOLD: Jack, what's the matter with you? You look uptight.[8]

   JACK: I am. My parents _____ into Manhattan tonight and
   (come)

   _____ me out to dinner. In a few minutes, I
   (take)

   _____ Molly and invite her to go with us, but I'm not
   (call)

   sure if my parents _____ her.
   (like)

   ARNOLD: You need something for your nerves, Jack. I have a great herbal

   tea. I _____ you some. It _____ you down.
   (get)   (calm)

   JACK: Thanks.

   ARNOLD: Here's your tea. Relax. But it's really hot, so don't drink it too fast.

   JACK: I _____ .
   (negative)

   ARNOLD: And don't worry about tonight.

[8]*Uptight* means "anxious and uncomfortable."

JACK: You're right. I _____ . This tea is making me feel better
(negative)
already.

■ ACTIVITY 2F

Madame Wiz knows everything. She sees into the future and reads minds. She
is a famous fortune-teller. She has a crystal ball that gives her amazing powers.

   You are Madame Wiz, and you have her amazing power. People come to see
you, and you look into your crystal ball and know everything. Tell the future of
each of the following people. (You can use the questions as a guide). Role play
this in class.

1. Molly is sitting in front of you and asking you a lot of questions. Answer
   her questions and tell her fortune.

   When will Jack ask me out again?

   Will we get married?

   Am I going to leave home this year?

   Am I going to get my own apartment?

   When am I going to get a job?

   Will I ever get rich?

   Will Jack and I be happy together?

2. You are the President of the United States. You are very worried about
   the future. You are asking Madame Wiz a lot of questions about your
   future, your country's future, and the future of the world. Your partner
   is Madame Wiz and will answer your questions.

3. Choose a name for yourself, and choose a new career that you are
   starting. Ask Madame Wiz about your future. She will answer you.

■ ACTIVITY 2G

You are the minister of economic development in your country. A journalist is
interviewing you about your country's future.

INTERVIEWER: What problems is your country facing nowadays?

        YOU: _____

INTERVIEWER: Will these problems become more serious in the future, in your
        opinion?

        YOU: _____

INTERVIEWER: What is the population of your country?

YOU: _____

INTERVIEWER: According to sociologists, is it going to increase?

YOU: _____

INTERVIEWER: What do you think your country's population will be in twenty years?

YOU: _____

INTERVIEWER: Is overpopulation a problem? What is your government doing about it now? What is your government going to do about this problem in the future?

YOU: _____

INTERVIEWER: What are the main industries of your country?

YOU: _____

INTERVIEWER: What industries do you think your country will develop in the next twenty years?

YOU: _____

INTERVIEWER: What products will your country export and import because of these new industries?

YOU: _____

INTERVIEWER: Is unemployment a problem at the present time? Is the government doing anything about this problem now?

YOU: _____

INTERVIEWER: Do you think unemployment in your country is going to increase or decrease in the next decade?

YOU: _____

INTERVIEWER: In your opinion, what role is your country going to play in the world?

YOU: _____

EXPRESSING YOUR IDEAS

1. Sociologists say that the relationship between men and women has changed a great deal in the last ten or twenty years. Often, both parents must work outside the home, and family life is changing as a result. Men have learned to help more in the home, but there still seem to be many

problems. The divorce rate is high, so more and more single parents are raising children nowadays.

What changes are taking place in your country nowadays? Discuss these changes.

What are your predictions for the future in your country? What other changes will take place? Will divorce become more or less common? Will children suffer because more and more women are working, or will they adjust easily? Will the size of the average family change?

2. Look at Activity 2G. Choose one area to discuss at length. For example, you could choose unemployment, or overpopulation, or industrial growth. Write about what is happening at the present time, and predict what will happen in the future.

3 THE SIMPLE PAST TENSE

Astronaut Aldrin posing for a photograph beside the flag of the United States on the moon.

Dialog

JACK, ARNOLD, YOLANDA, and MOLLY are sitting in a cafe having a cup of coffee together.)

YOLANDA: Where **did** you and Jack **meet**, Arnold?

ARNOLD: We **were** classmates at City University, but I **dropped** out[1] a year ago to play music.

YOLANDA: When are you going to finish your degree, Jack?

JACK: In two years.

YOLANDA: Astronomy is an unusual field. What are you going to do with your degree—teach?

JACK: Yes, I think so.

MOLLY: I think astronomy is fascinating. I guess you know a lot about the space program too. You know, I can never forget the *Challenger* accident.[2] **Did** you **follow** all the news on it the way I did? **Wasn't** that a terrible tragedy?

JACK: It sure **was.** The *Challenger* **blew** up, and with it we **lost** seven astronauts and a lot of our confidence in the space program.

YOLANDA: You're right. I guess everybody **watched** and **read** every piece of news on the *Challenger.* The news **showed** the explosion over and over again.

MOLLY: Tell me something, Jack. I know the old stereotype about how men aren't supposed to cry. **Were** your eyes dry when you **watched** the news, or **did** you **cry** too? I know my eyes sure **weren't** dry.

JACK: Yeah, I **cried.** I **felt** really bad for the family and the students of that schoolteacher who was on board.

ARNOLD: She **wasn't** even an astronaut.

MOLLY: When **did** they **start** allowing nonastronauts on the shuttle?

JACK: I don't know when exactly, but I know that a senator[3] and a congressman[4] **went** on previous trips.

YOLANDA: What exactly **was** the cause of the explosion? **Was** something the matter with the rocket boosters?[5]

---

[1]*Drop out* means "to leave school before graduation."

[2]*The* Challenger *accident:* The space shuttle *Challenger* exploded on January 29, 1986.

[3]A *senator* is a member of the U.S. Congress; each state elects two senators to the Senate.

[4]A *congressman* is a member of the U.S. Congress; each state elects representatives to the House of Representatives. States with larger populations have more representatives.

[5]*Rocket boosters* are rockets used to launch the space shuttle.

JACK: Yes. The O-ring seals[6] on the rocket boosters **didn't work** right because the weather **was** colder than usual. Some hot gases **escaped** and **caused** the explosion.

ARNOLD: Well, that sure **was** a terrible setback[7], but the space program **got** back on its feet fairly soon.[8] NASA[9] **was** much more careful with the next space shuttle, *Discovery.*

MOLLY: You know it! Much, much more.

Listening Comprehension Questions

1. Where did Jack and Arnold meet?
2. What is Jack's field?
3. How many astronauts did NASA lose in the *Challenger* accident?
4. Were all the *Challenger* passengers astronauts?
5. Why didn't the O-ring seals on the rocket boosters work?
6. Did the space program get back on its feet fairly soon after the *Challenger* tragedy?

REGULAR AND IRREGULAR VERBS

Use the simple past tense when you want to talk about something that happened at a specific time in the past. Here are some time expressions that we use with the simple past tense.

yesterday	last night	(_____) ago
the day before yesterday	last week	a minute ago
	last month	two hours ago
	last year	a few days ago

Affirmative Statements

REGULAR VERBS

In English there are both regular and irregular verbs. Most verbs are regular. To form the simple past tense of a regular verb, add *-ed* or *-d* to the base form.

---

[6]*O-ring seals* are giant black rubber Os that help stop gases from escaping from the four segments (pieces) of the rocket boosters.

[7]*Setback* means "some problem that stops progress."

[8]*Fairly soon:* After thirty-two months of hard work, the United States was back in space with the successful flight of the space shuttle *Discovery* on October 6, 1988.

[9]*NASA* is the National Aeronautics and Space Agency.

> ### *Examples*
>
> In October 1957, the Soviet Union launch**ed** the world's first satellite, *Sputnik I*. The success of *Sputnik I* shock**ed** Americans. After the Soviet success, the United States push**ed** ahead rapidly with its own space program.

IRREGULAR VERBS

Many common verbs have a completely different form in the simple past tense. They do not add *-ed* or *-d* to the base form to form the simple past. Turn to the Appendix for a list of the most common irregular verbs and their endings.

> ### *Examples*
>
> On April 12, 1961, the Soviet Union **sent** the first man, Yuri Gagarin, into space. Soon after, President John F. Kennedy **gave** his complete support to the U.S. space program. The space budget soon **grew** to $5.25 billion. Finally, on July 15, 1969, *Apollo 11* **took** off. This was the first spacecraft that carried men to the moon. Millions of people **saw** the takeoff on television. On July 20, 1969, the spacecraft landed on the surface of the moon with astronauts Neil Armstrong and Buzz Aldrin.

Negative Statements

Use *did not* (*didn't*) and the base form of the verb.

> ### *Examples*
>
> In the early years of the U.S. space program, some launchings **didn't go** smoothly. Some rocket ships **didn't** even **leave** the ground. Scientists solved most of these problems, but years later other problems came up on the *Apollo 11* moon shot. Some equipment **didn't work** properly. For example, the lunar module **didn't connect** perfectly with the command ship. Fortunately, the astronauts corrected their error, and they **didn't get** hurt.

Past Tense Chart—Affirmative and Negative Statements

Subject	Verb				
	Helping Verb	Not	Base Form	Past	
President Kennedy				gave	support to the space program.
President Eisenhower	did	n't	give		much support to the space program.

■ ACTIVITY 3A

Fill in the blanks with the simple past form of the verb below the line.

Neil Armstrong _grew up_ in Ohio. He was a very bright student.
(grow up)

In the first grade, he _____ ninety books. He _____
(read)   (negative, **attend**)

the second grade because he already _____ on a fifth-grade level.
(read)

In high school, he _____ in science and mathematics. He even
(excel)

_____ these subjects for a while when his science teacher was sick.
(teach)

In high school, he was very studious. He _____ very
(negative, **socialize**)

much. According to his brother, he _____ many dates.
(negative, **have**)

Neil Armstrong _____ interested in flying at a young age.
(become)

When he was six years old, he _____ in a plane for the first time.
(fly)

His hobby was building model airplanes. He _____ hundreds
(build)

of them. When he was a teenager, he _____ at a small airport in
(work)

his hometown. He _____ his pilot's license before he _____
(get)   (get)

his driver's license. He _____ his professional flying career
(start)

after college when he _____ a pilot for the navy.
(become)

■ ACTIVITY 3B

Fill in each blank with the past tense of the verb in parentheses. Some verbs are in the affirmative, and others are in the negative. Use the helping verb *did* for a short statement.

1. In the early days of the space program, American spaceships

   *splashed down* in the ocean. They _*didn't land*_ on solid
      (splash down)   **(negative, land)**

   ground. Soviet spaceships ____*did*____ .

2. The Soviets _____ the first man into space. They
                   (send)

   _____ the first man to the moon. The Americans _____ .
    (negative, send)

3. The Soviets _____ a woman into space. The Americans
                   (send)

   _____ .
       (negative)

4. A *Viking* spacecraft _____ to Mars. It _____
                 (go)   **(negative, go)**

   to the moon. The *Apollo 11* _____ .

5. The *Viking* spacecraft _____ equipment on Mars. It
                 (leave)

   _____ men. Only the *Apollo* flights _____ .
     (negative, carry)

Questions

WORD ORDER—REGULAR AND IRREGULAR VERBS

(Question word) + *did(n't)* + subject + base form?

> ### *Examples*
>
> **Did** the Soviet Union **send** a woman astronaut into space?
> Yes, it sent Valentina Tereshkova into space.
>
> **Did** the United States **launch** the world's first satellite?
> No, it didn't.
>
> **Did** the astronauts **leave** footprints on the moon?
> Yes, they did.

What else **did** the astronauts **leave** on the moon?
They left an American flag.

Where **did** Apollo 11 **splash** down?
It splashed down in the Pacific Ocean.

QUESTIONS WITH *WHO* AND *WHAT*

When *who* or *what* is the subject of the verb, do not use *did* in questions. Use the simple past form of the verb. Note that the short answer is: subject + *did*.

Examples

Who **walked** on the moon in 1969?
Neil Armstrong and Buzz Aldrin **did.**

Who **sent** the first woman astronaut into space?
The Soviet Union **did.**

What **protected** the astronauts from the extreme temperatures on the moon?
Their space suits **did.**

In questions, when *who* or *what* is the object of the verb, use *did* and the base form of the verb.

Examples

Who **did** Armstrong and Aldrin **leave** in the command ship when they walked on the moon?
They left Mike Collins in the command ship.

Who **did** the astronauts **talk** to from the moon?
They talked to President Nixon.

What **did** the astronauts **eat** on the *Apollo 11* flight?
They ate freeze-dried food, such as steak and eggs out of plastic bags.

NOTES

1. In more formal English, we use *whom* when the question is about the object of the verb. However, to many Americans, this sounds too formal for conversational English.

2. Notice that we frequently use a short answer with *did* for the *Who* subject question. It is impossible to do that for a *Who* object question.

QUESTIONS WITH *WHAT HAPPENED*

This is another kind of question in which you do not use *did* and the base form.

Example

What happened when the astronauts splashed down?
They went into isolation, and doctors examined them carefully.

Question Review Chart—Simple Past Tense

Wh- *Questions*	*Helping Verb*	*Subject*	*Base Form*	
	Did	the U.S.S.R.	send	a woman into outer space?
Where	did	*Apollo 11*	splash	down?
Why	did	the astronauts	go	into isolation?
What	did	the astronauts	eat	on the flight
Who(m)	did	the astronauts	talk	to from the moon?

	Wh- Questions as Subject	*Past Form*	
	Who	walked	on the moon in 1969?
	What	protected	the astronauts from the extreme temperatures on the moon?

Spelling Problems for the Simple Past Tense

1. When you add *-ed* or *-d* to many regular verbs, you need to double the final consonant. See page 9, and read the rules for doubling the consonant when you add *-ing*. The rules are the same when you add *-ed* or *-d*.

stop	→	stopped
rob	→	robbed
omit	→	omitted
admit	→	admitted
rip	→	ripped

2. When a verb ends with a consonant and *y*, change the *y* to *i* when you add *-ed*.

> hurry → hurried
> try → tried
> apply → applied

3. When a verb ends with a vowel followed by *y*, you don't change *y* to *i*.

> stay → stayed
> obey → obeyed
> play → played

Pronunciation of Regular Verbs in the Simple Past Tense

/əd/	/d/	/t/
Pronounce *-ed* as /əd/ only with verbs that end with a t or d sound.	Pronounce *-ed* as /d/ with— 1. verbs that end with these consonants: *b, g, j, l, m, n, r, v, z.*	Pronounce *ed* as /t/ with these consonants: *c, ch, f, k, p, s, sh, x.*
Examples	Examples	Examples
operate → operated /əd/	grab → grabbed /d/	kiss → kissed /t/
wait hand visit provide demand collect land	hug stare call starve dim buzz open	slice hope watch wash fluff fix talk
	2. verbs that end with vowel sounds.	
	Examples	
	stay → stayed /d/	
	cry allow veto agree argue review	

■ ACTIVITY 3C

Ask questions about Neil Armstrong. The verb is given in parentheses. Then answer the questions. Look back at Activity 3A on page 30 for the answers. Practice this exercise in pairs orally. Then write it.

1. Where *did Neil Armstrong grow up ?* _____
    (grow up)

    Neil Armstrong *grew up in Ohio.* _____

2. _____ many books in the first grade?
    (read)

    _____

3. What _____ in high school?
    (study)

    _____

4. _____ in high school?
    (teach)

    _____

5. _____ many dates in high school?
    (have)

    _____

6. _____ in a plane when he was young?
    (fly)

    _____

7. _____ a hobby?
    (have)

    _____

8. What _____?
    (do)

    _____

9. _____ when he was a teenager?
    (work)

    _____

10. When _____ his driver's license?
    (get)

    _____

◼ ACTIVITY 3D

Ask questions in the negative using the simple past tense. Use the verbs in parentheses in the questions.

1. Neil Armstrong and Buzz Aldrin walked on the moon.

   Didn't _____ the third astronaut _____ *go* _____ with them?
   (go)

   No, he didn't. He stayed in the command module.

2. President Kennedy gave more support to the space program than any other president did before him.

   Why _____ other presidents before Kennedy

   _____ as much support as he did?
   (give)

   Because the United States didn't realize that Soviet space technology was as advanced as it was.

3. Two astronauts walked on the moon on the *Apollo 11* space shot.

   Why _____ the third astronaut _____
   (walk)
   on the moon too?

   Because someone had to be in the command ship.

4. On the *Apollo 11* flight, the astronauts walked on the moon.

   _____ they _____ in a moon vehicle too?
   (ride)
   Yes, they did.

5. The lunar module and the command ship almost missed each other on the *Apollo 11* flight.

   Why _____ they _____ at first?
   (connect)
   Because the equipment didn't function properly.

5. The first woman to travel in space was Valentina Tereshkova, a Soviet.

   _____ the Americans _____ women
   (have)
   in their Apollo program?
   No, they didn't.

◼ ACTIVITY 3E

❑ Ask questions about these sentences with *Who* or *What* in the subject position. Phrase your questions so that they can be answered by the *Answers* below.

1. A French author wrote *Voyage to the Moon*.

   Who wrote Voyage to the Moon?

2. Two Americans flew the first airplane on December 17, 1903.

_____?

3. An American made the first flight from New York to Paris on May 21, 1927.

_____?

4. A special rocket lifted *Apollo 11* into space.

_____?

5. Something slowed down the space capsule before it splashed down in the ocean.

_____?

Answers

1. Jules Verne did.

2. The Wright brothers did.

3. Charles Lindbergh did.

4. A *Saturn* rocket did.

5. A giant parachute did.

❑ Ask questions with *Who* or *What* about the object of the sentence. Phrase your questions so that they can be answered by the *Answers* below.

1. The Soviets sent the first man into space.

   Who did the Soviets send into space?

2. King Ferdinand and Queen Isabella sent a famous explorer on a long voyage in 1492.

_____?

3. The Italian Amerigo Vespucci mapped part of a continent.

_____?

4. The Church persecuted a famous scientist because he believed the earth moved around the sun.

_____?

5. Thomas Edison invented many important things.

_____?

Answers

1. Yuri Gagarin.

2. Christopher Columbus.

3. Part of the Americas.

4. Galileo.

5. The first successful phonograph, for example.

☐ Read the sentence. Then write a question about it with *Who* or *What* in the subject or object position. Look at the correct answer to the question first, and write the correct question for the answer.

1. Homer, a Greek poet, wrote the *Odyssey*.

   a. _Who wrote the Odyssey?_
      Homer did.

   b. _What did Homer write?_
      The *Odyssey*.

2. Ptolemy, a famous ancient astronomer, believed that the Earth was the center of the universe.

   a. _____?
      Ptolemy did.

   b. _____?
      That the earth was the center of the universe.

3. Stanley Kubrick, an American filmmaker, made a famous film, *2001: A Space Odyssey*.

   a. _____?
      2001: A Space Odyssey.

   b. _____
      Stanley Kubrick did.

4. An apple fell from a tree. It hit Isaac Newton on the head.

   a. _____?
      An apple did.

   b. _____?
      It hit Isaac Newton.

5. Albert Einstein won the Nobel prize for physics in 1921.

   a. _____ ?
      Albert Einstein did.

   b. _____ ?
      the Nobel prize for physics.

❑ Test your classmates on their knowledge of history. Think of famous writers, artists, generals, inventors, and scientists. Ask subject or object questions beginning with *Who* and *What*.

Examples

Who invented the telephone?

Who painted the *Mona Lisa*?

Who did Romeo love?

What famous battle did Napoleon lose?

WAS AND WERE—PAST TENSE OF VERB TO BE

Statements

Affirmative: With *I, he, she,* and *it,* use *was.*
              With *you, we,* and *they,* use *were.*

Negative: *was + not = wasn't.*
          were + not = weren't.

Examples

American astronauts **were** the first men on the moon, but Americans **weren't** always in first place in the "space race." The first two men in space **were** Soviets. John Glenn **was** the first American in space. On February 20, 1962, he circled the earth three times.

Questions

Put *was* or *were* before the subject.

> ### *Examples*
>
> **Was** John Glenn alone in the space capsule?
>   Yes, he was.
>
> How long **was** he in space?
>   He was there for four hours and fifty-six minutes.
>
> **Were** Americans proud on this day?
>   They certainly were.

Questions with *Who*

When *who* is the subject of the verb, it is always singular.

> ### *Examples*
>
> *Who* **was** the first man in space?
>   Yuri Gagarin **was**.
>
> *Who* **was** in control of his spacecraft?
>   Soviet scientists on the ground **were**.

■ ACTIVITY 3F

Complete the following dialog by filling in the blanks. Use *was* or *were*. (Arnold and his father argue about almost everything. In this dialog, they are arguing about the moon shot.)

ARNOLD: Remember the moon shot?

FATHER: I remember. Three Americans landed on the moon.

   ___*Wasn't*___ that exciting?
      (negative)

ARNOLD: Only two landed on the moon. One stayed in the capsule.

FATHER: Oh, yes. That's right.

ARNOLD: How long _____ they on the moon? Do you

   remember exactly?

FATHER: I think they _____ there for a couple of days.

ARNOLD: No, that's impossible. They _____ there for only a

few hours.

FATHER: Oh, well. I guess you're right. Where _____ Neil

Armstrong when he spoke to President Johnson?

_____ he on the moon or back in the capsule?

ARNOLD: Johnson? Johnson _____ president then. Nixon
                              (negative)

_____ .

FATHER: All right, Mr. Know-it-all, how do you know so much?

ARNOLD: I _____ in a bar with friends. We

_____ there for hours. We watched the broadcast on

TV there. And where _____ you?

FATHER: I don't remember where I _____ .

◼ ACTIVITY 3G

Use the words in the correct sentence word order, and use the past tense. When
you finish, you will have a short paragraph about the life of John F. Kennedy. In
general, use this word order in your sentences.

subject + verb + object + place + time

subject + (*to be*) + (adjective or noun) + place + time

1. (be/   president/   John F. Kennedy/   during the first great
expansion of the space program)

   John F. Kennedy was president during the

   first great expansion of the space program.

2. (be/   he/   as a writer/   successful/   also)

   _____

3. (be/   Massachusetts/   his home state)

_____

4. (grow up/   Kennedy/   there/   and/   Harvard University/
   attend/   later)

_____

_____

5. (write/   at Harvard/   he/   *Why England Slept*)

_____

6. (be/   before World War II/   about England/   this book)

_____

7. (experience/   fifteen years later/   Kennedy/   severe back pain)

_____

8. (be/   he/   for many months/   in the hospital)

_____

9. (write/   he/   another book/   at this time)

_____

10. (describe/   famous Americans/   in this book, *Profiles in Courage*/
    he)

_____

11. (win/   in 1956/   it/   for literature/   the Pulitzer Prize)

_____

■ ACTIVITY 3H

Fill in the blank with either the present continuous or single past tense of the verb in parentheses.

Voice Communication: Sunday, July 20, 1969, 10:56 P.M.
(Neil Armstrong is already on the moon. Buzz Aldrin is still in the lunar module. He is getting ready to join Armstrong on the moon. They are talking to Ground Control in Houston, Texas.)

ARMSTRONG: I *am standing* on the moon. I _____
             (stand)   (look)
up at the windows of the lunar module.

GROUND CONTROL: We _____ a picture on the TV now. You
       (get)
_____ upside down in the picture.
  (stand)

ARMSTRONG: I'm not upside down here. Look, I _____
             (make)
footprints in the sand. Beautiful view here.

ALDRIN: (from the lunar module) Ready for me?

ARMSTRONG: Roger.[10] Take it easy now. You _____ my
             (see)
difficulties when I _____ down before.
      (step)

ALDRIN: I _____ on the top step now.
  (stand)

ARMSTRONG: OK. I _____ down the steps very slowly. I
     (come)
_____. That _____ comfortable
 (hop)   (be)
for me.

ALDRIN: Good. I _____ down now too. Here I
    (come)
_____. It _____ beautiful!
 (be)   (be)

ARMSTRONG: You _____ down easily. _____
    (come)   (negative, **be**)
it fun?

ALDRIN: It sure _____. I _____ any
    (be) (negative, **have**)
trouble. Hey, you _____ around like a
      (jump)
kangaroo!

ARMSTRONG: I _____ almost _____!
         (float)

ALDRIN: Hey, what _____? Why _____
     (happen)
you _____? _____ you
 (stop)
_____ something?
 (find)

ARMSTRONG: Yes, I _____ a purple rock. Look at it!
    (find)

GROUND CONTROL: Bring it back!

[10]*Roger* means "That's right. Yes."

USED TO

When we want to talk about an action that we did repeatedly in the past but that we don't do anymore, we use the expression *used to*.

Statements: subject + **used to** + base form
subject + **didn't use to** + base form
Questions: **Did(n't)** + subject + **use to** + base form?

Examples

People **used to believe** the earth was the center of the universe. They **used to think** the sun revolved around the earth.

Note: When we want to emphasize that something that happened repeatedly in the past continues in the present, we express the idea in this way.

The ancient Egyptians **used to tell** time by a sundial, and in some parts of the world, people **still do.**

When we want to show that something happened repeatedly in the past and we want to emphasize that it no longer happens in the present, we express the idea in this way.

People **used to think** that an eclipse of the sun meant the end of the world, but they **don't anymore.**

▪ Activity 3I

Answer the following questions. Write sentences with *used to*.

1. What are some things people used to believe about the universe that they no longer believe? (Write five sentences.)

Example

People used to believe the earth was flat.

2. Write five sentences about things that you don't do anymore but that you used to do in your country, either when you were a child or when you lived with your parents.

3. Pretend you are a reporter interviewing a 200-year-old man. Ask him questions about how the world used to be 100 years ago and how it is different today. Write both the questions and the answers.

> ### Example
>
> REPORTER: In your youth, how did you used to get around?
>
> OLD MAN: I used to walk everywhere, or I rode around in a horse and carriage. People don't walk enough anymore. They don't get enough exercise.

■ ACTIVITY 3J

Review all the information on Neil Armstrong and his famous moon walk. Look at Activity 3A, Activity 3F, and Activity 3H. Imagine that you are a reporter and that you are interviewing Neil Armstrong. Think of questions about his childhood and his trip to the moon. You can act out the interview in class with one student playing the role of Armstrong and the other students playing the role of reporters. Later you can write the interview as homework.

EXPRESSING YOUR IDEAS

1. What do you remember about the first walk on the moon? How old were you in 1969? Where were you? Did you watch it on TV? How did you feel about it? How did people in your country react?

2. You just returned from a space flight to Mars. Write a report on your expedition. Here is some vocabulary you might want to use.

to blast off	command ship
to orbit a planet	countdown
to land	space capsule
to make a soft landing	space suit
to travel through space	to set up scientific instruments
to collect rock samples	to see canals on Mars
to see signs of life	to communicate with ground control
to splash down in the ocean	to see other galaxies
Martians	to feel dizzy
vegetation	to experience weightlessness
spaceship	to travel into outer space

3. From the 1950s to the 1970s, the Soviet Union and the United States spent billions of dollars on their space programs. Why was the space race so important to these two countries? Was competition for power and prestige the main reason for the space programs? Was exploration of the new frontier the main reason? What's your opinion?

4. How did people benefit from the space program? What new advances in technology resulted from the program? How did it change our lives? In your opinion, was the space program valuable?

5. Did the United States and the Soviet Union spend too much money on the space program? Did they neglect social programs because of the space program? Was it worthwhile to put a man on the moon? Should we continue to spend money on the space program?

4 THE SIMPLE PRESENT TENSE

A tanker docked in Alaska.

ENERGY SOURCES AND ENVIRONMENTAL PROBLEMS

Dialog

ARNOLD: Hey, Jack. What **do** you **think** of that oil spill[1] near Valdez, Alaska? More than ten million gallons of oil all over the place! The newspaper says it's the worst oil spill in U.S. history.

JACK: Yeah, what a tragedy!

ARNOLD: Why **does** this kind of thing **happen** so often? Why **don't** we **find** another way to transport oil?

JACK: We **don't have** the technology to transport it any other way.

ARNOLD: But oil spills like this one **kill** thousands of birds and fish and other wildlife. They **ruin** the beaches.

JACK: How **do** they **clean** up all the oil from a major spill? **Do** they ever **clean** it all up?

ARNOLD: No. I read an article that says they usually **recover** only about ten percent of the oil from a spill. Some of the rest **evaporates,** but most of it **turns** into thick black stuff and **sinks** to the bottom of the ocean.

JACK: Then what **happens**? What kind of damage **does** the oil **cause** next?

ARNOLD: Well, the experts **don't know** for sure, but they **think** the oil deposits on the bottom **release** harmful chemicals for months or even years. Those chemicals **contaminate**[2] microorganisms[3] first. Then small fish **eat** the microorganisms. Then the larger fish, the birds, and the seals **eat** the small fish. How long **does** the damage **go** on? Who **knows**? And what **do** we **do** to stop these oil spills? Nothing! What's the matter with us?

JACK: Well, luckily it **doesn't happen** that often. And, besides, **don't** we **need** the oil? This country **depends** on oil imports. I **think** we **import** around forty billion dollars worth of oil a year. Look at that plastic pen in your hand. Where **does** it **come** from? Oil, right?

ARNOLD: True, but that **doesn't mean** that we can't be more careful about pollution. How often **do** we **hear** that the people in Washington[4] are working on alternative sources of energy[5]? **Does** the government really **care** that much about pollution?

---

[1]*oil spill* means "the accidental escape of oil into the ocean from a tanker."
[2]*Contaminate* means "to pollute; to make impure."
[3]*Microorganism* means "a living thing that can be seen only under a microscope."
[4]*The people in Washington* means "the members of the federal government."
[5]*Alternative sources of energy* means "other ways to produce energy besides oil, such as solar energy, gasoline made from alcohol, and so on."

JACK: I **don't know** how to answer that question. And, speaking of pollution of the oceans, what **do** you **think** of all that medical waste that washed up on the New Jersey beaches a couple of summers ago?

ARNOLD: It's scary all right. The oceans just **don't have** the ability to take care of all the world's garbage anymore.

Listening Comprehension Questions

1. How do oil spills like the one in Prince William Sound, Alaska, affect the environment?
2. How much oil do workers usually recover from an oil spill?
3. What happens to the rest of the oil?
4. Describe the damage caused by oil on the ocean floor.
5. In Jack's opinion, how often does a tragedy like the one in Alaska happen?
6. In Arnold's opinion, does the government really care about pollution?
7. Can oceans still take care of the world's garbage problems?

THE SIMPLE PRESENT TENSE

Use the simple present tense when you want to talk about the following actions:

1. an action that you do every day
   Yolanda gets up early every morning.
   Arnold smokes a lot.

2. an action that is a fact or general truth
   Water boils at 212°F or 100°C.

Affirmative Statements

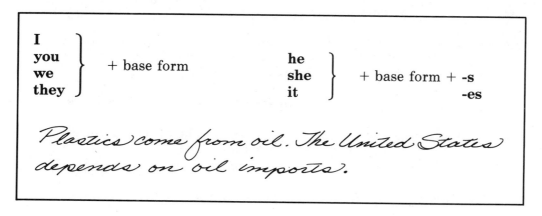

I
you
we
they
} + base form

he
she
it
} + base form + **-s**
   -es

Plastics come from oil. The United States depends on oil imports.

> ### Examples
>
> There are many sources of energy in the world today. Oil and coal **come** from under the ground. We **burn** coal and oil to make heat. We also **mine** uranium, a radioactive mineral, to produce nuclear energy. Solar energy **comes** from the heat of the sun. The sun **supplies** an enormous amount of energy. Wind also **produces** energy, and the ocean **does** too.

■ ACTIVITY 4A

❏ Fill in each blank with the correct form of the simple present tense.

Coal is a major source of energy in the United States. A lot of coal

mining ___*takes*___ place in the Appalachian Mountains in the eastern
(take)

part of the country.

A coal miner usually _____ long, hard hours. He or
(work)

she _____ into the mines when it is still dark, often before 6:00 in
(go)

the morning. The miner _____ a hat with a bright light on it so he
(wear)

or she can see. The miner _____ heavy tools when he or she
(carry)

_____ down in the mine. The miner _____ these tools to
(go)   (use)

break off pieces of coal. Sometimes the miner _____ explosives to
(use)

break up the coal. Then the miner _____ the coal onto railroad
(load)

cars. These railroad cars _____ the coal up out of the mine. When
(carry)

the coal miner _____ work and _____ back out of the
(finish)   (come)

mine, he or she is covered with black coal dust.

Coal mining is a dangerous occupation. One of the dangers is the

black coal dust that the miners _____. The dust sometimes
(breathe)

_____ black lung disease. Coal miners often _____
(cause)   (have)

trouble with their lungs as well as other health problems.

❏ Write a paragraph about someone you know who has an interesting (boring, dangerous, and so on) job.

ACTIVITY 4B

Fill in each blank with the correct form of the simple present tense.

　　　All power plants *produce* heat. The process _____ in
　　　　　　　　　　　(produce)　　　　　　　　　　　　　　　　(start)
different ways. Some plants _____ oil, and others _____
　　　　　　　　　　　　　　　(burn)　　　　　　　　　　　　　　(use)
coal or uranium. When these fuels _____, they _____ a
　　　　　　　　　　　　　　　　　　(burn)　　　　　　　(give off)
lot of heat. This heat _____ water and _____ steam. The
　　　　　　　　　　　　(boil)　　　　　　　　　(create)
steam then _____ a turbine, and this _____ electricity.
　　　　　　　(spin)　　　　　　　　　　　　(generate)
　　　　The fuels that _____ from under the ground—oil, coal, natural
　　　　　　　　　　　(come)
gas, uranium—_____ most of the energy we _____ in
　　　　　　　(supply)　　　　　　　　　　　　　　　(use)
our daily lives. But there are other sources that _____ energy.
　　　　　　　　　　　　　　　　　　　　　　　　(provide)
　　　　Every day, the earth _____ 10,000 times more energy from the
　　　　　　　　　　　　(receive)
sun than we _____ from all other kinds of fuel together. Many
　　　　　　(get)
countries _____ solar energy. In the United States, for example,
　　　　　(use)
30,000 homes _____ solar heat. In Israel, 200,000 homes
　　　　　　　(use)
_____ solar water heaters. In Japan, more than two million
　(have)
buildings _____ their heat from solar water heaters, and, in
　　　　　(get)
Australia, the law _____ solar water heaters on all new buildings.
　　　　　　　　(require)
A disadvantage of solar energy is that it _____ a very large area to
　　　　　　　　　　　　　　　　　　　　　(take)
collect solar heat for use by a small number of people. An advantage of

solar energy is that it is very clean and plentiful.

Negative Statements

I
you
we
they } + **do not** + base form

Oil spills don't happen that often.

he
she
it } + **does not** + base form

The United States doesn't import all its oil.

Contractions: **do**   + **not** = **don't**
       does + **not** = **doesn't**

Examples

The supply of oil in the earth is limited. Oil **doesn't exist** in infinite amounts. Most countries **don't produce** enough oil for their energy needs, so they import oil from other countries. The OPEC (Organization of Petroleum Exporting Countries) countries have the capacity to produce more oil, but they **don't want** to use up their oil too rapidly. For this reason, they limit their production.

■ ACTIVITY 4C

Look at the underlined parts of the sentences. Change each underlined part of a sentence to the negative so it makes sense in the blank space in the following sentence.

(The utility company, Con Elec, turned off YOLANDA'S electricity this morning. YOLANDA is talking to an official of the utility company.)

YOLANDA: Why did you turn off my electricity? You have my payment now.

OFFICIAL: I'm sorry. We ___*don't have your payment.*___
     We have <u>half</u> your payment.

YOLANDA: That's not true! You're wrong. Con Elec always <u>overcharges</u> me.

OFFICIAL: Con Elec _doesn't overcharge anybody_ , miss.
You probably <u>have three or four air conditioners</u> in your house.

YOLANDA: That's ridiculous! I _____ .
I have only one air conditioner.

OFFICIAL: Well, you probably <u>leave it on all day.</u>

YOLANDA: What are you talking about! I _____ .
It doesn't even work.

OFFICIAL: Well, you use something, Miss. You <u>probably have a lot of other</u>
<u>electrical appliances.</u>

YOLANDA: That's outrageous! I _____ .
All I have is <u>one</u> electric typewriter.

OFFICIAL: Well, I don't know what to say to you. <u>Con Elec tries to be fair.</u>

YOLANDA: _____ !
Con Elec raises its rates for no reason. Con Elec <u>makes a fortune!</u>

OFFICIAL: No, we _____ .
Con Elec <u>loses money</u> because of people like you.

YOLANDA: Con Elec _____ .
Con Elec makes money. Kindly turn my electricity back on. I
paid my bill.

Questions

(Question word) + do + { I / you / we / they } + base form?

How often do you read the newspaper?

(Question word) + does + { he / she / it } + base form?

How often does Jack read the newspaper?

Examples

Do U.S. oil companies **drill** for oil only in the United States?
No, they don't. They drill for oil all over the world.

Does the United States **use** other sources of energy besides oil?
Yes, it does. It uses coal, gas, nuclear, and solar energy.

Do the big oil companies also **own** a lot of coal and uranium mines?
Yes, they do. They own more than one billion tons of coal and a lot of the uranium in the United States.

Where **do** the big oil companies **get** crude oil?
They get it from Alaska, Norway, Venezuela, Nigeria, Mexico, the Middle East, and the continental United States.

What **does** an oil refinery **do?**
It takes crude oil and makes it into heating oil and gasoline.

Who and *What* Questions

When *Who* or *What* is the subject of the verb in the question, the verb is always singular. When *Who* or *What* is the object of the verb, the question formation is the same as with all other *wh-* questions. In formal English, we use *Whom* for the object questions.

Examples

Subject Questions

Who **mines** uranium?
A lot of the big oil companies **do.**

Who **regulates** the production of nuclear energy?
The government **does.**

What **powers** most modern submarines?
Nuclear reactors **do.**
Note: When you follow *What* with a plural noun, the verb is plural:

What companies operate nuclear power plants?
Utility companies **do.**

Object Questions

Who **do** the OPEC countries **sell** their oil to?
They sell it to countries all over the world.

Who **does** Mexico **sell** most of its oil to?
It sells it to the United States.

Simple Present Tense Charts

Affirmative and Negative Statements

Subject	Verb			
	Helping Verb Do/Does	*Not*	*Base Form* -s/-ses	
Oil			comes	from under the ground.
The big oil companies			own	a lot of coal and uranium.
Oil	does	not	exist	in an infinite supply.
The OPEC countries	do	not	want	to use up their oil.

Questions

Wh- *Question Word*	*Helping Verb* Do/Does	*Subject*	*Base Form*	
	Does	the United States	use	nuclear power?
What	does	an oil refinery	do	?
Who	does	Mexico	sell	most of its oil to?
		Wh- Questions as Subject	Third-Person Singular	
		Who	mines	uranium?

NOTES

1. When the base form of a verb ends in *ss, sh, ch, x, z,* or *o,* you add *-es* for the third-person singular (*he, she, it*).
    pass → passes   fix → fixes   go → goes   do → does

2. The verb *to have* is irregular in the simple present tense.
    I, you, we, they + *have*
    he, she, it   + *has*

■ ACTIVITY 4D

Write the correct question for each answer. Use the word in parentheses in the question.

(You are a reporter writing an article about solar energy. You are interviewing a producer of solar heaters.)

REPORTER: *Does your company produce* solar energy?
                                      (produce)

PRODUCER: Yes, we do. We make solar water heaters.

REPORTER: _____ solar energy _____ a lot of money?
                                                       (cost)

PRODUCER: Yes, it does at the present time.

REPORTER: Why _____ the government _____
                          (negative)   **(help)**
your company?

PRODUCER: It helps us a little. But solar energy isn't very profitable yet.

The technology isn't very developed.

REPORTER: _____ some countries _____ solar water
                                            (require)
heaters in new homes and office buildings?

PRODUCER: Yes, they do. They require them in new buildings in Australia.

REPORTER: _____ a solar water heater _____ a house
                                                     (heat)
after the sun goes down?

PRODUCER: Yes, it does.

REPORTER: What _____ a solar heater _____ ?
                                            (do)
How _____ it _____ ?
                                  (operate)

PRODUCER: It collects solar heat during the day and stores it so that you

have heat when there is no sun.

■ ACTIVITY 4E

Write two different questions beginning with *Who*. Write one about the subject of the sentence and one about the object. Remember that the *Who* subject question is always singular. Look at the answer first.

1. The United States buys oil from the Middle East producers of oil every day.

   Who buys oil from the Middle East producers?

   The United States does.

   Who does the United States buy oil from?

   It buys oil from the Middle East producers of oil.

2. The president often asks the American public for cooperation in conserving energy.

   _____

   The president does.

   _____

   He asks the American public.

3. Congressmen sometimes disagree with the president about his energy policies.

   _____

   Congressmen do.

   _____

   They disagree with the president.

4. Congress often funds groups interested in protecting the environment.

   _____

   Congress does.

   _____

   They fund groups interested in protecting the environment.

FREQUENCY ADVERBS

Frequency adverbs are often used with the simple present tense to indicate how often or how many times we do something. They are used with other tenses also. Frequency adverbs occur in different positions in the sentence.

Middle-Position Frequency Adverbs

always	rarely
almost always	hardly ever
usually	almost never
often	never
seldom	

AFFIRMATIVE STATEMENTS

These frequency adverbs usually go after the verb *be* and before other verbs.

> **Examples**
>
> *The Verb* Be
>
> The big oil companies **are** *always* interested in finding new places to drill for oil. The oil in Alaska is not easy to drill because it **is** *often* offshore and deep under the sea.
>
> *Other Verbs*
>
> Oil money is very important in Alaska. The state *usually* **gets** about eighty-five percent of its budget from oil sales and taxes from oil companies. Alaskans *always* **ask** themselves this question: How can we keep the oil money coming in and protect our beautiful state from oil spills at the same time?

NEGATIVE STATEMENTS

In negative statements, we usually place *always, almost always, usually,* and *often* after *not*. This is true of *be* and other verbs.

> **Examples**
>
> The production of oil does**n't** *always* increase from year to year. When companies drill for new oil wells, they do**n't** *always* find oil.

Frequency Adverbs in Initial or Middle Position

Sometimes, occasionally, and *frequently* can go at the beginning or in the middle of a sentence.

Frequency Adverbs in Middle or Final Position

The following expressions usually come at the end of the sentence. Sometimes they come in the middle.

once a day	every day	every now and then
twice a week	every year	every once in a while
three times a year	every summer	from time to time
five times a week	all the time	

Examples

The energy producers and environmentalists[6] disagree about nuclear energy *all the time.* Environmentalists say that nuclear plants give off small but dangerous amounts of radiation from *time to time.* Energy producers say that they check radiation levels *every day,* and there is no danger.

Questions and Short Answers

POSITION OF FREQUENCY ADVERBS

The frequency adverbs discussed on page 58 usually go after the subject in *yes/no* questions. In a short answer, they also usually go after the subject.

Examples

Are American homes and office buildings often overheated and over air-conditioned?
Yes, they *often* **are.**

Do American drivers frequently waste gasoline?
Yes, they *frequently* **do.**

---

[6]*Environmentalists* are people who work to protect the environment.

QUESTIONS WITH *EVER*

We often use *ever* in *yes/no* questions when we want to ask about frequency. *Ever* means "at any time." Don't use *ever* in the main clause of an affirmative statement. Use a frequency adverb to answer a question with *ever*.

Examples

Do people *ever* use solar energy to heat their homes?
 Yes, they *sometimes* do. About 20,000 American homes use solar heat.

Do people *ever* use windmills for energy in their homes?
 Yes, they *sometimes* do.

QUESTIONS WITH *How Often*

We also use *how often* in questions when we want to ask about frequency.

Examples

How often **do** American utility companies send out bills to their customers?
They send them out *once a month*.

How often **does** a new model of an American car come out on the market?
A new model comes out *every year*.

⊗ ■ ACTIVITY 4F

❑ Here is a paragraph about the climate of Alaska. To make it accurate, you need to add frequency adverbs. First read the paragraph.

   A lot of oil comes from Alaska. The climate of Alaska varies in different parts of the state and affects the lives of the oil workers. The Panhandle is an area in the southeastern part of the state next to Canada. (1) Winters there are mild. (2) It rains in the winter, (3) but it doesn't snow. The interior of Alaska has very different weather conditions. (4) The winters there are extremely cold. (5) The temperature reaches −40°C. (6) In this same area, however, the summers are very hot but short. The northern coast of Alaska is the area where oil was discovered. (7) This area isn't free of ice. (8) The ground there doesn't thaw; it is permanently frozen. With its different climates and types of terrain, Alaska is a land (9) where travel is a problem. Oil workers do not move about easily in the winter months. If they make a trip, (10) it is by air. Air travel is still the easiest form of travel in this state.

❑ Rewrite the paragraph (use a separate sheet of paper) and put the following frequency adverbs in the correct position in the sentence or part of the sentence that has the number in front of it. The first sentence is written for you as an example. Continue rewriting the paragraph, adding the frequency adverbs.

1. usually

2. often

3. seldom (remember that *seldom* is already negative, so you must change the verb to the affirmative for this sentence)

4. always

5. sometimes

6. almost always

7. rarely (remember to change the verb to the affirmative)

8. never (remember to change the verb to the affirmative)

9. frequently

10. often

1. *Winters there are usually mild.*

❑ Write some *yes/no* questions about the paragraph on the climate of Alaska. Put the frequency adverb in the correct position in each question. Then write a short answer using a frequency adverb.

(Look at 1.)   1. *Are winters usually mild in the Panhandle?*
Yes, they usually are.

(Look at 2.)   2. _____

_____

(Look at 5.)   3. _____

_____

_____

(Look at 8.
Use *ever* in
this question.)   4. _____

_____

(Look at 10.)   5. _____

_____

❑ Now write a paragraph (on a separate sheet of paper) about a season in a place in your country. Follow the example about Alaska and use frequency adverbs.

■ ACTIVITY 4G

Every person feels differently about the morning. Some people are in a bad mood and are very slow in the morning; others are happy and full of energy. Some do exercises. Some only need fifteen or twenty minutes to get ready for work or school; others need an hour or more. Some people are late every morning. Some people don't talk in the morning. Some need a cup of black coffee right away. Some eat a big breakfast; others eat nothing.

❑ Write a short composition about how you feel and what you do in the morning. Use a lot of frequency adverbs (*always, almost always, usually, frequently, often, sometimes, seldom, rarely, hardly ever, almost never, never, one/twice/three times* a _____, every morning, and so on).

❑ Write about a person who does the opposite of what you do in the morning. Now you will write in the third-person singular.

■ ACTIVITY 4H

❑ This is an imaginary meeting. The Nuclear Regulatory Commission (NRC) is interested in the safety of nuclear power plants. The NRC wants to know how often accidents happen, how often the company does a safety check on equipment, and so on.

Write questions for the NRC to find out information. Write some *yes/no* questions and some questions with *how often*. Ask how often the workers have accidents, how often the plant changes the uranium, how often it checks for radiation, how often it checks workers for exposure to radiation, how often it is dangerous to go into the plant, and how often they wash down the plant. Then answer the questions.

You may want to use some of this vocabulary in your questions or answers.

Vocabulary

wash down:	to clean the surfaces of the plant with water
nuclear power plant:	a factory where uranium is used to produce electricity
radioactivity:	rays of energy that are dangerous to people
accident:	something wrong that happens in some part of the plant
overheated:	too hot; unsafe. When the uranium isn't cool enough, it becomes dangerous.
shutdown:	the closing of a plant because of safety problems
routine shutdown:	the closing of a plant on a regular schedule
exposure:	nearness to the dangerous rays of energy. When these rays get absorbed by the body, we say the person has been *exposed* to radiation.

CHAIRMAN OF THE NRC: _How often do you have accidents in the plant?_

OFFICIAL OF NUCLEAR POWER PLANT: _We almost never do._

CHAIRMAN: _How often do the workers go for medical checkups?_

OFFICIAL: _They see our doctors almost every three months._

CHAIRMAN: _____?

OFFICIAL: _____

CHAIRMAN: _____?

OFFICIAL: _____

CHAIRMAN: _____?

OFFICIAL: _____

☐ Person A is an official of a nuclear power plant. Person B is an environmentalist asking questions about this nuclear plant. Role play a meeting between these two people. Ask *how often* and *yes/no* questions.

STATIVE VERBS AND VERBS OF PERCEPTION

Stative Verbs in the Simple Present Tense—Nonaction

Certain verbs are rarely used in the present continuous (*-ing*) tense, even when they have a *now* meaning. These verbs are called stative verbs, or verbs of perception. They are *see, hear, know, believe, doubt, forget, remember, understand, want, desire, love, hate, like, dislike, own, belong, contain, seem, appear, prefer,* and *exist*.

Examples

(JACK, MOLLY, YOLANDA, and ARNOLD are driving to YOLANDA's house to listen to the president's speech on energy on TV.)

YOLANDA: Let's hurry. I **want** to hear the president's speech. It starts in fifteen minutes.

JACK: Oh, no! My gas gauge is on empty. Sorry, Yolanda, but I **need** gas.

MOLLY: There's a station on the corner. Why don't you pull over there?

JACK: My car is falling apart. It's so old.

MOLLY: Oh, I **like** it. It has character.

YOLANDA: Come on, let's go. You know we **need** to hurry.

Verbs That Express Action or Stative Meaning

Certain verbs have one meaning when used in the simple present tense and another meaning in the present continuous tense. These verbs are *think, look, have, taste, feel, smell,* and *see.* When they are used in the present continuous tense, they describe an action that is happening *now.* When they are used in the simple present tense, they have a stative meaning that can describe a quality (*feel, taste, smell, look*), an opinion (*think*), possession (*have*), or measurement (*weigh*).

Examples

(JACK, MOLLY, ARNOLD, and YOLANDA are at YOLANDA's house watching the president on television.)

JACK: The president **looks** very tired. Maybe he has a cold.

MOLLY: Yeah, he does. Why **is** he **looking** at something over the camera?

JACK: I **think** he's reading his speech from a screen.

ARNOLD: Jack, you're frowning. What **are** you **thinking** about?

JACK: **I'm thinking** about all the money I spend on gasoline, and prices are going up again.

ARNOLD: Why **do** you **have** a big car?

JACK: I bought it secondhand[7] a long time ago.

YOLANDA: Please stop talking. **I'm having** a hard time hearing anything. I **think** this is an important speech.

■ ACTIVITY 4I

YOLANDA is a reporter for a television station. She is interviewing a scientist about "the greenhouse effect." Fill in the blanks using the simple present tense of the verbs in parentheses.

YOLANDA: I'm happy to have here with me today Dr. Ernest Brock, who

is an expert on the environment, especially the climate. Dr.

Brock ___*does*___ research at Columbia University. Dr.
      (do)

Brock, many experts say that the 1980s had the four hottest

years in this century, and some of us probably remember the

heat wave in July and August of 1988. _____ you

_____ that the heat wave was the result of "the
   (believe)

greenhouse effect"?

[7]*Secondhand* means "previously owned and used by someone else."

DR. BROCK: Yes, I _____. I think we _____ to face the
(short answer)   (need)

truth here.

YOLANDA: What exactly _____ we _____ when we say
(mean)

"the greenhouse effect"? I _____ this term all the
(hear)

time, but I _____ it completely.
(negative, **understand**)

DR. BROCK: Well, "the greenhouse effect" refers to a layer of gases in the

air that is causing the earth to get warmer each year.

YOLANDA: How _____ this layer of gases[8] _____ that?
(do)

DR. BROCK: Well, certain gases _____ heat to escape into
(negative, **permit**)

the earth's atmosphere. Take carbon dioxide, for example. CO_2

_____ the earth's heat. Each year we _____
(trap)   (release)

more and more CO_2 into the air. We _____ it "the
(call)

greenhouse effect" because CO_2 _____ the same way
(work)

as the panes of glass in a greenhouse[9]; they _____
(allow)

the sun's heat to enter the greenhouse and warm it, but they

_____ part of that heat from escaping.
(prevent)

YOLANDA: _____ the burning of fuels[10] like oil and coal

_____ off CO_2?
(give)

DR. BROCK: That's right. The burning of these fuels _____ most
(cause)

of the problems.

---

[8]*Layer* is the subject of the verb here.
[9]A *greenhouse* is a building made of glass in which you can grow plants.
[10]*Burning* is the subject of the verb here.

YOLANDA: But what about the trees? _____ the trees
                (negative)

  _____ CO_2?
   (absorb)

DR. BROCK: Yes, but that _____ us to the second big problem—
              (bring)

deforestation. We are destroying the world's rain forests.

Every year, farmers in Brazil _____ down thousands
                   (cut)

of trees. Of course, they _____ to clear the land for
              (need)

farming. But every year, Brazil _____ fewer trees, and
              (have)

more CO_2 _____ in the air. Of course, I
      (remain)

_____ to blame Brazil for this problem. All countries
(negative, **want**)

_____ the responsibility.
  (share)

YOLANDA: Yes, that's true. What other gases _____ to the
               (add)

problem?

DR. BROCK: Well, methane _____ the escape of heat into the
          (block)

atmosphere too.

YOLANDA: What _____ methane?
    (produce)

DR. BROCK: Cattle. Cows _____ off a lot of gas as a product of
        (give)

digestion. Another greenhouse gas is nitrous oxide.

YOLANDA: And where _____ that _____ from?
           (come)

DR. BROCK: _____ you _____ a car?
        (own)

YOLANDA: Yes, I _____. _____ the exhaust
   (short answer)

_____ nitrous oxide?
 (contain)

DR. BROCK: That's right. You don't look like a gardener to me, but

_____ your dad _____ a garden?
         (have)

YOLANDA: My father _____ gardening, but my
 (negative, **enjoy**)

mother _____. She _____ hours in her
 (**spend**)

garden in the summer.

DR. BROCK: And _____ she _____ chemical fertilizers?
 (**use**)

YOLANDA: I think she _____. Is nitrous oxide in them too?

DR. BROCK: Uh, huh. So your mother's beautiful garden

_____ to the problem too.
 (**contribute**)

YOLANDA: And what about Freon[11] in our refrigerators? I heard

something about that.

DR. BROCK: Yes, and your air conditioner _____ Freon for
 (**use**)

cooling too. And sometimes when we _____ out our
 (**throw**)

old refrigerators or air conditioners, some of that Freon

_____ into the air and _____ the problem
 (**escape**)   (**make**)

worse.

YOLANDA: Well, thank you very much, Dr. Brock, for helping us all to

understand "the greenhouse effect." I certainly _____
 (**know**)

much more about it now.

☐ What predictions do scientists make about what will happen as a result
of the earth's becoming warmer each year? Do you believe the scientists
who warn us about the greenhouse effect? What can we do about this
problem?

☐ Review the vocabulary and the facts in the interview with Dr. Brock.
Then role play a similar interview between Dr. Brock and a reporter.
You can include more students in the interview if there are three or four
scientists and three or four reporters.

[11]*Freon* is a gas used for cooling.

■ **ACTIVITY 4J**   *Paragraph about me* → *terrible day*
                                        → *for past, present, future*

Fill in the blanks with either the <u>present continuous</u> tense or the simple
<u>present</u> tense of the verbs in parentheses. (A reporter is interviewing a
supervisor at a nuclear power plant.)

REPORTER: We are inside the control room of the Apple Core Nuclear

Power Plant. I *am interviewing* Mr. Wilkins and
                    (interview)

_____*Asking*_____ questions about nuclear power in general and
     (ask)

the Apple Core Plant in particular. What kind of material

_____*do*_____ power plants _____*use*_____ for nuclear fuel?
     (do)   **(use)**

MR. WILKINS: Well, for the most part we _____*use*_____ uranium.
                                          (use)

REPORTER: I'm going to follow Mr. Wilkins and ask him questions. Mr.

Wilkins, what _____*Are*_____ you _____*doing*_____ right now?
                                        (do)

MR. WILKINS: I *'m checking* the safety valves for the plant's
               (check)

cooling system.

REPORTER: How often _____*DO*_____ you _____*check*_____ them?
                                            (check)

MR. WILKINS: We _____*check*_____ them several times a day.
                 (check)

REPORTER: How many men usually _____*work*_____ in this room? *NO AUXILIARY with*
                                (work)   *how many*

MR. WILKINS: Half a dozen or so.

REPORTER: What _____*Are*_____ those men _____*doing*_____ over there in
                                            (do)

the corner?

MR. WILKINS: They _____*Are putting*_____ on protective clothing. When
                        (put)

we _____*go*_____ into many areas of the plant, we
       (go)

_____*wear*_____ this protective clothing.
     (wear)

REPORTER: _____*DO*_____ supervisors _____*monitor*_____ the men and the
                                        (monitor)

plant for radioactivity every day?

MR. WILKINS: Oh, yes. Whenever a worker ___leaves___ the plant,
(leave)

he ___checks___ himself for radioactivity at the door. The
(check)

man over there ___is record___ radiation levels in this room
(record)

right now. We ___re monitoring___ radiation all the time. In fact,
(monitor)

the equipment shows that nothing ___is leaking___ into the
(leak)

environment right now.

REPORTER: ___DOESN'T___ your plant ever ___HAVE___ leaks?
(negative)   (have)

MR. WILKINS: Well, occasionally a small amount of radiation

___escapes___ into the environment. But this
(escape)

___Doesn't happen___ very often.
(negative, **happen**)

REPORTER: Thank you very much, Mr. Wilkins. This has been most

interesting.

EXPRESSING YOUR IDEAS

1. Does your country produce oil? Does it import or export oil? Are there energy problems in your country? What are they?

2. Is there a conflict between big oil companies and people who want to protect the environment in your country? Describe it.

3. Why are there so many oil spills from tankers? How can we prevent them?

4. Are oil prices very high in your country? Are they controlled by the government? Do the prices increase every year? What problems or benefits does this create for the average person?

5. How is electricity produced in your country? Is there a shortage of energy to produce electricity? If so, does your country have a plan to deal with this problem?

6. What are some other sources of energy in addition to oil?

7. Does your country operate or plan to operate nuclear power plants? What are the advantages and disadvantages of nuclear power?

8. Does your country use or plan to use solar energy? What are some of the advantages and disadvantages of solar power?

9. Does your country waste energy? If you think it does, describe how. Many people say Americans waste a great deal of energy. Do you agree? Do you know any examples of this? Describe what you have noticed.

10. What do you know about the pollution of the oceans? What are the different sources of this pollution? What are the negative results? What laws do we have now to stop the pollution? What else can we do about this problem?

5

THERE + BE AND COUNT AND MASS NOUNS

Unknown Indian from a southeastern Idaho Reservation, 1897.

NATIVE AMERICANS AND IMMIGRANTS

Dialog

(ARNOLD, YOLANDA, JACK, and MOLLY are sitting in a coffee shop. YOLANDA is planning to visit her parents in New Jersey in the afternoon.)

ARNOLD: How about another cup of coffee, Yolanda? **How much time** do you have before your train leaves?

YOLANDA: **Not much.** There's a train in about thirty minutes.

ARNOLD: It only takes you about ten minutes to get to the train station from here. **There's time** for another cup of coffee.

JACK: Yolanda, were your parents born in this country?

YOLANDA: No, they came here in the fifties.[1] **A great many Puerto Ricans** immigrated to New York around that time.

MOLLY: **How many Puerto Ricans** are there in New York now?

YOLANDA: I don't know exactly, but **there are** more **Puerto Ricans** here than in San Juan.

JACK: It's really amazing to think about the number of different ethnic groups in this country. Just in New York alone **there are thousands** of Greeks, Italians, Chinese—

MOLLY: Jack, how about you? Where are your parents from?

JACK: My parents were born here, but my grandparents came over here from Poland around 1915.

ARNOLD: Immigrants really had **a lot of problems** in those days, didn't they? Did your grandparents know **much English** when they came here?

JACK: No, they knew **very little.** They just knew **a few words** like "hello," "good-bye," "thank you," and "how much."

MOLLY: How did they manage?[2] Did your grandfather have **much trouble** finding a job?

JACK: **There weren't many good jobs** in those days if you couldn't speak English. Luckily my grandparents already had **a few relatives** in this country, and they helped my grandfather find a job.

YOLANDA: What kind of job did he get?

JACK: He worked in a shoe factory for **many years.** He saved every penny and finally bought his own business. They're living a very comfortable life today.

[1]*In the fifties* means "from 1950 through 1959."
[2]*How did they manage?* means "What did they do to overcome all the problems they had?"

MOLLY: That's a typical American success story, isn't it?

JACK: It sure is. My grandparents are Americans now, but they take **a great deal of pride** in where they come from.

ARNOLD: **A lot of people** today are interested in tracing their roots.[3] Most people in this country have an immigrant background. **Very few Americans** can say that their ancestors came over here on the *Mayflower.*[4]

Listening Comprehension Questions

1. Were Yolanda's parents born in the United States?
2. When did a great many Puerto Ricans immigrate to New York?
3. How much English did Jack's grandparents know when they came to the United States from Poland?
4. Did Jack's grandfather have much trouble finding a job?
5. Do his grandparents take a great deal of pride in their roots?
6. How many Americans can say that their ancestors came to the United States on the *Mayflower*?

THERE + BE

There + be is an extremely common structure in English. We can use it with all tenses. Here we show only the present and past tenses.

Statements

> There $\left.\begin{array}{l} \textbf{is} \\ \textbf{was} \end{array}\right\}$ **(not)** + singular noun
>
> There $\left.\begin{array}{l} \textbf{are} \\ \textbf{were} \end{array}\right\}$ **(not)** + plural noun
>
> *There are many different ethnic groups in this country.*
>
> Contraction: **there is = there's**

[3]*Roots* means "family background; where your ancestors came from."

[4]*The Mayflower* is the ship that brought the first European settlers to Massachusetts in 1620.

Questions

Is
Are
Was
Were
} **there** + subject?

Are there many different ethnic groups in your country?

Examples

The United States is a nation of immigrants. However, the American Indians lived in this country long before the first European immigrants arrived in the fifteenth century. At this time, **there were many Indian tribes** in all parts of the country. Each tribe had its own language, its own religion, and its own customs. When the white settlers pushed west, **there were many conflicts** between them and the various Indian tribes. Partly because **there was never a united Indian nation** of all the different Indian tribes, the Indians gradually lost their lands to the settlers.

Questions

Why **was there a conflict** between the Indians and the settlers during the settlement of the West?
Because the settlers wanted the Indian land to raise cattle and crops, but the Indians wanted to keep the land for hunting.

Were there any peace treaties between the U.S. government and the Indian tribes?
Yes, **there were.**

Is there land in the United States today that belongs to the American Indians?
Yes, **there is.**

Are there still **many disputes** over land between the U.S. government and the Indians?
Yes, **there are.**

Today **there are** still **many Indian tribes** that live all over the United States. For the most part, they live on reservations. This is land that the federal government gave the Indians to live on after the Indians lost the conflicts with the white settlers. Many Indians are dissatisfied with these reservations. **There is a movement** among American Indians today to reclaim some of their lost land.

Contrast *There Is/There Are* with *It Is (It's)/They Are*

Don't confuse *there is* with *it is* (*it's*) or *there are* with *they are* (*they're*).

Examples

Every year, **there is** an Indian festival in Anadark, Oklahoma. **It is** very popular with tourists. **There are** several performances that deal with Cherokee Indian history. **They are** always very emotional performances because the Indians dramatize a tragic period in their history when the United States government forced them to move away from their land in Tennessee to a reservation in Oklahoma.

■ ACTIVITY 5A

Fill in the blanks with *there is, there are, there was,* or *there were.*

Before 1840, *there weren't* many white people in the western
                    (negative)

part of the United States. In the 1840s, white people began to move out

West. _____ many fights between the settlers and the Indians

over the land. _____ also fights between white hunters and

the Indians. The white hunters killed millions of buffalo. In 1865,

_____ 15 million of these animals. By 1885, _____ only

a thousand. The Indians needed the buffalo to survive. Without the buffalo

and the land, _____ any way for the Indians to keep their old
                 (negative)

way of life.

Many terrible battles took place between the Indians and the settlers. Many lives were lost on both sides. During the last part of the nineteenth century, fighting was especially intense. The Indians made a great effort to try to maintain their way of life. However, they did not have very modern weapons.

In 1880, _____ a tragic confrontation between the U.S. Army and a group of Sioux Indians in Wounded Knee, South Dakota. The U.S. Army ordered all the Indian men to give them their guns. Two or three of the Indians refused, and the soldiers started shooting.

The fight was very bloody. After it was over, _____ many
(negative)
Indian survivors. An Indian chief, Red Cloud, said, "_____ no hope on earth." Another chief, Black Elk, said, "_____ no center any longer, and the sacred tree is dead."

_____ 1,500,000 Indians in the United States today.

_____ still many different tribes, each with its own language and traditions. _____ 300 different Indian languages and dialects that are spoken today. _____ many tribes today that still make their
(negative)
living in the same ways they used to before the white settlers came, but a few have preserved their old ways. For example, _____ a tribe in Arizona called the Navajo that still makes beautiful silver and turquoise jewelry. The Navajo use the traditional designs that have been in their tribe for hundreds of years. _____ also a revival of interest in Indian art forms, such as pottery, rugs, and baskets. _____ some Navajo baskets that sell for over a hundred dollars.

The Navajo are also an example of a tribe that wants to become part of industrialized society. _____ valuable deposits of oil, coal, and uranium on Navajo land. The Navajo want control of the development of these resources.

■ ACTIVITY 5B

❑ Choose a place that had special meaning for you at some point in your past. Describe this place and what you used to do there. Use *there is, there are, there was,* and *there were.*

❑ Choose a place that has changed over the years. Describe what it was like in the past. Use *there was* and *there were.* Then write about what it is like today. Use *there is* and *there are.*

■ ACTIVITY 5C

❑ Use the past tense. Fill in the blanks with *there was, there were, it was,* or *they were.*

Thanksgiving is a national holiday that people in the United States celebrate in November. In the early seventeenth century, _____ a small community of people in Massachusetts. _____ people who had left England to find religious freedom in the New World.

_____ called Pilgrims. In 1621, at the end of their first year in the new country, _____ a big feast and celebration to give thanks to God. _____ the first Thanksgiving. At this feast, _____ also many Indians. _____ guests of the Pilgrims at this feast because they had helped the Pilgrims during the long and difficult first year in New World.

❑ Use the present tense to describe the picture on page 79. Fill in the blanks with *there is, there are, it is,* or *they are.*

This is a scene of the first Thanksgiving Day celebration. The Pilgrims are preparing the feast. *There are* also two Indians in this picture.

They are guests of the Pilgrims. One of the Indians is carrying a

basket. _____ some fish in it for the feast. _____ a gift

from the Indians. The man in the right-hand corner of the picture is

carrying something in his arms. _____ logs for the fire. Most of

the food for the feast was probably cooked over an open fire outdoors. On

the table, _____ a large basket of vegetables. _____ native

to North America, not to Europe. The Indians taught the Pilgrims how to

grow these new kinds of food. Beside the basket of vegetables,

_____ a large turkey. All the turkeys at the first Thanksgiving

were wild. Even today, no Thanksgiving dinner is complete without a

turkey. However, _____ very few wild turkeys left. Today's

Thanksgiving Day turkeys come from the supermarket, not the forest.

COUNT AND MASS NOUNS

A count noun is a noun that has a plural form (usually *s* or *es*). It is always possible to put a number in front of a count noun. For example, *one* table, *two* tables. Mass nouns (noncount nouns) do not have a plural form. They are almost always singular, but we never use the indefinite articles *a* or *an* before a mass noun. Here are some common examples.

water	oil	pollution
coffee	gold	advice
rice	money	

Statements about a Large Quantity

Look at the following lists.

For Count Nouns	For Mass Nouns
a lot of	a lot of
many	a great deal of
a great many	quite a bit of
quite a few	

Note: We use the expression *a lot of* when we talk about a large quantity of both count and mass nouns. *A lot of* is conversational. It is not the preferred written form.

Examples

Count Nouns

The only native Americans are Indians. The United States is really a country of immigrants. Europeans began to arrive in the United States in the seventeenth century. Immigrants are still coming to the United States.

One of the major periods of immigration was during the nineteenth century. **A lot of people** came to the United States to escape the economic or political problems in Europe at that time. In those days, the sea journey from Europe to America was very difficult. **Many passengers** became sick. **A lot** died before they reached America. **Quite a few** arrived with nothing but the clothes on their backs. **Many of these new Americans** found a better life in the United States. Some of them later became rich. **A great many famous Americans** are immigrants or the descendants of immigrants.

Mass Nouns

Immigrants came for a number of reasons. America was a land of promise. **There was a great deal of available land** ready for farming. The Midwest attracted many settlers because it has **a lot of rich, fertile soil.** The Midwest is known as the "breadbasket" of the country. Despite the abundance of good farmland, the newcomers who settled here suffered **quite a bit of hardship.** For example, there were prairie fires, droughts, and harsh winters.

NOTES:

1. It is not always necessary to repeat the noun. When you don't repeat the noun, don't use *of* after *a lot*.

2. In general, we don't use *much* before a mass noun in affirmative sentences because it will usually sound too formal or incorrect.

Statements about a Small Quantity

Use the following expressions to talk about small quantities of count and mass nouns.

For Count Nouns	For Mass Nouns
not many	not much
(very) few	(very) little
just / only } a few	just / only } a little
a few	a little

Examples

Mass Nouns

Immigrants came to this country because they had **very little hope** of making a better life for themselves in their native land. The difficult conditions in Europe forced them to emigrate. In the 1840s in Ireland, for example, there was a great potato famine. Potatoes were the staple of the Irish diet. Without potatoes, there **wasn't much food,** and many people starved. The journey to America did**n't cost much money** in those days—only about twenty dollars.

Count Nouns

Sometimes there weren't **many opportunities** for the immigrants in America. For example, when the Irish first arrived in Boston, **very few jobs** were open to them, and **only a few** were high paying. **Not many American workers** liked these "new Americans" because they worked for low pay. Because of this, wages for all workers went down. There were many disagreements and problems between the "old" Americans and the "new" ones.

Note: Sometimes you see *not a lot* in negative statements. However, the most common pattern is *not much* or *not many* when the sentence is negative.

Contrast of *Few/Little* with *A Few/A Little*

Few
or   has a different meaning from { a few.
Little   a little.

Few
or   has a meaning similar to { not many.
Little   not much.

A few
or   has a positive meaning similar to *some* when we are talking
A little about a small quantity.

Notice the difference in meaning.

1. *Very few good jobs were open to the immigrants.*
    (In this sentence, we mean that this was a real problem for the immigrants because the number of jobs was very limited.)

2. *Most of the immigrants had very little education.*
    (In this sentence, we mean that this was a real problem that made it difficult for them to find jobs.)

3. *A few good jobs were open to the immigrants.*
    (In this sentence, we mean that there were some good jobs for immigrants and that at least some immigrants had good job opportunities.)

4. *Some of the immigrants had a little education.*
    (In this sentence, we mean that these immigrants had some education.)

Questions

1. Use *how many* + count noun or *how much* + mass noun.

> ### *Examples*
>
> **How many immigrants** came to the United States during the nineteenth century?
> A great many did. Millions came then.
>
> **How much English** did they know when they arrived?
> In general, they didn't know much.
> They knew just a little.
> They knew only a few words.

2. In *yes/no* questions, follow these patterns.

$$\left.\begin{array}{l} \textit{many} \\ \textit{a lot of} \\ \textit{a large number of} \\ \textit{quite a few} \end{array}\right\} + \text{count noun}$$

$$\left.\begin{array}{l} \textit{much} \\ \textit{a great deal of} \\ \textit{a lot of} \end{array}\right\} + \text{mass noun}$$

> ### *Examples*
>
> Did they have **a great deal of knowledge** about the geography of the land they had to cross?
> No, they had **only a few crude maps.**
>
> Did settlers have **much trouble** crossing the country in covered wagons?
> Yes, they had **a great deal of trouble.**
>
> Did **many immigrants** settle in big cities?
> Many did, but many went west to farm also.
>
> Did **a large number of immigrants** become rich?
> No, they didn't, but a few did.

Ways to Count Mass Nouns

It is almost always possible to describe specific quantities of mass nouns—in other words, to count mass nouns. Here is a list of vocabulary to do this.

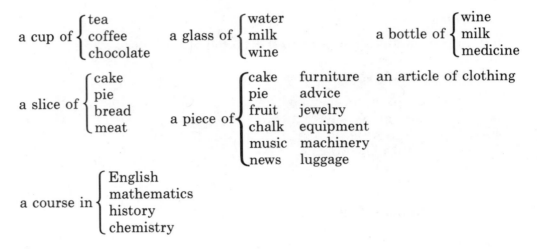

a cup of { tea, coffee, chocolate }

a glass of { water, milk, wine }

a bottle of { wine, milk, medicine }

a slice of { cake, pie, bread, meat }

a piece of { cake, pie, fruit, chalk, music, news, furniture, advice, jewelry, equipment, machinery, luggage }

an article of clothing

a course in { English, mathematics, history, chemistry }

To talk about a specific quantity of some mass nouns, we can also use other vocabulary.

Mass Nouns	Count Nouns
trouble	a problem
luggage	a suitcase
homework	a homework assignment, homework exercise
information	a fact
mail	a letter
jewelry	a ring, a necklace, a bracelet

Examples

How much English do you know?
 I know quite a bit.

How many courses in English have you taken?
 I've taken several.

How much information do you have on how California was settled?
 I think I know a great deal.

How many facts do you know about how California was settled?
 I can only give you a few specific facts.

■ ACTIVITY 5D

Write sentences (use your own paper) beginning with *there is* or *there are*. Use the expressions *many, quite a few,* and *a great many* for count nouns and the expressions *a great deal of* and *quite a bit of* with mass nouns.

1. mountains in Switzerland

   There are a great many mountains in Switzerland.

2. pollution in the oceans of the world

   There is a great deal of pollution in the oceans of the world.

3. people in the People's Republic of China

4. diamond mines in South Africa

5. nightlife in New York City

6. nice weather in California

7. oil wells in Iran

8. gambling in Monaco

9. cowboys in Texas

10. banking in Switzerland

11. traffic in Tokyo

12. earthquakes in California

(Remember, *a lot of* is correct in all these sentences.)

■ ACTIVITY 5E

Write sentences beginning with *there is* or *there are*. Use *not many, very few,* and *only a few* with count nouns. Use *not much, very little,* and *only a little* with mass nouns.

1. rain in the Sahara Desert

2. illegal drugs in the U.S.S.R.

3. daylight in Scandinavian countries in the winter

4. women political leaders in the world

5. agriculture in Saudi Arabia

6. tourism in Antarctica

7. things you can buy for five cents in the United States

8. peace in the world today

■ ACTIVITY 5F

Complete the questions by filling in the blanks with *much, many, how much,* or *how many*. Then answer the questions using *a lot, a great many, a great deal, quite a few, quite a bit, very few, very little, only a few, only a little, a few, a little, not many,* or *not much*. Add *of* when it is necessary. When you see an asterisk (*) next to a question, try to add specific information to tell exactly how much. Use a number.

1. *Do you drink ___*much*___ coffee?

   Yes, I drink a lot. I drink about five cups a day.

2. Did you have _____ problems when you got your visa to come to the United States?

   _____

3. Did your parents or relatives give you _____ advice when you left home?

   _____

4. *Did you bring _____ luggage with you when you came to the United States?

   _____

5. *Do you receive _____ news from home?

   _____

6. _____ letters do you send home each week?

   _____

7. *_____ cash do you usually carry?

   _____

8. Do you have _____ American friends?

   _____

9. _____ times a week do you go to class?

   _____

10. Are there _____ students in your class?

_____

11. Do you have _____ interest in politics?

_____

■ **ACTIVITY 5G**

Fill in the blanks with *a few, very few, a little,* or *very little.* Read the entire sentence before you make your choice.

Many Scandinavians immigrated to this country in the last half of the nineteenth century and the first part of the twentieth century. For example, more than a million Norwegians came during this time. Most of these immigrants settled in the northern central part of the United States. These settlers left their native land with *very few* resources because they were not allowed much room for storage during the voyage. Of course, they needed _____ help when they arrived, and fellow countrymen were often there to give advice and aid. As newcomers, they quickly learned _____ words of English so they could buy what they needed. From the East Coast, where they landed, they traveled west to some of the best farmland in the country.

In 1862, President Lincoln signed the Homestead Act, which provided that a man could buy 160 acres of land. The government charged _____ money because it wanted this area to be settled quickly. By this time, there were _____ settlements in the Midwest, so settlers could meet, exchange news, and buy goods. When the Scandinavians arrived, there were _____ hostile Indians remaining in this territory. As a result, the settlers didn't have to worry about war; they only had to worry about their survival. However, because the Scandinavians had come from a cold climate, they had _____ trouble adjusting to the very hot summers in that part of the country. Another problem was medical care. There were _____ doctors, so people had to rely on home remedies. Most of these settlers became farmers. At that time, there were _____ people in this area, so the nearest neighbor probably lived miles away. _____ farm help was available, so families did most of the work themselves. They usually began farming with _____ livestock and equipment. As soon as the farmers earned _____ dollars, they bought farm equipment with the money and invested their profit in the farm. Many eventually became some of the most prosperous citizens in the area.

■ Activity 5H

Fill in the blanks with *much* or *many* and/or use one of the following for the answer: *bottle, bag, package, box, pound, loaf (loaves)*. Use *of* when necessary.

(Yolanda is planning to invite her coworkers to her apartment for a party in the evening. Molly is at Yolanda's apartment now. They are making a shopping list.)

Molly: How ___*many*___ people are going to come tonight, Yolanda?

Yolanda: About twenty, I think.

Molly: How _____ soda do you want me to get?

Yolanda: Get three _____ of cola and two _____ _____ seltzer, and get some orange juice.

Molly: Okay. How _____?

Yolanda: Only two _____.

MOLLY: How _____

ice do you want?

YOLANDA: Get me three.

MOLLY: How _____ cheese did you say? I forgot.

YOLANDA: One _____ Swiss cheese and

two _____ Brie.

MOLLY: And how _____ bread?

YOLANDA: Two _____ rye bread and four

_____ French bread.

MOLLY: And how_____ Alka Seltzer?

YOLANDA: You're funny! Actually, I need some. Get me a _____.

■ ACTIVITY 5I

☐ Fill in the blanks with *much, many, (very) few, (very) little, (only) a few,
(only) a little, a lot (of), quite a bit (of),* or *quite a few.* Try to use all of
these expressions one or more times.

California

California is the most populous state in the United States, and it is the

third largest in area. Americans have always considered California a kind of

"Promised Land." Some have gone there hoping to find gold, some to find

fame and fortune in Hollywood, and others to find the easy life of

California's golden sunshine and white beaches. Some have found their

dreams, but most Californians work hard to make a living from their

state's abundance of natural resources.

California has a diverse geography and economy. There ___*is a*___
                                                        (is/are)

___*great deal of*___ commercial fishing, and there _____
                                                        (is/are)

canning factories. In fact, California leads the nation in the area of fishing.

California has _____ excellent vineyards and

produces _____ wine. In the past, wine from California was

considered inferior to European wine, but today _____ California

wine is exported to Europe.

Agriculture is a major part of California's economy, particularly in the

interior valleys. However, California has a serious problem with its water

supply. The southern part of the state does not get _____ rain and

has _____ major rivers. The coastal region has to bring in

_____ water from the Colorado River 200 miles away. California

agriculture depends heavily on irrigation. Without its complex irrigation

system, the state would have _____ agriculture. It could not

produce the wonderful fruits and vegetables for which it is famous.

There _____ citrus groves in California. The
                    (is/are)

California navel orange is famous all over the country.

And what about the gold that the gold miners of 1849 rushed to the

state to find? How _____ gold _____ there in California
                                        (is/are)

today? There _____ gold left, but it is not a
                        (is/are)

significant part of the economy. Today California has "black gold."

Petroleum is now the state's most valuable mineral. Oil companies are drilling

_____ new oil wells, especially off the coast of Santa Barbara.

California is also famous because it has _____ natural

disasters. There _____ earthquakes in California.
                            (is/are)

Not _____ of the earthquakes do serious damage, but

_____ people predict that one day California will fall into the

ocean. In addition to the earthquakes, there _____
                                                    (is/are)

floods and mud slides. Despite these problems, very _____

California residents choose to leave their beautiful state.

☐ Now prepare a talk for your classmates on an interesting region of your country. Use the article on California as a model for your talk.

■ ACTIVITY 5J

☐ Interview a classmate about life in his or her country. Use the different question forms on page 83 for count and mass nouns. Give answers using the following expressions: *a lot, many, a great many, a great deal, quite a few, quite a bit, not many, not much, (very) few, (very) little, (only) a few,* or *(only) a little.* Use *of* when necessary. After you ask a question with one of the count or mass nouns, you may want to ask for additional information on the subject. For example, if you ask, "Is there much pollution in the big cities of your country?" you can also ask, "What causes this pollution? Is the government trying to control pollution?"

Here is a list of count and mass nouns that the interviewer can ask about.

1. Life in the Big Cities

    Mass Nouns: traffic   **Count Nouns:** foreigners
    pollution   skyscrapers
    dirt   museums
    noise   restaurants
    crime   nightclubs
    modern   theaters
      architecture   public
                                             universities
                                             private
                                             universities

2. Politics and Social Problems

    Mass Nouns: unemployment   **Count Nouns:** political parties
    poverty   economic
    interest in politics   problems
    terrorism   student
    power   demonstrations
    religious   strikes
      discrimination   unions
    racial discrimination   programs to help
    illiteracy   poor people

3. The Economy

Mass Nouns:	manufacturing	Count Nouns:	factories
	fishing		resorts
	mining		tourists
	industry		highways
	import/export trade		railways
	tourism		airports
	oil		mines (gold,
	steel		silver, coal,
	coffee		copper)
	wheat		steel plants
	rice		

❑ Now write a summary of what you have learned from your classmate about his or her country.

EXPRESSING YOUR IDEAS

1. Does your country have many different ethnic groups? What are they? Are there many immigrants in your country? From which countries? When did they come? What attracts immigrants to your country? Do many people emigrate from your country? Why? To what countries do they usually immigrate? How many immigrants does your country accept each year?

2. Is it easy to become a citizen in your country? What does a person have to do to become a citizen?

3. Are there many jobs and other opportunities for newcomers to your country?

4. Is there much unemployment among immigrants or certain minority groups? Do immigrants generally hold certain kinds of jobs? If so, what are they?

5. Is there much discrimination against immigrants or minority groups? If so, why? Which groups? Are there laws that attempt to limit discrimination? How successful are these laws?

6. Are there many famous people in your country who are immigrants or the descendants of immigrants? Name some.

7. If you decide to remain in the United States as an immigrant, how might this affect your life?

6 VERB + INFINITIVE, VERB + OBJECT + INFINITIVE, AND VERB + GERUND

Roger Daltrey and Pete Townsend of The Who.

Content Focus / ROCK MUSIC

Dialog

(ARNOLD and his father, MR. CALHOUN, are talking on the telephone.)

ARNOLD: Hello?

MR. CALHOUN: Hello, Arnold. This is Dad. How are you?

ARNOLD: Fine, and you?

MR. CALHOUN: Okay. I **invited you to come** to dinner Saturday night, remember? I **expect to see** you this weekend.

ARNOLD: Well, I'm not sure I can make it.[1] I **forgot to tell** you I got a job at a nightclub Friday and Saturday nights.

MR. CALHOUN: You **don't need to do** that, Arnold. I'll give you the money to go back to school. I'**d like you to go** back and **finish** your degree.

ARNOLD: I'm **sick of**[2] **going** to school, Dad. I **want to be** on my own.[3] I **don't want you to give** me money all the time, and besides, I **enjoy playing** my guitar.

MR. CALHOUN: The guitar, the guitar, the guitar! I **don't want to hear** about that guitar!

ARNOLD: Look, Dad, I'm **tired of fighting** about this. I **decided to drop out** of school[4] and **try** my luck with music, and that's that![5]

MR. CALHOUN: All right. Let's **stop talking** about it. What about next Monday or Tuesday? **Would** you **like to come** for dinner then?

ARNOLD: I'm sorry, Dad. I'**d like to**, but I **need to practice.**

MR. CALHOUN: You can never **hope to make** any money as a musician. **Don't expect me to help** you every time you need money.

ARNOLD: Dad, I appreciate your advice, but please **stop treating** me like a child.

MR. CALHOUN: All right, I'll **try to mind** my own business,[6] but I **urge** you **to think** very carefully about your decision.

---

[1]*Make it* means "to be able to accept an invitation to a party, dinner, or appointment."
[2]*Sick of something* means "to be very tired of something or very bored with something."
[3]*On (your) own* means "to be independent and responsible for yourself."
[4]*Drop out of school* means "to leave school before you get a degree or diploma."
[5]*That's that!* means "That's final! Let's not discuss it anymore."
[6]*To mind (your) own business* means "to worry about your own problems; not to interfere in another person's problems or decisions."

Listening Comprehension Questions

1. Do Arnold and his father agree about Arnold's interest in music?
2. Does Arnold want to make his living as a rock musician or to return to college?
3. What does Arnold's father want Arnold to do with his life?
4. Why can't Arnold go to dinner at his father's house next week?
5. What does Arnold want his father to stop doing?
6. What is Arnold's father going to try to do in the future?

VERB + INFINITIVE, VERB + OBJECT + INFINITIVE, AND VERB + GERUND

Some verbs in English are often followed by a second verb. The second verb can be in two different forms: the infinitive (*to + be*) or the gerund (*be + -ing*). The first verb can be in any tense.

VERB + INFINITIVE

Affirmative Statements

When certain verbs—such as *want, need,* and *hope*—are followed by another verb, the second verb must be in the infinitive form. Here is a list of verbs and verb phrases that require the infinitive form for the second verb. This list is not complete. Only the most common verbs have been selected.

afford	dare	hesitate	mean	refuse
agree	decide	hope	need	seem
appear	deserve	intend	offer	threaten
ask	expect	learn	plan	try
attempt	fail	long	prepare	want
choose	forget	manage	promise	would like

Examples

Rock music is an important part of American culture. Rock music first became popular during the 1950s, and it is still popular today, mainly among teenagers and young adults. Teenagers often **want to establish** their own identity and **need to express** their own feelings. Rock music does this for them. Some teenagers even **hope to become** rock stars.

Reduced Infinitives

Look at the examples below. Notice that, in the answers to the questions, you use *to* after the first verb, but it is not necessary to include the second verb or verb phrase. All of the verbs in the above list are used in this way.

Examples

Do many women become rock stars?
Some **manage to,** but there are many more men than women in rock music.

Note: It is not necessary to say **some manage to become rock stars.**

Do parents like the rock music that their kids like?
Some **try to.**

Negative Statements

It is possible to make either the first verb or the second verb negative, depending on your meaning. When you want to make the meaning of the first verb negative, follow the general rules for forming negatives.

Example

Many parents and teenagers disagree about rock music. Many parents **don't want to listen** to loud rock music in their homes all the time.

When you want to make the meaning of the second verb negative, put *not* after the first verb and before the infinitive (before *to*).

Examples

Many parents **prefer not to listen** when their teenagers turn on rock music.
Note: Don't confuse these two different negative forms. The meaning is different.

Some parents **try not to let** loud rock music bother them because they know it's important to their kids.

Other parents **don't try to understand** and don't permit loud rock music in their house.

> Arnold's father **promised not to nag** him about dropping out of college.
>
> He **didn't promise to pretend** that he was happy about his son's decision to drop out.

VERB + OBJECT + INFINITIVE

Verb + (Optional Object) + Infinitive

Some verbs can be followed by an infinitive (for example, *want to do*) or by an object and then the infinitive (for example, *want someone to do* something). The following verbs and verb phrases operate in this way.

ask	dare	prepare
beg	expect	want
choose	need	would like

> ### *Examples*
>
> The Beatles were probably the most popular group in the history of rock music. Even Queen Elizabeth of England **wanted to meet** them and **wanted them to visit** Buckingham Palace. She **asked them to accept** a special medal of honor.
>
> From about 1964 to 1970, every Beatles record sold over a million copies. Every album was new and innovative and had a strong influence on other musicians and young people everywhere. When the Beatles broke up in 1970, people were shocked. They **expected the Beatles to stay** together forever.

Verb + Object + Infinitive

One group of verbs *always* takes an object before the infinitive when the sentence is in the active voice. Here is a list of these verbs.

advise	forbid	order	teach
allow	force	pay	tell
challenge	hire	permit	urge
command	instruct	persuade	warn
convince	invite	remind	
encourage	motivate	require	

Examples

One of the Beatles, George Harrison, became especially interested in Indian music and philosophy. Ravi Shankar, a famous Indian musician, **taught Harrison to play** the sitar. The sitar is an Indian instrument.

In 1970, there was a war in Bangladesh, East Pakistan. Harrison wanted to help the war victims, so Ravi Shankar **encouraged him to give** a concert. Harrison **invited several other rock stars to play** at the concert. He **convinced everyone to give** the money from the concert to the people of Bangladesh.

■ ACTIVITY 6A

Choose the correct tense for the first verb below each blank. Then put the second verb in the infinitive form.

Stevie Wonder is one of the best-known "pop" musicians in the United States. His record albums have won many awards, and many of his songs, such as "You Are the Sunshine of My Life," are popular all over the world.

Stevie was born in a poor section of Detroit. He was born blind. Even as a child, he _refused to allow_ his blindness to interfere with his life.
(refuse, allow)

As a young child, he _learned to play_ the bongos, drums, piano, and
(learn, play)

harmonica, and he _learned to write_ songs. When he was twelve, a
(learn, write)

record company _offered to give_ him a recording contract. His record
(offer, give)

became a hit!

Today Stevie experiments with many different kinds of music, and he

tried to include different rhythms in his songs, such as Brazilian
(try, include)

bossa nova, samba, rock, jazz, and soul. He _expected to have_ perfect
(expect, have)

sound on his records and works long hours for this. Sometimes he

decides to get up in the middle of the night to rush down to a
(decide, get up)

recording studio.

Stevie has an active life. He ___doesn't + to use___ a cane or Seeing
(negative, **need, use**)
Eye dog to get around.

Stevie Wonder can't see with his eyes, but he says, "My mind

___wants to see___ to infinity."
(**want, see**)

■ ACTIVITY 6B

Fill in each blank with the correct tense of the first verb. Use the infinitive for
the second verb. In some of the sentences, an object separates the two verbs.

Last month Arnold ___invited___ his father ___to come___ to the
(**invite, come**)
nightclub where Arnold works. He ___wanted___ his father ___to hear___
(**want, hear**)
him play the guitar. Arnold's father ___refused to go___ to the
(**refuse, go**)
nightclub. He said he ___didn't like to listen___ to noise. Two weeks later,
(negative, **like, listen**)
Arnold and his father had an argument about Arnold's decision to make

music his career. Arnold ___decided not to visit___ his father that weekend
(**decide,** negative, **visit**)
and ___did not to be___ money from him either because he
(negative, **take**)
___wanted to be___ independent.
(**want, be**)
Arnold's father ___didn't want___ Arnold ___to earn___ a living from music.
(negative, **want, earn**)
He ___would like___ Arnold ___to be___ a doctor or a banker, but Arnold
(**would like, be**)
___didn't choose to listen___ to his father and ___followed___ his interest in music.
(**choose,** negative, **listen**)   (**follow**)

■ ACTIVITY 6C

Fill in the blanks with the verbs below using the simple past tense or the simple
present tense for the first verb and the infinitive for the second verb. You must
add an object pronoun between the first verb and the infinitive.

1. Madonna started many new fashion trends. Her fans always ___want___
(**want, wear**)
___her to wear___ something outrageous and original.

2. Mick Jagger of the Rolling Stones studied at the London School of Economics. He also sang in a rock group at that time. His parents

_____ his studies. They _____ a
    (encourage, continue)   (negative, **want, be**)

rock star.

3. George Michael is the rock star who started the fashion of wearing three or four days' growth of beard. His fans thinks he looks sexier that way.

They _____ clean shaven.
        (negative, **expect, be**)

4. In 1988, William Morrow wrote a biography of John Lennon, *The Lives of John Lennon*. In the book, Morrow said some very negative things about Lennon. For example, he wants readers to believe that Lennon was a heroin addict. John Lennon's widow, Yoko Ono,

_____ these negative things about her husband. She
(negative, **want, believe**)
never spoke with William Morrow before he wrote the book. She

_____ her for the book because Morrow had written
  (negative, **allow, interview**)
a biography of Elvis Presley several years before that was very negative.
    Imagine: John Lennon is a film documentary that was released in 1988. Ono says fans should see this film instead of reading Morrow's

book. She _____ *Imagine* because she believes it gives
            (encourage, see)
a more accurate picture of what Lennon was really like.

5. Many rock stars need to hire bodyguards so that they will not be crushed by a crowd of fans who want to touch them or grab their hair or a piece of their clothing as a souvenir. Michael Jackson always travels with bodyguards who protect him from his fans. The bodyguards

_____ too close to Michael.
  (negative, **allow, get**)

■ ACTIVITY 6D

Use the grammar pattern verb + object + infinitive and write sentences (on a separate sheet of paper) with the verbs given in parentheses.

1. (*remind*)
   Arnold is very absentminded. He forgets everything. What things did his mother always have to remind him to do when he lived at home?

2. (*warn*)
   Molly's mother worries about her a lot because she thinks New York City is very dangerous. What things does her mother always warn Molly to do or not do?

3. (*want*)

What things do language teachers want their students to do? What don't they want their students to do?

4. (*order, encourage, advise, urge, tell*)

Arnold's father went to the doctor for a checkup last week. He smokes a lot; he is overweight; he doesn't get much exercise; he never relaxes or takes a vacation. What did the doctor say to him?

ACTIVITY 6E

Look at the examples. Notice that, in the first answer, it isn't necessary to use a long sentence. Use a reduced infinitive (for example, *want to*). Answer the questions that ask *when* or *where* or *what kind* by using a full sentence. Use these verbs in both short and long sentences.

want   need   expect   plan   intend   hope   would like

Examples

Is Arnold going to buy a new guitar?
Yes, he plans to.

When?
He plans to buy one next month.

You may also use a negative answer. In this case, do not answer in a complete sentence.

Does Arnold want to find a part-time job for extra money?
He needs to, but he doesn't want to.

Now ask a classmate about his or her plans.

1. Are you going to find a part-time job for extra money?
   What kind of job?

2. Are you going to take another course in English?
   When?

3. Are you going to travel abroad this summer?
   Where?

4. Are you going to get a job after this course or after you return to your country?
   What kind of job?

5. Are you going to get married?
   When?

VERB + GERUND

When some verbs, such as *enjoy, avoid,* and *dislike,* are followed by another verb, this second verb is in the gerund form (base form + *-ing*). Here is a list of verbs that require the gerund form for the second verb. This list includes only the most common verbs.

appreciate	dislike	have	postpone	resume
avoid	enjoy	(trouble, problems, difficulty)	practice	spend
consider	escape		quit	(time, two hours, several months)
delay	finish	miss	regret[7]	
deny			report	waste
			resent	(time)

Examples

The music of the Beatles and other famous groups of the 1960s is based on the music of black rhythm-and-blues singers of the 1950s like Fats Domino, Little Richard, and Chuck Berry. Little Richard's music was very shocking for the middle class of the 1950s. He **enjoyed singing** about sex and fast cars. Some radio stations **avoided playing** his music, but teenagers loved him. In later life, Little Richard became a Christian preacher. Today he **dislikes listening** to the sexy songs he recorded in his youth.

Preposition + Gerund

1. Some verbs in English are followed by a preposition (*on, up, off, for* example). When you follow these two-word phrases with a second verb, you must use the gerund form. This is true for any verb that follows a preposition.

Examples

Little Richard **gave up singing** rock music when he became very religious. He didn't **feel like singing** this kind of song anymore. However, Chuck Berry **kept on singing and writing** songs through all the changes in rock.

[7]There is one exception to this rule. In formal letters, we often use the expression *We regret to inform you that....*

Here is a list of some common verbs that are followed by a preposition. If the preposition is followed by a second verb, use the gerund form. This list is not complete.

succeed   in
keep   on (means "continue")
put   off (means "postpone")
give   up (means "stop")
concentrate   on
think   about   +   base form   +   **-ing**
prevent (someone) **from**
believe   in
feel   like
discourage (someone) **from**

The following verbs are especially confusing because they have the preposition *to* in front of the gerund:

look forward to (means "anticipate with pleasure")
get used to (means "get accustomed to")
be used to (means "be accustomed to")
confess to
admit to   } + base form + **-ing**

Examples

Many young people **look forward to going** to their first rock concert. Most parents want their children to save money. However, many teenagers **admit to spending** their entire allowance on records.

2. Some adjectives are followed by prepositions. When you want to use a verb after these adjective phrases, you must use the gerund form.

Examples

"Oldies but goodies" is a common rock expression. It means records that are old but still popular. People are still **interested in hearing** Chuck Berry's songs today. They never get **tired of listening** to his rock classics like "Johnny B. Goode," "Sweet Little Sixteen," and "Roll Over Beethoven."

Here is a list of some common adjectives that are followed by prepositions.

afraid of	tired of	sick of
interested in	worried about	responsible for
		bored with

Negative Statements

If you want to make the meaning of the first verb negative, follow the general rules for forming negatives.

Example

Little Richard **doesn't enjoy listening** to his old records anymore.

If you want to make the meaning of the second verb negative, put *not* immediately in front of the gerund.

Example

Many radio stations **considered not playing** the first rock records of the 1950s because the records shocked many people.

Look at the following sentences. Notice the use of the same verb, *dislike*. Yolanda often eats in restaurants. She **doesn't dislike cooking** for herself; it's just that she often does not have the time, and her kitchen is very small. She **dislikes not having** enough space to cook in.

■ **ACTIVITY 6F**

Using the words in parentheses, make some general statements about the life of rock stars. Use the gerund form for the second verb.

1. (appreciate, hear, applause)

   Most rock stars _appreciate hearing applause._

2. (avoid, use, the main entrance of a theater)

   Rock stars _avoid using the main entrance of a theater_ because their fans surround them and ask for autographs.

3. (deny, take, drugs)

   Most people think that all rock stars use drugs, but rock stars _deny taking drugs_

4. (dislike, sing, the same hit songs)   (enjoy, hear, their favorite songs)

   Rock stars _dislike singing the same hit songs_

   over and over again in concerts, but the fans always _enjoy hearing their favorite songs._

5. (negative, finish, play, until 2:00 or 3:00 A.M.)
   When rock stars perform, they usually give two concerts a night, so they

   don't finish playing until 2:00 or 3:00 AM.

6. (miss, see, their families)
   Rock stars have to travel a lot. When they are married and have

   children, they _miss seeing their families._

7. (regret, have, so little time)

   They _regret having so little time_

   to spend at home and they (get tired of, travel) _get tired of traveling_

VERB FOLLOWED BY EITHER THE INFINITIVE OR THE GERUND

Verb + Infinitive or Gerund (Little Change in Meaning)

After the following verbs, you may use either the infinitive or the gerund form. In most situations, there is not much difference in meaning.

begin	hate	love	start
continue	like	prefer	

Example

People all over the world like to listen/like listening to rock music.

Verb + Infinitive or Gerund (Change in Meaning)

Certain verbs have one meaning when they are followed by an infinitive and a different meaning when they are followed by a gerund. The most common of these verbs are *stop* and *remember*.

1. *Remember to do.* If we say we *remembered to do* something, we mean that we had something to do and we did it.

Example

When Elvis Presley first appeared on TV, the cameramen were told not to show Elvis moving his hips. During the show, they **remembered to focus** on Elvis's face.

2. *Remember doing.* When you use the gerund form after *remember*, you mean that you recall an event or an action.

Example

Today a lot of people **remember watching** Elvis's first television appearance.

3. *Stop doing.* When you use *stop* with a gerund, you mean you are stopping an action.

> ### Example
> The Beatles **stopped performing** together in 1970.

4. *Stop to do.* When you use *stop* with an infinitive, you mean you are stopping in order to do something.

> ### Example
> I was on my way to the bank, and I **stopped to talk** with a friend. Unfortunately, the bank was closed when I got there.

■ ACTIVITY 6G

Choose the correct tense of the first verb below each blank. Choose the infinitive or the gerund form for the second verb. For some verbs in this activity, both infinitive and gerund are correct.

During the summer of 1969, one of the most important events in the history of rock music took place in Woodstock, New York. Around half a million people traveled to this small town for a weekend rock music festival. Many more people *wanted to come* but couldn't get near
(want, come)
the area because of all the traffic. People _____ traffic backed up for
(report, see)
ten miles.

The weather was bad on the weekend. It rained every day except for the last one. When the promoters of the concert heard the weather forecast, they _____ the festival, but finally they
(consider, negative, have)
_____ ahead with their plans. Some people
(decide, go)
_____, but most _____ and
(choose, leave)   (prefer, stay)

_____ the rain to spoil their weekend. They
(refuse, allow)

_____ to the music even in the rain.
(enjoy, listen)

Many of the young people who came to Woodstock believed in a world

of music, drugs, and free love. They _____ an example
(hope, set)

for a new world, and they _____ society. They called
(expect, change)

themselves the Woodstock Nation.

Many of the local townspeople _____ so many
(negative, **appreciate**, have)

hippies in their town and _____ nudity and drugs so
(resent, see)

near their homes. Some people _____ a lot of trouble
(expect, see)

with so many people living together in a small area for three days, but

the visitors _____ everything with one another and
(enjoy, share)

_____ with one another or with the residents of
(avoid, argue)

Woodstock. The local townspeople _____ the extra
(appreciate, have)

business, but _____ up after the weekend.
(negative, **look forward to**, clean)

In the years after Woodstock, many rock promoters

_____ this rock festival, but they all
(attempt, copy)

_____ the same spirit of happiness, peace,
(fail, achieve)

and good music that the Woodstock festival symbolized.

■ ACTIVITY 6H

❏ Your instructor will read you the following biography of Elvis Presley
two or three times. Before the instructor begins, you may wish to
preview the Listening Comprehension Questions at the end of this
activity. The first time that you listen to your instructor, just try to
catch the information, but don't write anything. The second or third
time that you listen, you may take notes. Also, try to pay attention to
the verb forms (infinitive or gerund). When your instructor finishes, try
to answer the questions. After that, go back and fill in the blanks in the
activity. Sometimes you need to add an object between the two verbs. If
you see the abbreviation *prep,* supply the correct preposition.

Elvis Presley is one of the most famous names, if not the most famous name, in the history of rock 'n' roll music. He was born on January 8, 1935, in Tupelo, Mississippi. He first *became interested in singing*
(become interested + prep, sing)
when he was a very young child. His parents took him to church every Sunday. He always _____ because he
(like, go)
_____ the hymns.[8]
(enjoy, sing)

Elvis was very close to his mother, whose name was Gladys. Gladys was an overprotective[9] mother who worried a lot about her son and never _____ out of her sight for very long. She
(want, be)
_____ to school by himself even when he was in high
(negative, permit, walk)
school. She walked him to school every day until his senior year. Like most young children, Elvis _____ a bicycle, but his
(want, have)
parents _____ one for him because his mother
(refuse, buy)
_____ himself. Instead _____ him a bike, they
(negative, want, hurt)   **(prep, buy)**
bought him a guitar and _____ most of his free time
(encourage, spend)
_____ it. He _____ the music he heard on the radio
(practice)   **(spend hours, imitate)**
and became very good at it.

Also, like most other boys, Elvis _____ football, so in
(enjoy, play)
high school he joined the football team. But again his overprotective mother

_____ himself, so she did everything that she could
(negative, want, hurt)
in order to _____. Finally, she _____
(discourage + prep, play)   **(convince, quit)**
the team, and he _____ football anymore. She also
(promise, negative, play)
_____ an after-school job because she thought it
(force, quit)
interfered with his schoolwork.

[8]*Hymns* are church songs.
[9]*Overprotective* means "trying too hard to protect." An overprotective parent is one who tries to protect a child from every possible danger or small hurt.

In 1953, Elvis _____ his first album. Soon after, disc jockeys

(decide, record)

_____ the album on their radio stations. Elvis _____

(start, play) (negative, **have much trouble, persuade, play**)

it. His album was almost an overnight success because Elvis was the only

white singer at that time who could sound like black singers. It was these

black singers who were coming out with the best new rock 'n' roll music.

Elvis's first television appearance was on "The Ed Sullivan Show," the

most popular TV show of the fifties. TV was very conservative about

sex at that time. Because Elvis _____ his hips so erotically

(keep + prep, **wiggle**)

when he sang, the TV cameras _____ him from the

(avoid, show)

waist down. It was hard for conservative audiences of the 1950s to

_____ such openly sexual behavior on TV. Elvis

(get used + prep, **see**)

was given the nickname "Elvis the Pelvis."

Elvis Presley earned millions of dollars from his records and

movies and became known as the King of Rock 'n' Roll. However,

he _____ with his fame and the national attention

(have trouble, cope)

that went with it. He developed psychological problems. He

_____ drugs and became very overweight. In 1976,

(start, use)

his doctors _____ because his health was so bad.

(order, stop, perform)

In 1977, Elvis died of a heart attack at the age of forty-two. His mother

had died at the same age.

Listening Comprehension Questions

1. Where and when was Elvis Presley born?
2. How did he first become interested in singing?
3. Did Elvis have a good relationship with his mother?
4. Give one or two examples to show that Gladys was an overprotective
   mother.
5. Why did Elvis's parents buy him a guitar?

6. What did Elvis's mother discourage her son from doing when he was in high school?

7. When Elvis made his first album, did he have much trouble persuading the radio stations to play it? Why or why not?

8. When Elvis first appeared on "The Ed Sullivan Show," why did the TV cameras avoid showing him from the waist down?

9. What were Elvis's two nicknames?

10. What effect did fame and national attention have on Elvis?

11. What did Elvis's doctors order him to do in 1976? Why?

12. What caused Elvis's death in 1977?

13. How old was he when he died? Why is this fact a little surprising?

☐ Reread the first part of the activity and study the information about Elvis's life. One student will role play someone who knew Elvis very well, such as his wife or a friend who grew up with him. The other students will role play reporters who are interviewing this person for a TV show about The King of Rock 'n' Roll. Plan which questions you want to ask and in what order you want to ask them. Then role play the interview.

■ ACTIVITY 6I

☐ Fill in the correct form for the second verb: infinitive or gerund. When you see *prep*, fill in the correct preposition.

Tina Turner has been singing rock 'n' roll for more than thirty years. Rock stars come and go. It is unusual for them to have a career last that long. Tina Turner's story is the story of a woman who refused *to give up*.
(give up)

Tina Turner's real name was Anna Mae Bullock. She was a country girl from Nutbush, Tennessee. Her childhood was not easy. Her parents had a very unhappy marriage. Anna Mae was their second child. She always felt that her mother never wanted *to have* her because she knew her
(have)
marriage was breaking up. She and her mother had trouble *communicating*
(communicate)
But Tina now says that she loved her mother very much. She remembers
watching her mother's face when she was making dinner on Sundays.
(watch)
She remembers *thinking* how beautiful her mother was.
(think)

When Anna Mae was ten years old her mother left her father. After several years, when her father realized that his wife didn't intend ___to come___ back to him, he sent his daughters to live with a relative,
(come)
and he left too. When Anna Mae was fifteen, her mother returned to Tennessee and offered ___to take___ her daughters to live with her in
(take)
St. Louis, Missouri. In St. Louis, Anna Mae started ___going___ to a
(go)
nightclub where her older sister worked as a barmaid. The hottest band[10] in town, Ike Turner and the Kings of Rhythm, was performing there. Night after night, Anna Mae listened to their music. She knew that she could sing as well as any of Ike's singers. Even as a child, she had enjoyed ___singing___ in front of the mirror. As a teenager, she had spent hours
(sing)
___imitating___ the singers on hit records. She wanted ___to have___ a
(imitate)   **(have)**
chance to show Ike what she could do, but she didn't dare ask him. One night during a break, Ike's drummer was teasing Anna Mae's sister. He put the microphone in front of her and asked her ___to sing___. She refused
(sing)
___to take___ the microphone, so Anna Mae grabbed it and began
(take)
___singing___. When Ike heard her, he was so impressed that he invited
(sing)
her ___to join___ his band. He didn't have a hard time ___persuading___ the
(join)   **(persuade)**
seventeen-year-old Anna Mae. She jumped at the chance to become a singer.

So began Tina Turner's career. Ike convinced her ___to change___ her name
(change)
to Tina. In 1960, they had their first hit, "A Fool in Love." It was one of the first truly black records to become popular on white radio stations; it was a crossover hit.[11] This record started Tina on the road to becoming a star. Not long after, she became Mrs. Ike Turner.

[10]*The hottest band* means "the most popular band."
[11]*A crossover hit* means "a hit record that is popular with both black and white people."

Tina was happy about her success, but she wasn't happy with her life. Ike Turner was a workaholic.[12] He never stopped _____touring_____ *(tour)*. They traveled from city to city, from club to club. Tina became tired _____of living_____ *(prep, live)* in hotels and _____leaving_____ *(leave)* her children behind at home. In addition, Ike and Tina had a very stormy relationship.[13] She says that he had a violent temper and attempted _____to control_____ *(control)* her completely. Many times she considered _____leaving_____ *(leave)* him, but she was too dependent on him. It was Ike who had made her a star, and she had no other career.

Ike and Tina Turner stayed together for more than fifteen years. They had a long and successful career together, with many hit records. Tina's strong voice, her energy, and her amazing long legs were famous throughout the United States and Europe, especially during the 1960s. But, during the seventies, people stopped _____buying_____ *(buy)* Ike and Tina's records, and their popularity dropped.

In 1976, Tina made a change in her life. She decided _____to end_____ *(end)* her relationship with Ike. She admitted _____to being_____ *(prep, be)* afraid, but she was curious to see if she could work alone. Some people tried _____to discourage_____ *(discourage)* her _____from leaving_____ *(prep, leave)* Ike. They told her that a woman in her forties couldn't make a successful comeback.[14] But Tina wanted _____to show_____ *(show)* everyone that she could make her own decisions and achieve recognition as a result of her own talents. She formed her own group, changed her image, and started _____touring_____ *(tour)*. After some hard times, she came out with a spectacular album in 1983 titled *Private Dancer*. The album stayed among

[12]*A workaholic* is a person who can't stop working, just as an alcoholic can't stop drinking.
[13]*A stormy relationship* means "a relationship with a lot of fighting."
[14]*Make a comeback* means "to regain popularity after a star has lost it."

the top one hundred albums for more than two years and sold more than 10 million copies around the world. At the 1984 Grammy Awards[15] ceremony, Tina won three awards, including Best Record of the Year. When she accepted the award, she said, "We're looking forward ___*getting*___ (prep, **get**) many more of these." The audience cheered and cheered because Tina Turner had survived in one of the most fickle[16] industries that there is and because she had succeeded ___*reaching*___ the top of that industry for a (prep, **reach**) second time all on her own.

☐ Go back and carefully read the information about Tina Turner's life again. Then form groups of three or four students. See if someone in your group can answer the following questions without looking back at the text.

1. About how long has Tina Turner been singing? Is this typical or unusual?
2. Describe her background. Where was she born? What kind of a childhood did she have? What was her relationship with her parents like?
3. How did her career as a rock 'n' roll singer get started?
4. How did Tina feel about her life with Ike Turner?
5. Why did she decide to leave Ike Turner in 1976? Did she have any trouble making that decision? What did some people say when they tried to discourage her from going out on her own?
6. Did she succeed in making a successful comeback?

■ ACTIVITY 6J

Ask a classmate these questions.

1. What did your parents advise you to be?
2. What did you hope to be?
3. What did your teachers encourage you to do?
4. How did you decide? Did you have trouble making up your mind?
5. Did anyone ever discourage you from doing what you wanted to do? How? Why?
6. Do you expect to be successful? Make a lot of money?
7. Do you expect your family to help you? Why or why not?

[15]*The Grammy Awards* are awards that are given for the best records and singers each year.
[16]*Fickle* means "changeable."

8. Do you plan to have children?

9. Do you plan to have a career? Will you postpone having children until you establish yourself in a career?

10. At what age do you expect to retire?

11. What do you look forward to doing after you retire?

EXPRESSING YOUR IDEAS

1. Arnold and his father have trouble understanding each other. They are from two different generations. We call this lack of understanding or lack of communication between generations the "generation gap."

   a. Do you have trouble talking with your parents? Do they seem to understand your problems? Do you usually agree or disagree with them? If you are a parent, do you have trouble talking with your children?

   b. Is there a generation gap in your country? Is this problem greater in the United States? Why or why not?

   c. What are some of the differences between people your own age and people your parents' age? Are there many similarities?

   d. Do your parents approve of the way you dress, talk, and behave? If you are a parent, how do you feel about how your children and their friends dress, talk, and behave?

   e. Do parents often expect their children to spend more time at home than the children want to spend there?

   f. Do parents usually give financial help to their children who are over the age of eighteen? At what age do they stop helping them? Do you think parents sometimes use money to control their children when they are trying to become independent? Give examples.

2. What are popular professions among young people in your country? In the United States? What professions do parents usually want their children to choose? Do parents often try to force their children to become something that they don't want to be? Did your parents encourage you to be something you didn't want to be?

3. What kind of music do you like? What kind of music did you enjoy listening to when you were a teenager? Do you and your parents have different tastes in music?

4. Is rock music popular in your country? What other kinds of music are popular? Which rock stars or groups are famous in your country? Who are your favorites?

5. Do you think rock stars have a positive or a negative influence on young people? Explain your answer by giving examples.

7

TIME CLAUSES
AND THE REAL
CONDITIONAL

PHYSICAL FITNESS— START RUNNING AND QUIT SMOKING

Dialog

(YOLANDA and MOLLY are jogging in the park. MOLLY started jogging about two months ago, but today is YOLANDA's first day.)

YOLANDA: Molly, I'm exhausted. It's only seven in the morning! Let's stop for a few minutes.

MOLLY: Don't quit yet. Push yourself a little. Just a few minutes more. **When I started jogging, it was really difficult for me too.**

YOLANDA: Have pity on me then. This is my first time.

MOLLY: Come on, Yolanda. **After you jog another month or two, you'll be ready for the marathon.**

YOLANDA: The marathon! How many miles is the marathon?

MOLLY: It's about twenty-six miles. **If I jog every day, I'll enter it next fall.**

YOLANDA: Count me out.[1] I'm tired now after only half a mile. I'm going to stop.

MOLLY: Okay, but don't sit down. Keep on[2] walking for a while. That's important. **When you stop exercising suddenly, sometimes you get muscle cramps.**

YOLANDA: I'm in terrible shape.[3] **I'm going to go back to bed as soon as I get home.** Is jogging really good for me?

MOLLY: Yes, but you won't feel the benefits right away. Doctors say that **the heart gets stronger after you jog regularly for a month or so.**

YOLANDA: I know. Everybody's talking about how wonderful jogging is.

MOLLY: That's true. Look. The park is full of joggers. Everybody jogs nowadays.

YOLANDA: Well, **unless you come by my apartment every morning and drag me out of bed, I won't do it.**

MOLLY: Okay. I'll come and get you. It's nice to have company. I really want to lose some weight and get in shape.[4] I'm tired of being out of condition.

YOLANDA: The new Molly!

MOLLY: **I'm going to do this until I look and feel the way I want to.**

---

[1]*Count me out* means "I don't want to be part of this. Don't include me."
[2]*Keep on* means "continue."
[3]*I'm in terrible shape* means "I am not in good physical condition." We say someone is in bad or terrible shape when his or her physical condition is poor, usually because he or she has not been exercising.
[4]*Get in shape* means "get your body in good physical condition by exercising."

Listening Comprehension Questions

1. How does Yolanda feel? Does she want to keep jogging, or does she want to stop?
2. When Molly first started jogging, was it difficult for her?
3. In Molly's opinion, when will Yolanda be ready for the marathon?
4. Why is it important to walk for a while after jogging?
5. What is Yolanda going to do as soon as she gets home?
6. Yolanda says she won't go jogging regularly unless Molly does something. What does she want Molly to do?

TIME CLAUSES

A time clause is a part of a sentence that has its own subject and verb and begins with a time expression such as *before, after, when, as soon as,* or *until.* It is not a complete sentence.

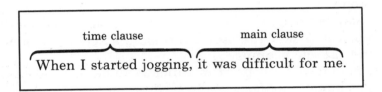

time clause   main clause

When I started jogging, it was difficult for me.

We can place the time clause at the beginning or end of the sentence.

About the Past

Examples

Jesse Owens is a famous name in the history of American sports. **When he was a student at Ohio State University,** he broke several world records in track. Later, at the 1936 Olympics, he broke the world record for the 200-meter race and the broad jump. The 1936 Olympics took place in Munich **when Hitler was in power.** Hitler was angry **when Jesse Owens, a black man, won several gold medals.** Hitler wanted Germans to win in order to prove his theories of racial superiority. **Before Owens received his medals,** Hitler left the stadium. Owens didn't receive full recognition for his victory **until he returned to the United States. As soon as he arrived in New York,** crowds of reporters and people greeted him.

About the Present

> ### *Examples*
>
> Americans love to watch spectator sports. They are also becoming more and more interested in participatory sports and physical fitness for reasons of health. Some studies show that **when people exercise properly** they have fifty percent fewer heart attacks. **After a person jogs regularly for a period of time,** his or her pulse rate and blood pressure go down.

About the Future

Notice that in the examples for the past and present time clauses the tense of the verb in the time clause is the same as the tense of the verb in the main clause.

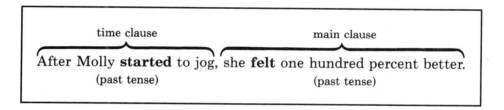

When we use time clauses to talk about a time in the future, the tenses in the two clauses are different. The verb in the time clause is in the simple present tense, and the verb in the main clause is in the future tense (*will* or *going to*).

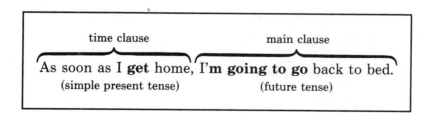

Questions

When you ask a question that contains a time clause, the question form is used only for the verb in the main clause. The time clause can come at the beginning or end of the question. Don't use the question form in the time clause.

Examples

main clause   time clause

MOLLY: How old **were you** *when you started smoking,* Arnold?
ARNOLD: Around thirteen or fourteen.
MOLLY: *When you're nervous,* **do you smoke** a lot?
ARNOLD: Yeah, and especially before I play.
MOLLY: **Do you reach** for a cigarette *as soon as you get up* in the morning?
ARNOLD: Yes, I have one or two cigarettes before I eat breakfast, but I won't tomorrow.

■ ACTIVITY 7A

☐ Fill in the correct tense of the verb—simple present, simple past, or future.

Physical fitness programs sponsored by corporations are a fast-growing trend in the American business world. More than 400 large corporations now offer exercise programs to their employees. The business world is fast becoming convinced that employees *work* more productively when

(work)

they *are* physically fit. When an employee _____ out

(be)   (stay)

because of illness, it _____ a company a lot of money. Employee

(cost)

health problems cost businesses more than $3 billion a year.

Many corporations build their own exercise centers. Xerox Corporation

_____ $3.5 million when it _____ its exercise center in

(spend)   (build)

Leesburg, Virginia, a few years ago. A large corporation in California is building a facility for 2,000 workers. When it _____ complete, the

(be)

center _____ two racquetball courts, a sauna, an exercise room, two

(have)

pools, a volleyball court, two tennis courts, a basketball court, and a track.

When a company _____ that it cannot afford to build its own
                   (decide)

center, it often _____ for its workers to enroll in independent
                  (pay)

exercise centers. Cardio-Fitness is an example of such a center.

Cardio-Fitness charges its members $550 a year. Most of the members are

sponsored by their corporations. The center always _____ the
                                                    (review)

applicants' medical histories very carefully before they _____ the
                                                          (begin)

exercise program. After the clients _____ a series of tests, the
                                     (take)

center _____ them an individual program to follow.
       (give)

Medical evidence that exercise makes for a healthy heart is growing.

When Dr. Ralph Paffenbarger, Jr., of Stanford University _____ a
                                                          (conclude)

fifteen-year study in 1979, he _____ that people who exercise
                               (find)

regularly have fewer heart attacks. Companies have found that workers

_____ with stress better when they _____ regularly. In
(cope)   **(exercise)**

Chicago a printing company called Excello Press _____ to build an
                                                 (decide)

exercise room after an angry employee _____ his lunch box into a
                                       (throw)

printing press and caused $100,000 in damage. When the president of the

company _____ about the incident, he _____ that his
        (hear)   **(realize)**

employees needed an outlet for their tensions and frustrations. One

employee of the federal government is delighted with her new exercise

program, which she participates in during work hours. Before she

_____ the program, she _____ tense all the time and
(start)   **(be)**

suffered from severe headaches. Now she feels much more relaxed.

The business world believes that company exercise centers are becoming

an important fringe benefit. Business experts predict that, in the future,

before an executive _____ accepting a job with a corporation, he or
                    (consider)

she _____ about exercise facilities in the same way that people now
(ask)

ask about other benefits, such as medical coverage or vacation time. Some

people predict that the employers' interest in the physical well-being of

employees will grow. In the future, employers _____ at several
(look)

other factors when they _____ health programs. They will consider
(consider)

such things as nutrition, weight control, and coping with stress in addition

to exercise programs.

   Others are not so optimistic. These pessimists say that the economy is

entering a very difficult period. They predict that when company profits

_____ the exercise programs _____ the first benefit to be
(drop)   (be)

eliminated.

☐ Read the exercise again. With your classmates, try to retell as much of
the information as possible without looking at it. Try to use time
clauses.

■ ACTIVITY 7B

Molly is going to run in a women's marathon in Central Park in two months.
Here are some of the things she is going to do *before* or *after* she runs the race.

1. buy a new running suit
2. practice extra hard
3. run an extra mile every day for practice
4. feel proud of herself
5. celebrate with her friends
6. take a long, hot shower
7. probably get new blisters on her feet
8. feel very, very tired
9. fill out an entry form
10. pay an entrance fee

Use the information above to make sentences with time clauses. Use these time expressions: *when, before, after, as soon as, until.* Use these verbs in your time clauses: *enter, run, finish, complete.*

> **Example**
>
> *Before Molly runs the marathon, she's going to pay the entrance fee.*

■ ACTIVITY 7C

☐ Your government is sending you to the moon. You are going to be one of the first settlers in a moon colony. Describe this adventure before takeoff, after takeoff, and after your arrival on the moon. Use time clauses.

Before I do anything else, I'm going to see a lawyer and make a will.

☐ You and your wife or husband have just visited the doctor. You're going to have your first child. How are you going to prepare for the birth of your child? What are you going to do after the child arrives? Make sentences using time clauses.

CLAUSES WITH *IF*—GENERAL TRUTHS AND HABITS

When we use an *if* clause to talk about general truths, facts, or habits, we use the simple present tense in both the *if* clause and the main clause.

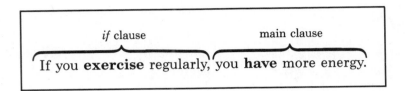

if clause   main clause

If you **exercise** regularly, you **have** more energy.

Examples

Smoking is very important to Arnold. If he **doesn't have** a cigarette in his hand at a party, he **doesn't know** what to do with his hands, and he feels very uncomfortable. He always has to have a cigarette after dinner, but he knows that Molly dislikes smoking in restaurants. If he **is** with Molly, he **doesn't smoke** after dinner in a restaurant. But he **feels** that dinner is not complete if he **doesn't have** a cigarette.

Note: In sentences that talk about general truths or habits, it is possible to substitute *when* for *if* and still express basically the same meaning.

CLAUSES WITH *IF* AND *UNLESS* IN THE FUTURE—PREDICTIONS ABOUT THE FUTURE

If Clauses

When we talk about a future time and use an *if* clause, we call this sentence a *real conditional* sentence. The actions in both the clauses will occur in the future. We use the simple present tense in the *if* clause and the future tense (*going to* or *will*) in the main clause.

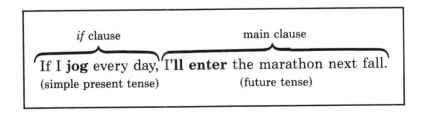

if clause   main clause

If I **jog** every day, I'll **enter** the marathon next fall.
(simple present tense)   (future tense)

Examples

ARNOLD: You know, it's going to be hard for me to quit smoking when I'm at the disco. Everyone smokes there. What'**ll** I **do** if someone **offers** me a cigarette?

MOLLY: If I'**m** there, I'**ll take** it away from you.

ARNOLD: Yeah, but when I play, I'm always very nervous. If I **don't have** a cigarette in my mouth tonight, I'**ll go** crazy.

MOLLY: If you really **need** something, we'**ll give** you chewing gum.

Unless Clauses

In many sentences, *unless* means "if not" when the verb in the *unless* clause is affirmative. Sentence 1 means the same as sentence 2.

1. **Unless** Molly comes to get Yolanda every morning, Yolanda won't jog.

2. **If** Molly does**n't** come to get Yolanda every morning, Yolanda won't jog.

We can't use *unless* with a negative verb when the verb in the main clause is negative.

Incorrect: I won't stop smoking unless you don't help me.

Correct: I won't stop smoking unless you help me.

Examples

YOLANDA: Listen, Arnold stopped smoking two weeks ago. Let's take him out to dinner to celebrate.

MOLLY: Okay. Unless we find a restaurant with a No Smoking section, Arnold **won't enjoy** his dinner at all. He still wants to light up when he smells cigarette smoke. When are we going to go?

YOLANDA: We'**ll go** Saturday night unless Jack and Arnold **have** other plans.

MOLLY: And let's treat him to a really nice dinner.

YOLANDA: We'**ll do** that unless we'**re** broke.[5] Let's check our purses first.

[5]*Be broke* means "to have no money."

A Note about Commas

When the time clause or *if/unless* clause is at the beginning of the sentence, it is followed by a comma.

After you jog regularly for a month or so, your heart gets stronger.

If Molly jogs every day, she'll enter the marathon next fall.

When the time clause or *if/unless* clause is at the end of the sentence, there is no comma.

Your heart gets stronger after you jog regularly for a month or so.

Molly will enter the marathon next fall if she jogs every day.

A Note about Other Modal Auxiliary Verbs

Will is not the only modal auxiliary verb that we use to talk about the future in a real conditional sentence. We can also use *should, may,* or *might.*

■ Activity 7D

Use the real conditional to talk about the future in this activity. It is possible to use the simple present tense in both clauses for many of the sentences, but practice making predictions about the future with *if* here.

In the United States, there is a bitter battle raging between smokers

and nonsmokers. Nonsmokers argue that, if they _breathe_ smoke
                                              (breathe)

from another person's cigarette, there's a good chance that this smoke

will have a negative effect on their health too. Most nonsmokers want
(have)

stricter laws to ban smoking in public places. Many smokers don't agree

with the strict new laws.

In the past ten or fifteen years, there have been numerous studies about

the effects of cigarette smoke on nonsmokers. One study researched

pregnant women who smoked. The study concluded that if a pregnant

woman _____ her baby probably _____ less than average at
       (smoke)   (weigh)

birth.

Another study was made on the wives of smokers in Japan. The study concluded that a wife _____ a greater risk of dying of cancer if her
(have)

husband _____.
(smoke)

According to a 1979 report, unless people _____ smoking, about
(stop)

320,000 people per year _____ prematurely.[6] The tobacco industry
(die)

is trying to show that smoking is not really that dangerous. Unless people

_____ to buy cigarettes, the tobacco industry _____ a great
(continue)   (lose)

deal of money. Many people want the government to stop all cigarette

advertising. The tobacco industry wants to continue advertising because it

_____ profits unless it _____.
(negative for **make**)   (advertise)

■ ACTIVITY 7E

Divide the class into smokers and nonsmokers. The nonsmokers will interview the smokers and then give a brief report to the class about their findings. Use these questions and/or any others that you want to add.

1. Why do you smoke?
2. How long have you been smoking?
3. Have you ever tried to quit? Were you successful? What method did you use?
4. Do you think that smoking has any bad effects on your health now? What bad effects do you notice?
5. What do you think about the reports that say that cigarette smoking can cause cancer and heart disease? Are you worried about these reports?
6. What do you think of some of the new antismoking laws in the United States? For example, in some states, you can smoke in a restaurant only if you sit in the smoking section, and there's no smoking in elevators. Are these laws fair or unfair?

[6]*To die prematurely* means "to die before the normal (average) age; to die too soon."

■ ACTIVITY 7F

Use the real conditional to talk about the future. Note that it is also correct here to use *if* sentences to talk about the general present and use the simple present tense in both clauses, but for practice use the future tense in the main clause.

Canadian athlete Ben Johnson was one of the best runners in the 1988 Olympic games. But drug tests showed that he was using steroids, so he had to give up his medal and withdraw from the games. Several other athletes in the 1988 Olympics tested positive for steroids and had to leave also.

Steroids can help an athlete. For example, if a runner _____
(take)
steroids, his or her muscles _____ bigger, and there _____
(get)   (be)
a remarkable improvement in performance over a very short period of time.

But steroids have some very dangerous side effects too. If a woman athlete

_____ these drugs, she _____ acne, her voice _____
(take)   (get)   (become)
deeper, and she _____ facial hair. If athletes—either men or
(develop)
women—_____ steroids, often their moods _____ very
(take)   (change)
suddenly, and sometimes they _____ violent for no good reason.
(become)
This is called a "roid rage." If a person _____ a tendency toward
(have)
high blood pressure, steroids _____ his or her blood pressure to
(raise)
dangerous levels. These drugs _____ liver damage too if an athlete
(cause)
_____ them over a long period of time.
(use)

Reread the activity. Then complete the following questions and ask a classmate to answer them.

1. If an athlete _____ steroids, _____ muscles

    _____ bigger?

2. If a woman athlete _____ steroids, what _____

    her face? What _____ her voice?

3. _____ violent if he or she _____ these drugs?

4. What _____ if a person _____ toward high

blood pressure and _____ steroids?

5. _____ liver damage if an athlete _____
steroids over a long period of time?

■ ACTIVITY 7G

What do you think about the issue of athletes taking steroids? Should the
Olympic Committee allow athletes to take them? Should we require all athletes
to take tests to determine if they are using steroids? Do you believe it was right
to take away Ben Johnson's medal and throw him out of the 1988 Olympics
because he used steroids?

■ ACTIVITY 7H

Discuss these problems in small groups in your class. Report back to the other
groups the pros and cons of each possible solution to the problem.

❏ The person you love is from a different country. She or he has a
completely different cultural and religious background. You are faced
with many choices.

whether or not to marry

whether or not to convert to this person's religion

what kind of marriage ceremony to have

where to live (in whose country)

how to raise your children (in what religion and with the values and
customs of which country)

Discuss each choice that you have to make, and tell what all the
consequences will be for each possible decision. For example, tell what
will happen if you marry the person and what will happen if you don't.

❏ Susan is a mother in her thirties. She has two children, aged two and
six. Susan is well educated and had a good job before she stopped work
to have children six years ago. Now she is beginning to feel frustrated
and bored with staying at home. She is trying to make a decision about
whether or not to start work again. She will feel more fulfilled if she
goes back to work, but she is concerned about her children, especially
the two-year-old. Discuss her choices in this situation and all the
consequences each decision will bring. Here are the choices.

whether to go back to work or to continue to stay at home as a
  mother and housewife

whether or not to leave the children in a day-care center or with a
  baby-sitter

whether to work part-time or full-time

whether to make a decision for herself or follow her husband's
  wishes (her husband prefers that she stay home)

■ ACTIVITY 7I

Write two sentences about each numbered person in the picture on page 130 using the real conditional to talk about the future. First write a sentence with *if*. Then write the same sentence using *unless*. You should have six pairs of sentences.

> ### *Example*
>
> **If** the woman doesn't tie her shoe, she'll trip over her shoelaces and fall.
>
> **Unless** the woman ties her shoe, she'll trip and fall.

EXPRESSING YOUR IDEAS

1. Are people in your country interested in physical fitness? What do people do to keep in shape? What do you do?

2. Is jogging very popular in your country? Why do you think jogging is so popular in the United States? What are some of the benefits of jogging? Which sports are most beneficial in helping a person maintain good physical condition?

3. What is your prescription for living a long and healthy life?

4. *Questions for a smoker:* Why do you smoke? Do you want to stop, or aren't you worried about doctors' warnings about the bad effects of smoking? What do you think of the new laws that restrict smoking in restaurants and public places in some parts of the United States? Is there a battle raging between smokers and nonsmokers in your country too? *Questions for a nonsmoker:* What do you think of smokers? Do you think many of them are thoughtless and inconsiderate? Were you ever a smoker? If so, how and why did you quit? What do you think of the laws against smoking in some parts of the United States?

Don Mattingly of the Yankees runs by Chris Bando of the Cleveland Indians to score a run.

Dialog

(JACK and ARNOLD are at a baseball game in Yankee Stadium. ARNOLD is a real baseball fan. JACK isn't.)

JACK: Look at Number 39. He **can't hit** anything.

ARNOLD: Yeah, the Yankees[1] are playing badly again this year.

JACK: What do you mean, again? I thought they won the World Series[2] last year.

ARNOLD: Yeah, they did, but they started the season[3] badly. They **couldn't win** anything in the first part of the season.

JACK: So how did they win the World Series?

ARNOLD: Well, finally they **were able to break** their losing streak.[4] They **were able to win** most of their games in the second half of the season.

JACK: Here comes Don Mattingly.

ARNOLD: He **can hit** almost anything.

JACK: **Can** he **play** outfield[5] well?

ARNOLD: I think he can. I was reading a story about him in a magazine last night. He could hit the ball out of the park even when he was just a kid.

JACK: Yeah? Let's hope he hits a home run today. The Yankees are behind. Say, didn't the Yankees lose one of their best players at the beginning of this season?

ARNOLD: Yes, he broke his finger, but they think he**'ll be able to play** in a few more weeks.

JACK: **Can** you **get** us tickets for next week's game?

ARNOLD: Sure, I **can. Can** you **give** me the money in advance? I'm broke,[6] as usual.

---

[1]*The Yankees* are a New York baseball team.
[2]*The World Series* is a group of games for the U.S. baseball championship.
[3]*Season* means "the time a sport is played." The baseball season is from April through October.
[4]*Break a losing streak* means "to stop losing one game after another."
[5]*Play outfield* means "to take one of three positions far out in the baseball field."
[6]*Be broke* means "to have no money."

Listening Comprehension Questions

1. In Jack's opinion, is Number 39 a good hitter?
2. How did the Yankees do last season?
3. Did Don Mattingly show any special skill in baseball when he was a kid?
4. How did the Yankees lose one of their best players at the beginning of this season?
5. Will he be able to play again before the season is over?
6. Does Arnold think he can get tickets for next week's game?

CAN, COULD, AND *BE ABLE TO*

The following are modal auxiliary verbs: *can, could, should, ought to, have to, must, might, may, had better, would rather.* A modal auxiliary is used before another verb. We often use modals when we want to give advice, prohibit something, give permission, or talk about ability.

CAN, COULD, AND *BE ABLE TO*—PRESENT TENSE

Can and *could* have many different meanings. In this chapter, we are going to talk about only a few of these meanings. We use the base form of the verb after *can, could,* or *be able to.*

Statements

can (not) + base form

Don Mattingly can hit almost any ball.

be (not) able to + base form

Don Mattingly is able to hit almost any ball.

Questions

Can + subject + base form?

Can Don play outfield?

Could + subject + base form?

Could you lend me your book on baseball?

Be + subject + **able to** + base form?

Is Molly able to play baseball?

Ability

When we have the capacity to do something, we usually use *can*. *Be able to* and *can* are frequently interchangeable in the present tense.

> ### Examples
>
> The Tarahumara Indians live in the Copper Canyon in the Sierra Madre Mountains of Mexico. They are excellent runners. They **can run** for forty-eight hours without getting out of breath. They play an unusual form of football. The game continues through the night. The players **are able to see** the ball at night because friends run next to them with torches. These people live in a canyon with very steep walls. Even donkeys **can't climb** up and down the canyon safely, but the Tarahumara Indians **can.**

Possibility

We also use *can* when we mean it is possible to do something. We usually don't use *be able to* for this meaning.

> ### Example
>
> Doctors think we **can learn** a lot about health and exercise from the Tarahumara Indians.

Permission and Prohibition

There are two ways to ask for or give permission—with *may* or with *can*. *Can* has the same meaning as *may,* but *may* is more formal. In the negative, *can't* means it is not permitted. For these meanings, we almost never use *be able to.*

> ### Examples
>
> MOLLY: I just read an article about the Tarahumara Indians in Mexico. Read it! Maybe they will inspire you to jog.
>
> YOLANDA: Okay. **Can I borrow** it? or **May I borrow** it?
>
> MOLLY: Sure, you **can take** it, but you **can't keep** it for more than a few days. It's due at the library next week.

Note: We often use *could* when we ask for permission. Some people think it is more polite than *can.*

Could I **borrow** that book?

COULD, WAS ABLE TO/WERE ABLE TO—PAST TENSE

We use *could* or *was able to/were able to* to express ability, possibility, and prohibition when we talk about the past. In negative statements, *couldn't* and *wasn't able to/weren't able to* are very similar in meaning. In affirmative statements, they are usually similar in meaning, but there are some cases in which we don't use *could.* When we want to talk about a specific event or a specific achievement, we don't use *could.* We use *was able to/were able to.*

> ### Examples
>
> Baseball is a favorite American sport. Jackie Robinson is one of the most famous players in the history of baseball. In high school, he was an all-round sportsman.[7] He **could play** baseball, basketball, football, and track. Of course, he **wasn't able to play** all of these professionally. So he chose baseball because he **could play** it the best. In 1945, he became the first black to join major-league baseball. He didn't start off the first

[7]*All-round sportsman* means "someone who can play many sports well."

season well, but by the end of the year, he **was able to finish**[8] with the highest batting average in the league.

Before 1945, only white baseball players **were able to join** organized baseball. When Jackie joined his first all-white team, the team **couldn't play** in several towns in the South because these towns didn't allow interracial teams to play. Because of Jackie's courage, more and more blacks **were able to join** organized baseball.

CAN, WILL BE ABLE TO, WON'T BE ABLE TO—FUTURE TENSE

We use either *can/can't* or *will be able to/won't be able to* to talk about possibility or ability in the future.

Examples

YOLANDA: Molly, some friends of mine organized a baseball game in the park for next Saturday. **Can** you **go?**

MOLLY: I **can go,** but I don't know how to play. I **won't be able to hit** the ball.

YOLANDA: I'll teach you. Practice with me for a few evenings. You'll **be able to play** by next Saturday.

QUESTIONS

Examples

1. **Can** women **play** for organized baseball today?
   No, they can't, but some women are fighting to change those rules.

2. **Are** women **able to earn** the same money as men in sports?
   No, they aren't. For example, women golfers earn much less than men.

---

[8]We cannot use *could* in this sentence because we are talking about a specific one-time achievement in a difficult situation. In all the other sentences in the example, it is possible to use *could* or *was able to/were able to*. Here are two more examples in which you cannot use *could*.

    a. I was sick yesterday, but I **was able to take** my math test in the afternoon because the doctor gave me some medicine.

    b. Molly had a cramp in her leg, but she **was able to finish** the marathon before it got really bad.

3. When **will** women **be able to compete** against men in the Olympics?
   Who knows?

4. **Could** women **compete** in the Olympics in ancient Greece?
   No, they couldn't. They finally organized their own Olympics.

■ ACTIVITY 8A

Read the following information and then ask a question using *can/can't* or *be able to* in the past, present, or future tense.

1. Molly can't beat Yolanda at tennis now.

   When _____*will she be able to beat*_____ her?
                    (beat)

   After she practices a lot.

2. Molly runs a lot more than Yolanda, and she runs more often.

   Who _____ in the next marathon?
            (participate)

   Molly _____

3. Who _____ faster, Molly or Yolanda?
            (run)

   Molly _____

4. Bob Hayes, a famous athlete, was sick when he was a child. He won an Olympic medal for running.

   Why _____ sports as a child?
           (negative, play)

   Because he had polio.

5. Girls didn't play on the same baseball teams as boys until 1978.

   Why _____ on boys' teams?
           (negative, play)

   Because the rules didn't allow them to.

6. Mickey Mantle was a great baseball hitter.

   What _____ that was unusual?
           (do)

   He hit left-handed and right-handed.

7. Mark Spitz was a champion swimmer.

   What _____ in the 1972 Olympics?
   (achieve)
   He won five gold medals.

8. Jim Thorpe won a gold medal in track and field. The Olympic
   Committee took it away from him.

   Why _____ the medal?
   (negative, **keep**)
   Because he had once played professional football and earned money.

   Only amateur athletes can participate in the Olympics.

■ **ACTIVITY 8B**

   ❑ Choose one of the superheroes from the following list.

   Superman   Wonder Woman

   Batman   The Incredible Hulk

   The Bionic Man/the Bionic Woman   Spiderman

Write five sentences about one of these superheroes. Tell what he or she can do.
Is there anything that he or she cannot do? Tell what.

> ### *Example*
> Superman can bend steel with his bare hands.

   ❑ Now you are one of these superheroes, and there are many things in the
   world that you want to change. What can or will you be able to do to
   bring about these changes?

> ### *Example*
> I am Wonder Woman. I work to eliminate crime and corruption. There is
> an international plot to steal all the gold at Fort Knox.[9] I will be able to
> stop this crime. I will be able to hear the conversation of the robbers with
> my superhearing. I'll be able to find their secret meeting place because I
> have X-ray vision. . . .

[9]*Fort Knox* is the place where the gold for the U.S. Treasury is kept.

1. Finish this story.
2. Now choose another superhero you want to be and write your own story.

> ❑ King Kong had enormous strength. He could do many things. For example, he could uproot a tree with one hand. What were some of the other things he could do? What were some of the things he couldn't do? Why?

◼ ACTIVITY 8C

Fill in the blanks with *could, was able to/were able to*. For many of the sentences, you can use both *was able to/were able to* and *could*, but remember that in some affirmative sentences you can use only *was able to/were able to*. After you finish this activity, go back and circle the blanks where *was able to/were able to* is the only correct answer. Your instructor may choose to do this activity as a listening comprehension exercise before you fill in the blanks. If so, look at the Listening Comprehension Questions at the end of the activity and keep them in mind as you listen to your instructor the first time. The second and third times that you listen, take notes in order to be able to answer the questions.

Florence Griffith Joyner was one of the superstars of the 1988 Olympics in Seoul, South Korea. She won three gold medals and one silver medal in track. In the trials for the 1988 Olympics, she broke a record for the 100-meter race. She *was able to* complete the race in 10.49 seconds— less time than any woman before her. Florence says that she _____ win these victories because she runs "more like a guy than a girl."

Florence didn't have an easy life as a child. When she was four years old, her mother took her eleven children and the thirty cents that was in her pocket and left the children's father. They moved to Los Angeles, California. They *couldn't* afford to live in a good neighborhood. Her
(negative)
mother searched for an apartment a long time until finally she

_____ move into a government housing project[10] in Watts, one of

---

[10]*Government housing project* means "a group of apartment buildings built by the government for poor people who can't afford high rents."

the poorest black slums in the United States. Florence remembers some

times when her mother went without food so that her children

_____ have enough to eat. Life wasn't easy, but somehow her

mother _____ keep her family together. There was strong discipline

in the Griffith family. The children _____ watch TV during the
(negative)

week so that they _____ study, and everyone had to be in bed with

the lights out by 10:00 P.M. Florence says she didn't know how poor they

were because they were rich as a family. This is why she _____

overcome all the difficulties and hardships of growing up in a place like Watts.

Florence's mother remembers that, as a child, Florence was very light

on her feet. When the girl went to visit her father where he lived in the

Mojave Desert, she used to chase rabbits. Naturally, most of the rabbits

_____ run faster than Florence, but she claims that once she

_____ catch one of them.

Florence is an unusual athlete. She attracted a great deal of media

attention at the 1988 Olympic games because of her eye-catching beauty,

brilliant smile, and sense of style. For the trials, she wore fashionable

bodysuits in electric colors with only one leg. She had six-inch fingernails,

each one polished a different color. In the 1984 Olympics, officials told her

that she _____ participate in the relay race because her nails were
(negative)

too long for passing the baton. She refused to cut them, and even her

family _____ make her change her mind. Some people thought that
(negative)

was ridiculous, but Americans enjoyed the glamour that Florence Griffith

Joyner brought to the 1988 Olympics.

Listening Comprehension Questions

1. What did Florence Griffith Joyner win in the 1988 Olympics?
2. Why did she attract so much media attention? How was she different from other athletes?
3. Florence didn't have an easy childhood. Explain.
4. What rules did the Griffith children have to follow?
5. Why was Florence able to overcome the difficulties and hardships of growing up in a slum like Watts?
6. Was Florence a good athlete as a child?

■ **ACTIVITY 8D**

Some of the sentences in the following reading are numbered. Change the numbered sentences, using the affirmative or negative form of *could* or *was able to/were able to* and the base form of the verb. (Use a separate sheet of paper.)

> *Example*
>
> (1) *At first, only runners could compete.*
>
> *The Olympic Games*
>
> The Olympics began in ancient Greece in the year 776 B.C. The Greeks held these contests during the summer months once every four years. (1)At first, only runners competed. Later there were competitions in boxing, chariot racing, and long-distance running. (2)In the Greek Olympics, only free men competed. (3)Women, foreigners, and slaves didn't participate. (4)Women didn't even watch the Olympics. (5)Later, however, women established their own games, which were called the Heraea. The Olympics and the Heraea disappeared when the Romans conquered Greece.
>
> In the nineteenth century, Pierre de Courbertin, a Frenchman, worked hard to revive these games. (6)Finally, he organized the first modern Olympics in Athens in 1896. Other Olympics followed. (7)Again, at first only men entered the competitions. (8)Finally, women participated in the Olympic games in 1912. (9)Nowadays, amateur athletes from many nations of the world compete in a variety of sports events, including track and field, water sports, gymnastics, skiing, and figure skating.

EXPRESSING YOUR IDEAS

1. Tell about a famous athlete or someone you know who had to overcome a difficulty. What could or couldn't the person do when he or she had this difficulty or handicap? How was the person finally able to overcome the difficulty? What can or can't this person do today?

2. In this chapter, you read about the special abilities of the Tarahumara Indians. Tell about a group of people who have a special or unusual ability.

3. Tell about a time in your life when you weren't able to do something that you very much wanted to do. What were some of the reasons for this? Were you finally able to solve this problem? How?

THE PAST CONTINUOUS TENSE

UFOS[1] AND OTHER UNEXPLAINED PHENOMENA

Dialog

MOLLY: Did you see that program about UFOs on TV last night? It was really incredible!

JACK: You don't believe in UFOs, do you?

MOLLY: I don't know what to think. The program was really convincing. They interviewed a man from New Jersey. He **was driving** through a park at night **when** a bright light **surrounded** his car and—

JACK: He was probably drunk.

MOLLY: —he got out of his car and saw a flying saucer[2] only fifty feet away from him.

JACK: And I suppose when it landed some little green men got out.

MOLLY: They weren't green, but when the door of the flying saucer opened, ten little creatures walked out.

JACK: Oh, sure they did. Tell me more, Molly. Then what happened?

MOLLY: Then they dug up some earth and put it into some little plastic bags.

JACK: Plastic! I suppose they have an oil industry on Mars too. And what **was** the man from New Jersey **doing while** all these little creatures from Mars **were digging?**

MOLLY: He **was** just **standing** there and **watching** them. Then all of a sudden one of the creatures started to walk toward him.

JACK: Did the creature introduce the man to all of his little friends? Did they shake hands . . . or antennae, I mean?

MOLLY: No! The man ran back to his car and drove away as fast as he could.

JACK: Come on, Molly. You don't really believe that story.

MOLLY: This man didn't seem like a kook.[3] He was just an average guy, just like you or me. You know, Jack, it *is* possible.

Listening Comprehension Questions

1. What did Molly watch on TV last night?
2. What was the man from New Jersey doing when he saw a flying saucer?
3. What did the man see when the door of the flying saucer opened?
4. What did the creatures do after they got out of the flying saucer?

[1]*UFOs* are unidentified flying objects.
[2]*Flying saucer* means "a spaceship from another planet"; another word for UFO.
[3]*Kook* means "a crazy or very peculiar person."

5. What did the man do when one of the creatures started to walk toward him?
6. Do Molly and Jack have the same opinion about UFOs? What does Molly think about UFOs? What is Jack's opinion?

THE PAST CONTINUOUS TENSE

We use the past continuous tense in several different ways. In this chapter, we will talk about several of the different meanings of this tense.

The form of this tense for statements is shown below.

subject + { **was** / **were** } **(not)** + base form + **-ing**

Molly was watching television at ten o'clock.

INTERRUPTED ACTIONS

Statements

When we want to say that we were in the middle of doing something when something else interrupted us, we use this pattern.

subject + past continuous + **when** + subject + simple past

A man was driving home when a bright light surrounded his car.

Example

In the summer of 1977, two young people **were walking** along a street in New York City *when* they **looked up** and **saw** a UFO above the World

Trade Center. It didn't look like an airplane, but it had blinking lights. The same night, another man **was jogging** on a beach near New York City *when* an object with flashing lights **appeared** above him.[4]

Sometimes the past continuous is used in the *when* clause. This does not change the meaning of the sentence. In this case, *when* has the same meaning as *while*.

Examples

Two young people **were walking** along a street in New York City *when* they **looked up** and **saw** a UFO.

When⎫
While⎭ two young people **were walking** along a street in New York City, they **looked up** and **saw** a UFO.

The *when* clause can come at the beginning or end of the sentence.

Examples

Muhammad Ali was jogging in the park *when he saw a flying saucer.*
or
When Muhammad Ali saw a flying saucer, he was jogging in the park.

Questions

(Question word) + ⎧ **was** ⎫ + subject + base form + **-ing?**
⎩ **were** ⎭

What was the man doing when he saw the UFO?

[4]Details on some of these and other sightings mentioned in this chapter are in *UFOs Exist!* (Putnam, 1976) by Paris Flammonde.

Examples

In 1972, a young man was climbing a mountain in Wyoming when he saw a flying saucer and strange creatures.

Was the flying saucer **coming** toward him when he saw it?
  Yes, it was.

What **was** he **doing** when he saw the flying saucer?
  He was resting from the climb.

Contrast of Simple Past Tense and Past Continuous Tense in Sentences with *When* Clauses

Notice the difference in meaning between these sentences.

1. In August 1952, a young man **was driving** a boat through a swamp in Florida when he saw a UFO.

2. The young man **drove** away quickly when he saw the UFO.

In the first sentence, the man was driving the boat through the swamp *first*. *Then* he saw the UFO. In the second sentence, the man drove away immediately *after* he saw the UFO. In this sentence, *when* means "after."
  Note the question formation.

1. What **was** the man **doing** when he saw the UFO?
      He **was photographing** wildlife.

2. What **did** he **do** when he saw the UFO?
      He **raced** away because he was afraid.

  Here are other examples.
Two boys **were skating** on a lake *when a bright object appeared* above the trees near the lake. The UFO remained there for several minutes. The boys **went** over to inspect the trees *when it took off*. The tops of the trees were cut off, and parts of the trees were burned.

What **were** the boys **doing** when the UFO appeared?
  They **were skating.**

What **did** they **do** when the UFO took off?
  They **went** over to inspect the trees.

■ ACTIVITY 9A

☐ Uri Geller is a famous Israeli psychic. A psychic is a person who has special mental powers. A psychic can do unusual things—read other people's minds or move objects without touching them. Some people believe in Uri Geller's special powers; others say Geller is dishonest and tricks people. Donald Singleton, a reporter for the *New York Post,* once spent several days with Geller. The following exercise is based on an article Singleton wrote after that experience. Fill in the blanks with the past continuous or the simple past form of the verb given. All of these sentences show interrupted action in the past.

Uri Geller says that when he is in a room strange things happen.

Frequently, he says, he is not trying to make these things happen. He gave

the reporter an example. One time he went to a friend's house for dinner.

This friend had a rare and beautiful rock on a shelf in the living room.

They __*were eating*__ dinner in the dining room when this rock
      (eat)

__*flew*__ through the dining room door and _____ to the floor
  (fly)   **(fall)**

with a loud noise. Geller says he _____ about the rock
                                    (negative, think)

when this _____.
          (happen)

Geller _____ this story to the newspaper reporter
                    (tell)

when the reporter _____ a fork on the table next to them. When he
                 (notice)

_____ at the fork a second time, it _____ from side to side
   (look)   **(move)**

on the table and _____. Geller was surprised when the reporter told
                 (bend)

him about the fork.

Later that same night, Geller and the reporter _____
                                                        (wait)

in the lounge of a theater when the reporter _____ a strange
                                    (hear)

noise. When he _____ across the room, the soda machine
             (look)

_____ ice all over the floor. Geller says that he didn't try
         (throw)

to make the machine do that.

After several days with Geller, the reporter didn't know how to explain all the strange things that he had seen.

☐ Ask questions to get more information about the situation.

1. One night in August 1952, a man from Long Island, New York, saw a UFO. It landed not far from him, and three small beings got out. They walked around for a few minutes and then got back in their ship and left.

What *was the man doing* when *the UFO landed?*
He was taking a walk.

2. In May of 1955, a New York photographer and his girlfriend were in a park when a huge object with a circular shape appeared above them. The man photographed the UFO, and the photograph later showed something that looked like a large doughnut.

What _____ when _____ ?
He was taking photographs of his girlfriend.

3. A woman from Brooklyn saw a UFO from her car window in January 1975. The UFO was in the sky above an apartment building. The ship had a circle of blinking lights around it.

Where _____ when _____ ?
She was going to visit some relatives.

4. On December 1, 1971, Muhammad Ali was in Central Park in New York City when he saw something bright with the shape of a light bulb in the sky.

Where _____ when _____ ?
No, he wasn't taking a walk. He was jogging.

5. A Manhattan man sighted a UFO in 1974. He saw something pink in the shape of a triangle in the clouds. After some time, it moved off to the north and disappeared.

What _____ when _____ ?
He was watching the sunset. It was a beautiful summer evening.

☐ Tell about your experience.

1. Think about some time in your life when something happened that frightened you or when something happened that you couldn't explain. Tell what you were doing when this happened. Try to think of more than one incident.

2. Invent a story about a day when everything went wrong from morning to night. Tell what you were doing when each of these things went wrong. Try to use two different patterns:

I was doing (something) when (something) happened.

or

While I was doing (something), (something) happened.

Example

Yesterday was a terrible day for me. The day was a disaster beginning with the moment that I got up. I was having a wonderful dream when the alarm clock woke me up. I tried to go back to sleep for a few minutes to finish my dream, but I couldn't. Later, while I was making my morning coffee, I knocked the can of coffee off the counter by accident, and it spilled all over the floor.

Now continue the story of your disastrous day. What mishaps happened while you were in these situations?

shaving or putting on makeup	getting on the bus
getting dressed	riding in an elevator
waiting for the bus in the rain	having lunch in a restaurant

If you have a real story about a day in your own life when everything went wrong, tell it.

◼ ACTIVITY 9B

UFOs and psychic powers like Uri Geller's are difficult to explain. Here are some other accounts of a strange creature. Some people believe that there is a strange creature called a "Bigfoot" that lives in the Pacific Northwest of the United States. A bigfoot is a hairy creature between 6 and 15 feet tall that is half man and half ape. Some people believe there are 200 of these creatures. Many residents of this area of the United States say that they have seen these creatures. Here are their stories.

The first incident happened on the Nooksak River in the state of

Washington. Early one morning, three men _were fishing_ when
                                          (fish)

they _heard_ some strange noises near the shore and _____
      (hear)   (smell)

something very unpleasant. When they _____ their flashlights at
(point)
the shoreline, they _____ a large hairy creature. The men had left
(see)
a bag of fish on the shore. When they _____ the bigfoot with their
(strike)
lights, it _____ to steal some fish from the bag. The bigfoot
(try)
_____ and _____ away when it _____ the men.
(turn)   (run)   (see)

In the spring of 1973, an Oregon high-school teacher _____ on a
(drive)
quiet country road when he _____ a bigfoot on the far side of a
(see)
lake. The creature _____ berries when the man _____ it.
(pick)   (see)
The man stopped his car and took his rifle out, but when he _____
(try)
to shoot the bigfoot, he _____ because the creature looked so human.
(negative, can)

A woman in the same area _____ in her living room and
(sit)
_____ television when a large hairy arm _____ through her
(watch)   (come)
window. When she _____, her husband _____ from the next
(scream)   (come)
room with a gun. When he _____ the front door, a bigfoot
(open)
_____ there. It _____ and _____ away
(stand)   (turn)   (run)
when it _____ the gun.
(see)

PAST CONTINUOUS TENSE WITH A SPECIFIC TIME

When we want to say that we were in the middle of doing something at a
specific time in the past, we use the past continuous tense.

Examples

Jack called Molly at 10:00 P.M. Molly **was watching** the news on TV then.

We use the past continuous (*was watching*) because we want to say that the action began before the specific time (10:00 P.M.) and perhaps continued after it. We can't use the simple past (*watched*) to express this meaning in this case.

Notice the difference in this situation.

Molly had a lot of things to do yesterday. She went shopping in the afternoon. She studied until about 8:00 P.M. At 9:00 P.M., she sat down and **watched** TV.

In this situation, we can't use the past continuous (*was watching*). Here we mean that Molly began watching TV at 9:00 P.M.

▪ Activity 9C

In the summer of 1977, there was a total blackout[5] in New York City and surrounding areas. The electricity went out at 9:25 P.M. New Yorkers were doing a variety of things that night at that time. Use your imagination and complete the following sentences about what people were doing at 9:25 on the night of the blackout.

1. *Some people were watching TV* at 9:25 that evening. They couldn't see the end of their favorite TV programs.

2. A number of people _____ were eating _____ at 9:25. They didn't know if they should pay for their half-eaten dinners or not. The waiters didn't know what to do either.

3. Some New Yorkers _____ were cooking _____ If they had an electric stove, they had to throw their half-cooked dinners in the garbage.

4. One man _____ was writing _____ He had to wait until the next morning to finish the last page of his murder mystery.

5. Quite a few people _____ were going up/down _____ They had to wait for hours until security men got them out of the elevators and helped them down blackened stairwells.

[5]*Blackout* means "a total failure of electricity in an area."

6. Some children _____ were reading LISTENING _____
   Their parents stopped reading the bedtime stories and let the children
   come into their bedrooms to sleep.

7. One journalist _____
   for *People* magazine. He had to finish writing the story by candlelight
   so that the story would be ready for publication the next morning.

8. Some people _____
   They had to come back another time to see the end of the movie.

9. Many New Yorkers _____
   They had to sit in the hot subway cars for hours before help came.

10. A teenage boy _____
    He couldn't find his dog in the darkness and ran home. Fortunately,
    the next day the dog returned.

11. A lot of children _____
    They didn't know about the blackout until the next day.

SIMULTANEOUS ACTIONS IN THE PAST

We often use the past continuous tense in both clauses to show that two actions
were happening at the same time in the past. We can use both *when* and *while*,
but we use *while* more often for this meaning.

> ### *Example*
> Jack didn't watch the program on UFOs last night because he was at the
> observatory. *While* Molly **was watching** the program, Jack **was looking**
> at the stars through a telescope.

■ ACTIVITY 9D

1. Think of a party that you went to where you did not have a good time.
   What were you doing while all the other people were enjoying themselves?

   While _____ , I _____

2. Arnold worked in a nightclub last night. He was annoyed because people
   didn't listen to his music very carefully. What were they doing while
   Arnold was playing?

   _____ while Arnold _____

3. The president of the United States gave a very long and boring speech to Congress yesterday. What were many of the congressmen doing while he was giving his speech?

_____ while _____

4. Yolanda's friend Lisa gave birth to her first baby a week ago. Lisa's husband was very nervous. What was he doing while Lisa was giving birth?

While _____, her husband _____

5. Yolanda decided to go on a diet for about a week. Last night she and Molly went out to a restaurant for dinner. Molly had a chocolate sundae for dessert; Yolanda had nothing. What was Yolanda doing while Molly was eating her chocolate sundae?

_____ while _____

■ ACTIVITY 9E

Imagine that you saw a UFO. A reporter is asking you to describe what you saw. Do this exercise with a classmate. One of you is the person who saw the UFO. The other person is the reporter. Invent a dialog. The reporter wants to know these things.

1. what the person saw

2. what the person was doing when he or she saw it

3. where it was

4. what it looked like

5. what time he or she saw it

6. what it was doing while he or she was watching it

EXPRESSING YOUR IDEAS

1. What do you know about UFOs? How do you explain them? Do you or anyone you know believe in UFOs or life on other planets?

2. Do you believe in some things that you can't explain rationally—for example, psychic phenomena? Tell why you do or do not believe in these things. Talk about any examples that you have from your own life or that you have heard about from a friend.

3. Do you or any people that you know believe in ghosts or other supernatural beings? Are there stories about supernatural creatures that most people in your country know about? Who are these creatures, and what do they do?

10 COMPARISON OF ADJECTIVES, ADVERBS, AND NOUNS

The Sears Tower in Chicago.

Dialog

ARNOLD: I'm sick and tired of living in New York City. It's dirty. It's noisy. It's crowded. I need **more space.**

JACK: That's true, but what city is really **better?** Where would you like to live instead?

ARNOLD: Maybe San Francisco. It's **much cleaner** and **much more beautiful than** New York.

YOLANDA: It's **less crowded,** and it's **safer** too.

JACK: I don't know if it's really **safer.** Maybe there's **less crime** in San Francisco, but if you think about it, San Francisco is **just as dangerous.**

ARNOLD: Oh, do you mean the earthquakes?

JACK: Yeah. California has **more natural disasters than** any other area of the country. It's got earthquakes, mud slides, forest fires—

ARNOLD: Okay. Forget San Francisco. What about Chicago?

MOLLY: Chicago? I lived there when I was a child. It was all right, but I'd rather live in a small town than a big city like Chicago.

YOLANDA: I wouldn't. A small town is**n't nearly as exciting as** a big city. There are**n't as many things** to do.

ARNOLD: Yeah. If I move, I want to go to a big city like Chicago.

MOLLY: Arnold, I don't think you'd like Chicago. You hate the winter in New York. The winters in Chicago are **worse than** they are here. It's **much windier** there.

ARNOLD: All right. Forget Chicago. What about New Orleans? It's **warmer than** New York. And it's a great city for musicians.

JACK: Yeah, it's great for jazz, but does it have **as many opportunities** for rock musicians **as** New York does?

ARNOLD: Probably not. I guess I'm stuck here in New York.

MOLLY: The grass always looks greener on the other side of the fence.[1]

Listening Comprehension Questions

1. How does Arnold feel about living in New York City?
2. Where would he like to live instead? Why?
3. Yolanda thinks San Francisco is safer than New York City. Does Jack agree?

---

[1]*The grass always looks greener* means "what you don't have always looks better than what you do have."

4. Why does Yolanda prefer to live in a big city rather than a small town?

5. According to Molly, why are winters worse in Chicago than in New York City?

6. Does New Orleans have as many opportunities for rock musicians as New York City does?

COMPARISON OF ADJECTIVES

Comparisons to Express the Idea of "More"

When we want to compare and contrast things, we often use these patterns.

---

short adjective (one syllable) + **-er** + **than**

San Francisco is cleaner than New York.

more + long adjective (two or more syllables) + **than**

San Francisco is more dangerous than New York.

Examples

San Francisco is built high on a hill overlooking the Pacific Ocean. Some of the streets are **steeper than** others. On some of these steep streets, people even have difficulty parking their cars. Almost every morning the fog rolls in from the Pacific. It is **foggier** in the morning **than** it is in the afternoon, when the sun burns off the fog. Most people who visit both New York City and San Francisco think San Francisco is **more beautiful than** New York, especially when they see the sunlight on the Golden Gate Bridge.

SPECIAL CASES

1. Spelling
   a. You must double the consonant when you add -*er* to some adjectives.

   > fat → fatter
   > big → bigger
   > slim → slimmer

   Please turn to page 9 on the present continuous tense to review the rules for doubling consonants. Use the same rules here.
   b. With one- and two-syllable adjectives ending in *y*, change *y* to *i* and add -*er*.

   > foggy → foggier
   > happy → happier
   > windy → windier

2. Some people use -*er* with some two-syllable adjectives (*narrow, handsome*). In general, you are correct if you use *more* with two-syllable adjectives (except for those that end in *y*).

Examples

The streets high up on the hill are *narrower than* the streets downtown.

The streets high up on the hill are *more narrow than* the streets downtown.

3. Do not add -*er* to adjectives with an -*ed* ending.

   > tired → more tired
   > bored → more bored

4. Look at this pattern.

$$\left.\begin{array}{l} \textbf{a} \\ \textbf{an} \end{array}\right\} \; + \; \text{comparative adjective} \; + \; \text{singular noun}$$

Examples

San Francisco is very cosmopolitan. It's famous for its ethnic diversity and different life-styles. San Francisco is **a more cosmopolitan city than** the other cities in California.

5. Some adjectives have irregular forms.

good → better than
bad → worse than
far → farther than

Examples

In the middle of San Francisco Bay is a famous island called Alcatraz. It used to be a federal prison. Many prisoners tried to escape by swimming to shore. The currents were **worse than** the prisoners thought they were. The shore was **farther away than** they expected.

6. When you want to express the idea of "very" with a comparison, use *much* or *a lot*.

Examples

There are no prisoners on the island of Alcatraz today. When Alcatraz was a prison, the island looked **a lot drearier than** now. Alcatraz is now a public park. The island is **much more attractive** than it used to be.

Comparisons to Express the Idea of "Less"

A common pattern for expressing a comparison that means "less" is shown below.

---

not as + adjective + **as**

A small town isn't as exciting as a big city.

Examples

Pittsburgh, the home of the steel industry, is an important industrial city in Pennsylvania. In the late 1940s, Pittsburgh had a very serious problem with air pollution. Pittsburgh burned a lot of cheap coal to make steel. Civic leaders decided that cheap coal was **not as important as** clean air. Industry had to put air filters on smokestacks. The cleanup was **not as difficult as** industry expected and **not as expensive.**

Today the air in Pittsburgh is actually **not as smoky or polluted as** the air was twenty years ago.

Note: In British English, the preferred pattern is *not + so + adjective + as.*

Another way to express a similar meaning to *not as* + adjective + *as* is this form.

---

less + long adjective (two or more syllables) + **than**

A small town is less exciting than a big city.

■ ACTIVITY 10A

☐ Fill in each blank with the correct comparative form of the adjective below the blank. Use these forms: *-er* (*than*), *more . . .* (*than*), *less . . .* (*than*).

The story of the North End of Boston is a story of great change.

In the early 1940s, the North End was a terrible slum. It was

older than the rest of Boston and *closer* to the area
    (old)   **(close)**

of heavy industry. Rents were less expensive they were in other
                               (expensive)

areas of Boston, so the North End attracted floods of new immigrants

every year. But this meant that the North End was more overcrowded
                                               (overcrowded)

any other part of Boston. Because of this overcrowding and because there

weren't adequate sanitary conditions, the North End of Boston was

dirtier any other area of Boston, and the residents of the
     (dirty)

North End were less healthy.
                    (healthy)

Between 1940 and 1960, the North End changed radically. The people

who lived there rehabilitated the neighborhood. They did many things to

make the neighborhood more attractive. They planted trees and painted
                            (attractive)

their houses. They cleaned the streets and alleyways. They became

more careful about garbage and in general took pride in making
       (careful)

the neighborhood look better. People did not want to leave the
                        (good)

North End because the rents were generally lower and because the
                                    (low)

North End was more appealing many other sections of Boston.
                 (appealing)

City planners were amazed and puzzled by this change. Bankers were

still hesitant to give out loans to the people from the North End. It was a

bigger risk than the bankers wanted to take because this
   (big)

section of Boston was still considered a slum. Nevertheless, the North End

was ___*cleaner*___ and the people were ___*friendlier* :___ in many
    (clean)   **(friendly)**

other neighborhoods of Boston. The North End became an example of how

neighborhoods can change when people really care about them.

☐ Describe a neighborhood or place you know that has changed. Compare
what it was like in the past with what it is like now.

Comparisons to Express the Idea of Equality or Near Equality

When we are comparing two things and we want to say that the two things are
the same in some way or close to the same in some way, we can use these
patterns.

	as	+	(adjective)	+	**as** ⎫
✗	**just as**	+	(adjective)	+	**as** ⎬ means "equal"
	nearly as	+	(adjective)	+	**as** ⎫
	almost as	+	(adjective)	+	**as** ⎬ means "almost equal"
	isn't quite as	+	(adjective)	+	**as** ⎭

Examples

Denver, Colorado, is another city with an air-pollution problem. Citizens
in Denver are **just as concerned** about their air **as** the citizens of
Pittsburgh were. The air in Denver doesn't look **nearly as dirty as** the
air in Pittsburgh did, but in fact it's more dangerous because it contains
many poisonous substances.

■ Activity 10B

Complete each blank with the correct comparative form of the adjective below
the blank. Use *as . . . as*.

Los Angeles is one of the largest and richest cities in the United States.

Yet it is not ___*as safe as*___ many other American cities. In fact, the crime
                          (safe)

rate in New York City or in Chicago is not ___as high as___ that in Los
                                              (high)

Angeles. Sociologists and urban planners have studied these cities to try to

understand their problems. Jane Jacobs, the author of *The Life and Death*

of Great American Cities, believes that a crowded area sometimes is not

___as * as___ a suburban area. She believes that city streets often aren't
   (dangerous)

___as * as___ or ___as as as___ dark suburban streets. Certain residential
   (empty)   (isolated)

areas can be just ___as * as___ inner-city streets. People in expensive
                      (dangerous)

neighborhoods are sometimes just ___as * as___ to come home alone at
                                      (afraid)

night ___as___ people in more crowded neighborhoods. According to

Jacobs, the North End of Boston is ___as safe as___ anyplace else because it
                                       (safe)
                                                      as
isn't ___as isolated___ and the people on the streets know each other. Even
         (isolated)

late at night, people can come home and not walk through empty streets.

Perhaps this is why the crime rate in the North End of Boston is not

___as high as___ the crime rate in all the other areas of Boston.
   (high)

Questions

We often use three different types of questions to make comparisons:

1. *Are large cities more interesting than small towns?*
    Arnold thinks they are. What do you think?

2. *Who is friendlier—people in cities or people in small towns?*
    People in small towns are. (short answer)
                      or
    People in large cities are.
    Which is more interesting—country life or city life?
    Country life is. (short answer)
                      or
    City life is.

3. *Are prices as high in small towns as they are in large cities?*
    In some small towns, prices are higher than in large cities.

◼ Activity 10C

Some people think their hometown is better or worse than other places in the world. Ask a friend about his or her hometown and its people. Study the examples and use the same patterns in your conversation.

> ### *Examples*
>
> (noisy)   Friend: Is your hometown as noisy as this city?
>
> You: Actually, my hometown is noisier during the day, but at night it's quieter.
>
> (crowded)   Friend: Are the streets of your hometown as crowded as they are here?
>
> You: No, the streets aren't as crowded because they're wider and there aren't as many cars.
>
> (industrialized)   Friend: Which is more industrialized, this city or your hometown?
>
> You: This city is.

You may want to use these adjectives.

expensive	decadent	ambitious	interesting
dangerous	big	outgoing	reserved
attractive	exciting	polite	overcrowded
polluted	lively	aggressive	unpleasant

Parallelism

Look at these two sentences for an example of parallel structure:

The architecture of New Orleans is more European than **the architecture of Chicago.**

The architecture of ~~New Orleans~~ is more European than **Chicago.**

We cannot say, "The architecture of New Orleans is more European than Chicago." We are comparing the architecture of two cities, not architecture and cities. This is an example of an incorrect sentence, because parallel structure is not used.

Sometimes we don't want to repeat the noun (*architecture*) a second time. We use a pronoun instead of the second noun if the referent (antecedent) is clear. These patterns are especially useful in written English.

❏ Use *that* to replace a mass noun.
Use *those* to replace a plural count noun.

Examples

The European architect Le Corbusier devised a dream city early in the 1920s. He called it the Radiant City. The skyscrapers in Le Corbusier's city were taller and more majestic than **those** of any city of the time. The design of the Radiant City was more formal than **that** of any real city. It had twenty-four skyscrapers and underground streets, which were all within a great park.

❏ Use *one* to replace a singular count noun preceded by an indefinite article. (For example: a *building,* a *city.*)
Use *the one* to replace a singular count noun preceded by a definite article and followed by an adjective clause. (For example: *the building (that) he designed as a young man. . . .*)

Examples

At the same time Le Corbusier was designing an ideal city in Europe, an American architect, Daniel Burnham, was planning **one** in Chicago. He called his ideal city the City Beautiful. Burnham wanted to build a whole city around a cultural center. The ideal city of Le Corbusier was more influential in the United States than **the one** *that Burnham designed.* Le Corbusier's city, with its skyscrapers and underground streets, was actually more practical and modern than **the one** *that was designed for beauty alone.*

■ ACTIVITY **10D**

Look at the following sentences. Some of them have a problem of comparing two things that are very different and therefore not really comparable. Correct each sentence that contains a faulty comparison. Some sentences are correct.

Example

The parks of Boston are not as dangerous as Chicago.

You should write this sentence this way.
   The parks of Boston are not as dangerous as the parks of Chicago.
                                    or
The parks of Boston are not as dangerous as those of Chicago.

1. The air of Denver is as dangerous to breathe as Los Angeles.

   _____

2. The public transportation system of San Francisco is more efficient
   than Los Angeles.

   _____

   _____

3. The population of New York City is greater than Chicago.

   _____

4. The suburban area of Los Angeles is larger than that of New York City.

   _____

5. The parking problem in New York City is much more severe than New
   Orleans.

   _____

   _____

6. The museums and cultural centers in large cities are more numerous
   than small towns.

   _____

   _____

7. The people in small towns are friendlier than most big cities.

   _____

8. The jazz of New Orleans is more exciting than that of New York City.

   _____

9. The bridges of San Francisco are more beautiful than New York City.

   _____

10. Earthquake tremors in San Francisco are more frequent than
    northeastern cities.

    _____

■ ACTIVITY 10E

❏ Choose the correct comparative form of the adjective in each group of words. Choose from these patterns: -*er than, more . . . than, as . . . as, less . . . than,* and *not as . . . as.* You must use each of these forms at least once.

1. (New York/ large/ Montreal.)

   _____ *New York is larger than Montreal.* _____

2. (Paris/ old/ Cairo.)

   _____

3. (In 1940, Shanghai/ industrialized/ Marseilles.)

   _____

4. (Dublin/ far from London/ Naples.)

   _____

5. (Cairo's climate/ dry/ London's.)

   _____

6. (Tokyo/ crowded/ Hong Kong.)

   _____

7. (London/ famous for its Renaissance art/ Florence.)

   _____

8. (For swimming, the Mediterranean/ good/ the North Sea.)

   _____

9. (A first-class hotel room in Paris/ expensive/ a first-class hotel room in Geneva.)

   _____

❏ Now write a paragraph about apartments in New York City and in your hometown. Use these expressions and add some of your own.

| expensive | difficult to find |
| spacious | convenient to shopping areas |

ADVERBS AND COMPARISON OF ADVERBS

Adverbs

A word that describes or gives more information about a verb is called an *adverb*. We don't use adverbs after the verbs *be, seem,* and *feel*. We use adjectives after these verbs because an adjective gives information about the subject of the sentence, not the verb. When you add *-ly* to many adjectives, they form adverbs.

$$
\begin{array}{l}
\textbf{strong} \ + \ \textbf{-ly} \ \rightarrow \ \text{strongly} \\
\textbf{quick} \ + \ \textbf{-ly} \ \rightarrow \ \text{quickly}
\end{array}
$$

There are a few common adverbs that don't end in *-ly*. The adjective and adverb forms of the following words are the same.

hard	long	straight
fast	high	
late	wrong	

Examples

In the 1960s, many people worked **hard** to clean up Pittsburgh. (*Hard* tells you how they worked.) They believed **strongly** in a clean environment.

GOOD AND BAD

The adverb form of *good* is *well*.

The adverb form of *bad* is *badly*.

Examples

In some cities of the United States, the highways are built **very well,** but they *are* maintained **very badly.**

Note: Some adjectives end in *-ly*. Do not confuse these with adverbs.

friendly

lively

These adjectives do not become adverbs. We form adverbial expressions with these adjectives in this way.

The people in Boston greeted me *in a friendly manner.*

The people in the streets of New Orleans danced *in a lively fashion.*

Comparison of Adverbs

Many adverbs end in *-ly.* To make a comparison, use this form.

$$
\begin{array}{ccc}
\left.\begin{array}{l}\textbf{more}\\\textbf{less}\end{array}\right\} + & \text{adverb} + & \textbf{than}\\
(\text{not}) \quad \textbf{as} \quad + & \text{adverb} + & \textbf{as}
\end{array}
$$

Examples

The London Underground System is older than the New York City Subway System. The London subways run **more smoothly than** the New York City subways and **more efficiently** too. However, the London subways do**n't** stop **as frequently as** the New York City subways, and they don't run all night.

Some very common adverbs do not end in *-ly*: for example, *hard, fast, late.* To make a comparison, use this form.

adverb + **-er** + **than**
harder than
faster than
later than

Example

Trains of the Japanese National Railways run **faster than** American and British trains.

◼ ACTIVITY 10F

Here is a list of adjectives that you are going to match with the descriptions below.

slow	happy	fast	creative
careless	graceful	hard	obsessive

Read each sentence. Then finish the sentence by forming an adverb from one of the adjectives above. Do not use any adverb more than once.

1. In some cities, people drive their cars and pay no attention to the rules

   of the road. These people drive _carelessly_ .

2. At rush hour, traffic moves very _____.

3. The Concorde is an airplane that travels across the Atlantic Ocean in

   record time. The Concorde travels very _____.

4. A person who studies with a dictionary all the time and has to translate

   every single word studies _____.

5. Some students spend a lot of time studying before an examination. The

   night before their examination, they study very _____.

6. Yolanda is a wonderful dancer. People watch her on the dance floor

   because she moves _____.

7. Arnold likes to invent new rhythms and songs. He is always coming up

   with new ideas. He writes _____.

8. Fairy tales often end with the princess finding the prince. They live

   _____ ever after.

◼ ACTIVITY 10G

❑ Fill in each blank with the adjective or the adverb form of the word below it. Decide whether you need *-ly*.

People who travel abroad to large cities often have a hard time,

especially if they do not speak the language _well_ . The people in a
                                              (well)

big city often seem _____ and _____ . The foreigner often
                    (unpleasant)   (cold)

feels _____ and _____ during his or her first days. Some
      (confused)   (unhappy)

visitors have a _____ time asking for directions. People often look
              (hard)

at them _____, answer _____, or walk away _____.
     (contemptuous)   **(abrupt)**   **(quick)**

When foreigners call a phone operator for information, the operators often

speak _____ and in a _____ voice. Often it is
     (fast)   **(strange)**

_____ to understand the operator's accent. If they ask the operator
 (difficult)

to repeat something, the operator sometimes answers _____ and
              (angry)

hangs up _____.
     (sudden)

   Many foreigners respond _____ to these experiences because
            (emotional)

they are not accustomed to such behavior. They speak _____ about
           (passionate)

how they are treated. They say people should try to treat foreigners

_____ and _____.
 (polite)   **(friendly)**

❑ Have you ever traveled abroad? Tell about the experiences you had.

COMPARISON OF NOUNS

Sometimes we want to compare the number or amount of two nouns.
Remember that count nouns can be plural and that mass nouns are always
singular. (See Chapter 5.)

Comparisons to Express the Idea of "More"

When the number or amount of one thing is greater than the number or
amount of some other thing, we use this pattern.

> **more** + plural count noun + **than**
>   mass noun

Examples

New York City has **more skyscrapers than** San Francisco.
There is **more smog** in Los Angeles **than** in San Francisco.

Comparisons to Express the Idea of "Less"

When the number or amount of one thing is smaller, we use these patterns.

$$1.\quad \textbf{not} \;+\; \textbf{as} \left\{ \begin{array}{l} \textbf{many} \\ \textbf{much} \end{array} \right\} + \left\{ \begin{array}{l} \text{plural count noun} \\ \text{mass noun} \end{array} \right\} + \;\textbf{as}$$

Examples

There **aren't as many museums** in Los Angeles **as** in New York City.

Washington, D.C., **doesn't** have **as much nightlife as** San Francisco (does).

$$2.\quad \left. \begin{array}{l} \textbf{fewer} \\ \textbf{less} \end{array} \right\} + \left\{ \begin{array}{l} \text{plural count noun} \\ \text{mass noun} \end{array} \right\} + \;\textbf{than}$$

Examples

Columbus, Ohio, attracts **fewer tourists than** Denver (does).

There is **less tourism** in the Midwest **than** (there is) on the West Coast.

■ ACTIVITY 10H

Choose two cities you know well. Compare them, using the words in parentheses. Try to use all the patterns for comparison of nouns.

1. (*big office buildings*) _There are more big office buildings in New York than in Athens._

2. (*expensive restaurants*) _____

   _____

3. (*pollution*) _____

   _____

4. (*traffic*) _____

_____

5. (*crime*) _____

_____

6. (*noise*) _____

_____

7. (*interest in art*) _____

_____

8. (*boutiques*) _____

_____

9. (*hospitals*) _____

_____

10. (*crazy people*) _____

_____

11. (*nightclubs*) _____

_____

12. (*cockroaches*) _____

_____

13. (*cultural life*) _____

_____

14. (*manufacturing*) _____

_____

■ ACTIVITY 10I

Fill in the blanks with the correct form of the adverb or the comparative form of the adverb, adjective, or noun.

Chicago is one of the most important cities in the United States.

Located on Lake Michigan, Chicago is _____ in area _____
(big)

any other city in the United States except New York City. Before 1871,

most of the buildings in Chicago were made of wood. Then, in the Great

Fire of 1871, flames swept through Chicago _____ fire fighters
(quick)

could put them out. This fire killed several hundred people and left almost

90,000 homeless. Afterward, the city was rebuilt _____. The new
(rapid)

buildings, made of stone and steel, were _____ the ones built
(safe)

before the fire. They were also architecturally _____. The
(innovative)

architecture of Chicago became famous in the early 1920s. The first

skyscrapers were built then. There were _____ there _____
(skyscrapers)

in any other city of the time.

Between World War I and World War II, Chicago became famous

because of its underworld[2] activities. Chicago was the home ground for Al

Capone, one of the world's most famous gangsters. There was

_____ in Chicago at this time _____ at any time in the
(crime)

city's history. Many gangster movies of the time were set in Chicago. Some

of them glorified the life of a gangster. In fact, the gangsters were

_____ in real life _____ they were in the movies that were
(ruthless)

made about them. They controlled the bars and illegal gambling houses.

At that time, Chicago had _____ any other city in the
(speakeasies)[3]

United States, and the Mafia controlled them.

---

[2]*Underworld* means "the world of gangsters and organized crime."
[3]*Speakeasies* were nightclubs in the 1920s that served liquor when it was against the law to buy and sell liquor.

After World War II, things quieted down in Chicago. Today there are

_____ and _____ there was in Al
    (gang wars)   **(street violence)**

Capone's time. Most people think there isn't _____
                 (organized crime)

there was before. Certainly, gangland violence was _____
                  (visible)

in Al Capone's time.

Why else is Chicago famous? There is _____ at
          (air traffic)

O'Hare International Airport _____ in any other airport in the

country, and Chicago is _____ for its shipping industry
         (important)

_____ any other United States city because it is on Lake Michigan.

The meat-packing industry is _____ it is in many other cities in
       (large)

the United States. Although Chicago doesn't have _____
              (skyscrapers)

New York City, it does have the tallest skyscraper in the world, the Sears Tower.

■ ACTIVITY 10J

1. Compare yourself now with how you were at some time in the past. For example, are you happier now? Why or why not? Are you more comfortable with people? More confident? Thinner? Heavier? Kinder? Wiser? Explain.

2. Compare yourself with someone in your family. For example, are you more intelligent? More practical? More concerned about politics or social issues? Choose someone in your family, and write about him or her, comparing yourself with this person. You might want to use some of these adjectives.

conservative	rich	good in school	absent-minded
creative	practical	neat	timid
serious	imaginative	friendly	shy
ambitious	good in business	considerate	attractive

3. Describe a city a hundred years from now in comparison to what the city is like now. Compare the people, the buildings, the stores, the hospitals, and the taxes. For example, are the people happier? Busier?

More relaxed? Are jobs easier to find? Are schools more or less plentiful? Are there as many public services? Talk about the technological changes, the transportation system, the communications systems, the food, the living arrangements, and the types of family structures.

4. Two people are talking about a problem in American cities. One person is you. The other person is a banker. The banker believes the city is in danger of going bankrupt and is suggesting ways to solve the city's problems. The banker wants higher taxes, fewer public services, and less government interference in business. You are agreeing or disagreeing. Write a dialog.

5. Make up a questionnaire for a singles dating service. You need to get a lot of information about each person and about what he or she likes so you can match people up. Make up a list of questions such as these:

Is strength as important to you as beauty?

Is an intelligent person more exciting to you than an attractive person?

Is a good conversation as interesting to you as a good movie?

Now get several people to fill out your questionnaire. Then write a report explaining which two people match up the best. Explain in your report why these two people are good for each other.

EXPRESSING YOUR IDEAS

1. What are some of the problems in the city you are living in now? For example, is traffic a problem? Air pollution? Health care? Noise? Housing? Are these problems more serious than they are in your hometown? Are there solutions? If so, what do you think they are?

2. If you moved to another city, where would you prefer to live? In what ways would that city be better than the city you're living in now? What other differences would there be?

3. Do you remember your first impression of the city you're now living in? Did you expect things to be different? Explain how.

4. Do you like to travel? Do you think most big cities resemble each other, or are there major differences?

5. What are some of the advantages and disadvantages of living in the city?

6. How do people in your country feel about Americans and the way they live? What do you think Americans feel about people from your country and the way they live? Where do you think these ideas come from? Are they stereotypes?

7. Did your family ever move from one city or town to another when you were growing up? What was the new city like? Did you like it better than the city or town you lived in before? How did the move affect you? Was it difficult to leave your friends and make new friends?

11 THE SUPERLATIVE OF ADJECTIVES AND NOUNS

A clown with the Clyde Beatty-Cole Brothers Circus.

THE BEST AND THE WORST

Dialog

MOLLY: Hi, Yolanda. Hi, Arnold. What did you do today?

YOLANDA: We took my niece Susie to the circus.

ARNOLD: It's called "**The Greatest** Show on Earth."

YOLANDA: I had **the most fun** I've had in ages.[1]

MOLLY: Where's the circus?

ARNOLD: It's at Madison Square Garden.[2] It has **the most seats** of any place in the city.

YOLANDA: We sat in **the least expensive seats** in the Garden, but we could see everything.

MOLLY: Did Susie like it?

ARNOLD: She loved it, especially the trapeze acts.[3] They had **the most** incredible trapeze artists in the world.

YOLANDA: And **the funniest clowns.**

ARNOLD: **One of the best trapeze artists** was dressed as a clown. He did wonderful stunts[4] without a net under him.

YOLANDA: He wore a ridiculous outfit,[5] really—**the baggiest pants** in the world. I don't know how he balanced on the tightrope.[6]

ARNOLD: He was actually **one of the most talented athletes** in the whole show.

YOLANDA: And **the silliest.** Susie couldn't stop laughing.

ARNOLD: There was a fat lady. They claimed she was **the fattest woman** in the world. She weighed more than 800 pounds!

YOLANDA: They had **the skinniest man** too. He looked like a string bean.

MOLLY: It sounds like fun. I bet Susie ate a lot of junk.

ARNOLD: Yeah. She ate cotton candy and hot dogs and popcorn.

YOLANDA: I ate a lot too. I ate **the most hot dogs** of the three of us. I ate four, and I feel a little sick now.

MOLLY: No wonder, four hot dogs!

[1]*In ages* means "for a very long time."

[2]*Madison Square Garden* is an indoor stadium in New York City. Large rock concerts, the circus, and a wide variety of sports events take place there.

[3]*Trapeze acts* are acts performed on ropes and swings high up in a circus tent.

[4]*Stunts* are very difficult, highly unusual acts that require a lot of skill.

[5]*Outfit* means "everything that someone is wearing." Usually an outfit is coordinated in color and style.

[6]A *tightrope* is the rope high at the top of a circus arena or tent. This is also referred to as the *tightwire* or *high wire*. It is the rope that people walk across to show skill in balancing.

Listening Comprehension Questions

1. What did Arnold and Yolanda do today?
2. Did they enjoy themselves?
3. Did they buy the most expensive or the least expensive tickets?
4. According to Arnold, who was one of the most talented athletes in the whole show?
5. How much does the "fattest woman in the world" weigh?
6. Why does Yolanda feel a little sick?

THE SUPERLATIVE

We use the superlative when we want to show that one person or thing out of a group of three or more is unique in some way.

SUPERLATIVE OF ADJECTIVES

To form the superlative of adjectives, use these patterns.

---

the + short adjective + **-est** + noun

The clown wore the baggiest pants of anyone in the circus.

the + **most** + long adjective + noun

The clown was the most talented athlete in the circus.

the + **least** + long adjective + noun

They sat in the least expensive seats in Madison Square Garden.

Examples

The Ringling Brothers' Barnum and Bailey Circus is **the biggest circus** in the United States. It has **the most spectacular acts** of any circus in the country. **The most popular clown** in the United States, Emmett Kelly, worked for the Ringling Brothers' circus for many years. He was never **the funniest** or **liveliest clown** in the circus, but there was something in his sad face that touched people's hearts.

It is possible to give the same information in the superlative and comparative forms.

Emmett Kelly was **the most popular clown** in the United States.

Emmett Kelly was **more popular than** any other clown in the United States.

The meaning of these two sentences is the same, but the grammatical structure is different.

SUPERLATIVE OF NOUNS

$$
\textbf{the} \quad + \quad \left\{ \begin{array}{l} \textbf{most} \\ \textbf{fewest} \end{array} \right\} \quad + \quad \text{count noun}
$$

$$
\textbf{the} \quad + \quad \left\{ \begin{array}{l} \textbf{most} \\ \textbf{least} \end{array} \right\} \quad + \quad \text{mass noun}
$$

Examples

Ringling Brothers gives **the most performances,** sells **the most tickets,** and makes **the most money** of any circus in the United States. Some of the attractions of the Ringling Brothers' circus include freak shows, clown shows, animal acts, trapeze acts, juggling acts, and parades. Which of these acts has **the most appeal** for adults? For children? Which of these acts holds **the least appeal** for adults? For children? Why?

ONE OF THE, TWO OF THE, THREE OF THE + PLURAL COUNT NOUN

Look at this pattern.

> **One** (**of the** + superlative adjective + plural count noun) + singular verb

Note that the noun is *plural*. The verb is singular because the subject of the verb is *one*.

Examples

One of the trickiest stunts of all time was performed on a high wire in New York City. In 1974, Philippe Petit walked across a wire between the towers of the World Trade Center. Then he walked back and forth several times. Finally he was arrested for trespassing.

Some people felt he was **one of the most foolish people** of all time, since this is **one of the windiest places** in New York. Others said he was **one of the bravest people** in the world because he accomplished such a difficult stunt. What do you think?

MORE INFORMATION ABOUT SUPERLATIVE FORMS

Prepositional Phrases

We frequently use prepositional phrases with *in* and *of* when we use the superlative. Here are some common expressions.

in the family	of the men in my family
in the class	of the women in my class
in the United States	of the major cities in the United States
in the world	of the industrialized countries of the world
	of these three things
	of all time
	of all

Present Perfect and the Superlative

We often use the superlative with the present perfect. This structure is discussed fully in Chapter 16.

> ### *Example*
> Michu is *one of the shortest men* who **has ever lived.** He is less than forty inches (100 centimeters) tall. He is with the Ringling Brothers' circus.

Special Cases

1. Some adjectives form the superlative in an irregular way.

adjective	*comparative*	*superlative*
good	better than	the best
bad	worse than	the worst

> ### *Examples*
> Many children dream of running away from home to join the circus. The life of a circus performer seems very glamorous. Some of **the best things** about circus life are the excitement, the applause, and the romance. However, there are also drawbacks to this life. One of **the worst aspects** of circus life is the lack of stability caused by the constant moving from town to town.

2. Some adjectives form the superlative with either *-est* or *most*.

> ### *Example*
>
> handsome → { the handsomest
> { the most (least) handsome
>
> narrow → { the narrowest
> { the most (least) narrow

■ ACTIVITY 11A

Here are some facts about the United States. Supply the superlative form of the adjective below the blank: the _____-est, the most _____, or the least _____.

1. The highest _____ mountain in the United States is Mount McKinley
   (high)
   in Alaska. It is 20,320 feet (6,194 meters) high. ✓

2. The largest _____ lake in the country is Lake Superior. It is 31,820
   (large)
   square miles. ✓

3. Several years ago, Lake Erie, another of the Great Lakes, was

   the most polluted _____ lake in the United States. It was so polluted that
   (polluted)
   nothing could live in it, and it was pronounced a dead lake. However,

   government and business have been working to clean it up, and life has

   begun to return to Lake Erie. ✓

4. The oldest _____ city in the country is St. Augustine. It was founded
   (old)
   in 1565 by a Spanish explorer. ✓

5. The least populous _____ state in the United States is Nevada. It has
   (populous)
   approximately 500,000 inhabitants for 110,540 square miles (286,299

   square kilometers).

6. The smallest _____ state in the United States is Rhode Island. It is 44
   (small)
   miles (70 kilometers) long and 35 miles (56 kilometers) wide.

7. Some of the richest _____ farmland in the world is in Bucks County,
   (rich)
   Pennsylvania.

8. Although the cost of living in New York City is very high, it is not

   The most expensive _____ city in the United States. For example, the average
   (expensive)
   price of a house in San Francisco is higher than it is in New York City.

9. Some of ___most spectacular___ caves in the eastern part of the United
   (spectacular)

   States are the Mammoth Caves in Virginia. There are fantastic natural

   sculptures of stalactites and stalagmites in the caves. One of

   ___most interesting___ is a stalactite that drips magical water. The guides
   (interesting)

   say that if a bald man puts his head under this stalactite, his hair will

   grow back.

10. One of ___more spectacular___ sights in the United States is the Grand
    (spectacular)

    Canyon. The Colorado River rushes through a deep, colorful gorge. The

    gorge is 1 mile (1.6 kilometers) deep and 4 to 18 miles (6.4 to 29

    kilometers) wide.

11. ___The BIGGEST___ city in the United States is New York. It has
    (big)

    approximately 8 million people.

12. ___The Oldest___ university in the United States is Harvard
    (old)

    University in Cambridge. It was founded in 1636 to train Puritan ministers.

13. Salt Lake in Utah is ___the saltiest___ lake in the United States.
    (salty)

    When a person jumps in, his or her body immediately floats to the surface.

14. Macy's Department Store in New York City is ___The bigger___

    (big)

    department store in the world. It covers one city block.

ACTIVITY 11B

Complete the sentences below. Use the correct superlative form of the adjective
you choose. You can work in a group and share your knowledge or look up the
information in a dictionary.

1. The Nile ___is the longest river in the world.___

2. Mount Everest ___is the highest mountain in the word___

3. Rolls-Royces ___is the most expensive car in frenetien___

4. China ___is the most crowded city in the word___

5. The cheetah _is the_ *faster* _animal in the world_

6. The lion _is the most dangerous animal in the world_

7. The giraffe _is the most tallest animal in the world_

8. The blue whale _is the most interesting animal in the world_

9. The great white shark _is the most horrible animal in the world_

10. The Great Wall of China _is the largest wall in the world_

11. The Sears Tower in Chicago _are the ~~most~~ to llest construction in the world_

12. The Alaska pipeline _is the longest pipeline in the world_

13. The Caspian Sea _is the more beautiful sea in the world_

14. The Verrazano Narrows Bridge _is the most longer in the world_

15. Greenland _is the coolest land in the world_

■ ACTIVITY 11C

Fill in the blanks with *the most/the fewest* or *the most/the least.*

1. Alaska produces ____the ~~fewest~~ most____ oil of any state in the United States.

2. New York, California, Ohio, and Massachusetts have an unusually large

   number of colleges. Ohio is the leader. Ohio has ___~~fewest~~ the most___ colleges of these four states.

3. Death Valley, California, is one of the driest places in the United States.

   Some years it has ____the ~~most~~ least____ rain of any area—less than two inches (five centimeters) of rain per year.

4. California has ____~~fewest~~ the most____ inhabitants of any state. In 1970, the population was approximately 20 million.

5. Nevada has ___the least___ representatives in Congress of any state in the country. Because of its small population, it has only one representative.

6. California grows ___the most___ lettuce of any state in the country.

   Lettuce, along with celery and radishes, has ___the least___ calories of any food.

7. Florida gets ___the least___ snow of any state in the United States.

■ ACTIVITY 11D

Complete the following questions by filling in the blanks with the superlative form of an adjective. Choose any adjective that you think is appropriate for the question. Then answer the question.

1. Who is *the best* cook in your family?

   _____

2. What is one _____ things that happened in your life today?

   _____

3. What is _____ problem in your country today?

   _____

4. In your opinion, why is an oil crisis one _____ crises in the world today?

   _____

5. Where are some of _____ mountains in the world?

   _____

6. Who is _____ leader in the world today?

   _____

7. Is the United States _____ country in the world?

   _____

8. What do you think is one of _____ political issues in the United States today?

   _____

9. Is pollution one of _____ problems?

   _____

◼ ACTIVITY 11E

Here are some adjectives.

beautiful	good	bad	convincing
sexy	funny	famous	interesting

Here are some famous people in movies.

Charlie Chaplin	Alain Delon	Ingmar Bergman
Marilyn Monroe	Woody Allen	Akira Kurosawa
Elizabeth Taylor	Robert Redford	Sergei Eisenstein
Jean-Paul Belmondo	Paul Newman	Toshiro Mifune
Marlon Brando	Jane Fonda	Jean Renoir

Write sentences about these people or others you know. Tell about what you think is the most striking quality of the actor, actress, or director. You may use other adjectives and write about other people.

Example

Marilyn Monroe had the sexiest figure of any actress in the world, but she wasn't the most beautiful. Elizabeth Taylor was more beautiful.

◼ ACTIVITY 11F

Fill in the blanks with the correct comparative or superlative form of the adjective or noun. Read the entire statement before you fill in the blank.

1. Although the Mississippi River is *longer than* any river in the
   (long)
   United States, it isn't *the longest* river in the world. The Nile is.
   (long)

2. Texas used to be _____ state in the United States, but
   (large)
   today it isn't _____ state. Alaska is.
   (large)

3. The Empire State Building in New York City used to be

   _____ in the world, but today it isn't _____
   (tall)   (tall)
   in the world. The Sears Tower in Chicago is.

4. The United States used to produce _____ oil of any

   country in the world, but now it doesn't produce _____

   Kuwait or Saudi Arabia.

5. Although the Caspian Sea is _____ freshwater lake in the
                                        (large)
   world, it isn't _____ of all lakes in the world.
                          (deep)

6. Mount McKinley is _____ point in North America, but it
                              (high)
   isn't _____ Mount Everest. Mount Everest is
              (high)
   _____ mountain in the world.
          (high)

7. The Arctic Ocean is one _____ of all the oceans in the
                                      (cold)
   world, but it isn't _____ it used to be. It has been warming
                              (cold)
   up each year.

8. Greenland is _____ island in the world, but it isn't
                        (large)
   _____. The island of Honshu is in Japan.
          (populous)

9. The King Ranch in southern Texas is _____ ranch in the
                                                  (large)
   United States. It is 1 million acres (404,700 hectares). It is larger than

   the state of Rhode Island.

10. The North Pole is completely dark on December 22. It has

    _____ sunshine of any area in the world on December 22.

    On June 22, the opposite is true. The North Pole has

    _____ sunshine of any place on earth on June 22. The

    "midnight sun" is famous.

11. Death Valley, California, has recorded some of the _____
                                                              (high)
    temperatures in the world. Sometimes the air temperature reaches

    134°F (57°C). The air temperature isn't _____ the ground
                                                    (hot)
    temperature, which sometimes reaches 165°F (74°C). Some rocks are

_____ a frying pan. You can fry an egg on them.
(hot)

_____ point in the United States is also located in Death
(low)

Valley. It's 282 feet (86 meters) below sea level.

12. Mount St. Helens is a volcano in the state of Washington. There was a

small eruption in 1857. In 1980, the volcano erupted again. This was

_____ eruption in the continental United States. It was
(destructive)

one of _____ natural disasters in United States history,
(bad)

causing over a billion dollars in damage. The destructive force was

_____ than that of the first atomic bombs. In fact, it was
(great)

almost as great as the force of the largest atomic bombs. It rained

down almost _____ mud and ash _____

Vesuvius did in A.D. 79. People in nearby Yakima, Washington, reported

that it was almost _____ night at noontime on the days of
(dark)

the eruption. The streetlights automatically turned on. Fortunately, it

did not cause _____ deaths _____ other

volcanic eruptions, such as Vesuvius, Mount Etna (1669), or Krakatoa

(1883). Krakatoa was _____ eruption in history, taking
(bad)

36,000 lives.

EXPRESSING YOUR IDEAS

1. Tell about the hardest choice you have ever had to make. Tell why it was so difficult to make this choice and how it was important in your life.
2. Describe the most unusual person you've ever met (or the richest, smartest, most naive, most sophisticated, or nastiest person).
3. Talk about the best or the worst day of your entire life. What happened?
4. Describe one of the most embarrassing moments of your life. Tell what made it so embarrassing and what happened as a result.

5. Talk about a famous person in the world today or in history. Who in your opinion is or was the most interesting person in politics? The most or least intelligent ruler of a country? The most impressive actor or actress? The most creative person you've ever met?

6. Describe the most frightening (or most fascinating or most beautiful) place you have ever seen.

7. Talk about the most expensive present you have ever bought for someone. Tell about what this person meant to you and why you bought this present. Tell how the person reacted to the gift.

8. Describe the most unpleasant experience or the most pleasant experience you have had since you came to the United States.

HAVE TO AND MUST

Dialog

(Molly, Yolanda, Arnold, and Jack are walking through Central Park in New York City.)

YOLANDA: Look at that homeless person over there. I guess that park bench is his home. Isn't it awful that he **has to make** his home in a park? This country **has to do** something about its homeless people.

JACK: I agree that we have a serious problem, but, you know, that guy **doesn't have to** sleep in the park. There are shelters[1] where he can go.

ARNOLD: Yeah, but sometimes those shelters are dangerous places. Some of the homeless people there are really crazy or even violent. There are fights in those places all the time. A lot of the homeless[2] say it's safer to sleep outside.

YOLANDA: The government just doesn't do enough to help the poor.

JACK: What are you talking about? What about all the money the government spends on welfare?[3]

YOLANDA: That's a drop in the bucket.[4]

ARNOLD: I agree with you. The government spends billions of dollars on the military, but, by comparison, it doesn't spend much on social programs. Why does this country **have to spend** so much on making war? We **must do** something to cut back on military spending.

JACK: Hold on![5] The military is vital to our defense. Social programs aren't.

ARNOLD: You sound like my father. Why **do** you **have to be** so conservative all the time?

JACK: All I'm saying is that we **mustn't weaken** our military defense system too much. I mean, I know relations with Russia are improving, but somehow I just don't trust the Soviets.

ARNOLD: Listen, the Russians want to stop the arms race just as much as we do. You don't know what you're talking about!

JACK: Come on, Arnold. You **don't have to be** so insulting. My opinions are valid too. We just have a different point of view.

MOLLY: Hey, why don't we all stop arguing? We **don't have to** fight about our ideas.

---

[1]*A shelter* is a place where homeless people can get out of the cold and sleep for the night. It is usually operated by the city government.

[2]*The homeless* means "homeless people." (*The poor* means "poor people.")

[3]*Welfare* is money the government gives to a person without a job so that he or she can pay the rent and buy food and clothing.

[4]*A drop in the bucket* means "something so little that it doesn't help much."

[5]*Hold on!* means "Wait a minute! Stop and think about what you're saying!"

Listening Comprehension Questions

1. In Jack's opinion, do homeless people have to sleep in the park, or do they have some other place where they can go at night?
2. According to Arnold, why do many homeless people prefer to sleep outside instead of in a shelter?
3. Do Arnold and Jack agree that the government must cut military spending?
4. Why does Jack think the United States mustn't weaken its military defense system too much?
5. Is Molly enjoying this argument?

HAVE TO

Affirmative Statements

We use *have to* and *has to* to talk about something that is necessary to do. We use *had to* to talk about something in the past that was necessary to do.

Examples

Today the United States has a volunteer army. A volunteer **has to do** many things. He **has to go** through basic training for seven weeks. During basic training, the volunteers **have to get up** between four-thirty and five A.M. They **have to learn** the discipline and routine of army life.

Before 1973, the army was not voluntary. Most men eighteen years and older **had to serve** in the army for two years.

FUTURE TIME

Sometimes we form the future of *have to* with *will*; sometimes we just use *have to*.

Examples

1. The army **will have to do** more studies to decide if the new volunteer army is better than the old army.

2. The army **has to do** more studies in the future to decide if the new volunteer army is better than the old army.

Negative Statements

We use *don't have to* and *doesn't have to* to talk about something that is not necessary to do. When you say that someone *doesn't have to do* something, you mean that there are other possibilities or choices. We use *didn't have to* to talk about something in the past that was not necessary to do.

Examples

Today's army gives the men more freedom. Today a man with a mustache **doesn't have to shave** it off. Volunteers today **don't have to get** short haircuts. Before 1973, they had to.

Questions

Examples

1. **Do** men **have to get** short haircuts in the army?
   No, they **don't.**
      or
   No, they **don't have to.**

2. **Do** people **have to have** a high-school diploma for the army?
   Yes, they **do.**
      or
   Yes, they **have to.**

3. How old **does** a volunteer **have to be?**
   He or she has to be eighteen or older.

4. Do volunteers like to get up at 4:30 A.M.?
   No, they don't, but they **have to.**

5. Why **did** men **have to join** the army before 1973?
   Because it was the law.

Affirmative and Negative Statements

Subject	Helping Verb	Has to Have to	Base Form	
A volunteer		has to	go	through basic training for seven weeks.
A volunteer	doesn't	have to	shave	his mustache.

Questions

Question Word	Helping Verb	Not	Subject	Have to	Base Form	
Why	did		men	have to	join	the army before 1973?
How old	do		volunteers	have to	be?	
Why	do	n't	volunteers	have to	shave	their mustaches nowadays?

■ **ACTIVITY 12A**

Arnold's older brother, Sam, was in the old army from 1971 to 1973. He hated it. He had to do many things that he didn't want to do.

☐ Look at the five pictures that follow and make sentences for each about what Sam had to do when he was in the army.

1. *Sam had to salute his officers.*
   He had to wear a uniform.

2. _____

3. _____

4. _____

5. _____

☐ Ask questions using *have to* or *has to*. Write an answer for each question. Use your imagination for the answers.

1. (Picture 1) (*always*)

   Did Sam always have to salute his
   officers? Yes, he did.

2. (Picture 2)

   How often _____

   _____

3. (Picture 3)

   What time _____

   _____

4. (Picture 4)

How long _____

_____

5. (Picture 5)

Why _____

_____

☐ Arnold has a friend whose younger brother, John, is in the volunteer army today. Some things about army life are the same today. Some things are different. Write a sentence about John. Then tell what Arnold's brother, Sam, had to do in the old army.

These things are the same.

1. (salute his officers)

John has to salute his officers.
Sam did too.

2. (get up early)

_____

_____

3. (go to rifle training)

_____

_____

4. (peel potatoes)

_____

_____

5. (obey orders)

_____

_____

These things are different today.

1. (get a short haircut)

   John doesn't have to get a haircut, but Sam had to.

2. (shave his mustache)

   _____

   _____

3. (get a pass to leave the base)

   _____

   _____

4. (eat army food all the time)

   _____

   _____

■ ACTIVITY 12B

Do this exercise with a partner. One of you is an angry sergeant. One of you is a rebellious soldier who has realized he or she doesn't like army life. The sergeant has many unpleasant duties for the soldier to do. The soldier insists that he or she doesn't have to do all of these unpleasant things. Act out an argument.

■ ACTIVITY 12C

❑ Tell or write about a time when your life changed and you took on increased responsibilities. What additional things did you have to do? (For example, you had a child, and you had to get up during the night to feed her or him.)

❑ Tell or write about a time when a change took place and you didn't have to do things you had to do before. (For example, you left home, and you didn't have to tell your parents what time you came home at night.)

MUST

Affirmative Statements

Must also means that it is necessary to do something. Its meaning is similar to *have to* and *has to*. We often use *must* to talk about rules or to give a strong order. Americans use *have to* and *has to* in more situations than *must* for this meaning. Use the base form of the verb after *must*.

> #### *Examples*
>
> It is the first day of basic training. The sergeant is telling the new volunteers the rules for the army.
>
> SERGEANT: All right, men. You're in the army now, and don't forget it. You **must obey** all orders. You **must salute** every officer.
>
> We can also use *must* + the base form to talk about the future.
>
> SERGEANT: Tomorrow you **must get up** at 4:30 A.M.
>
> To express this meaning of *must* in the past, we use *had to*.
>
> When Arnold was in the army, his sergeant told him that he **had to get up** at 4:30 A.M.

Negative Statements

We use *must not* (*mustn't*) to say that something is not permitted. In the negative, *must* and *have to/has to* are very different in meaning. Remember that *don't have to/doesn't have to* means that it is not necessary. Look at these sentences for a contrast of *must not* and *doesn't have to/don't have to*.

1. In the United States, all drivers must have a driver's license. A person **mustn't drive** unless he or she is carrying a valid license. (It is prohibited by law.)

2. A foreigner can drive with an international driver's license for a year. The foreigner **doesn't have to get** an American license right away. (It isn't necessary for him or her to get a license for one year.)

> #### *Examples*
>
> SERGEANT: Men, here are some things you **must not do.** They are against the rules. You **must not drink** when you are on guard duty. You **must not leave** your rifle anywhere. You **must not be**

> late for anything. One rule is different now. You **don't have to
> get** a pass when you leave the army base anymore, but you
> **must not stay** out all night.

Questions

We do not use *must* in questions very often. We usually use *do/
does* + *subject* + *have to* for questions.

> ### Examples
>
> 1. **Must** volunteers **wear** uniforms in today's army?
>   Yes, they must.
>
> 2. **Do** volunteers **have to wear** uniforms in today's army?
>   Yes, they do.

Sentence 1 is grammatically correct, but we do not use this form very often.
The form in sentence 2 is much more common.

■ ACTIVITY 12D

An experienced soldier who fought in World War II is speaking to a group of
young, inexperienced soldiers about war. They're going to fight their first
battle tomorrow.

Write sentences using *must* or *must not* and the words or phrases in
parentheses.

1. (*keep alert*)

   You must keep alert.

2. (*get your gun wet*)

   _____

3. (*try to be brave*)

   _____

4. (*panic*)

   _____

5. (*walk alone*)

_____

6. (*obey all orders*)

_____

◼ **ACTIVITY 12E**

Rewrite the following sentences. Decide which is correct—*must not* or *don't have to/doesn't have to.*

1. Muslims and Jews are not permitted to eat pork.

   Muslims and Jews mustn't eat pork.

2. Muslims must pray five times a day. It isn't necessary for Christians to pray five times a day.

   Christians *don't have to pray five times a day.*

3. One of the Ten Commandments says that people are not permitted to kill other human beings.

   One of the Ten Commandments says _____

4. A religious Muslim must go to the mosque on Friday. It isn't necessary for Christians to go to church on Friday.

   _____

5. It is prohibited for a member of the Roman Catholic clergy to marry.

   _____

6. It isn't necessary for a member of the Protestant, Jewish, or Muslim clergy to stay single.

   _____

7. A religious Muslim is not permitted to drink alcohol.

   _____

■ ACTIVITY 12F

☐ You are the dictator of an imaginary country. You have just gained power. You are announcing the new laws of the land. Make sentences using *must, has to/have to, mustn't,* and *don't have to/doesn't have to.*

These things are prohibited.

1. (have pictures of anyone but me in your homes)

   You must not have pictures of anyone but me in your homes.

2. (go out on the streets after 9:00 P.M.)

   _____

3. (hold political meetings without written permission)

   _____

4. _____

   _____

5. _____

   _____

These things are absolutely necessary to do.

1. (report any change of address to me)

   _____

2. (get permission to work)

   _____

3. (turn over fifty percent of all your income to the state)

   _____

4. _____

   _____

5. _____

   _____

These things are not necessary to do.

1. (worry about anything ever again)

   _____

2. (go to school)

   _____

3. (do military service if you're sixty-five or older)

   _____

4. _____

   _____

5. _____

   _____

❑ It's one year later. Because of your unpopular laws, there is a strong possibility of revolution in your country. The revolutionary leaders are demanding many changes. You are answering their demands. Write a dialog between you and one of these revolutionary leaders.

❑ Interview a classmate. Is there anyone in your class who has lived in a country under a military dictatorship? You and your classmates can ask this person questions about what it was like to live under a dictatorship.

■ ACTIVITY 12G

❑ Arnold's father, MR. CALHOUN, is at the doctor's office because he doesn't feel very well. The doctor, DR. NORMAL, is telling MR. CALHOUN that he must change certain bad habits. For example, MR. CALHOUN smokes too much, drinks four martinis a day, gets very little sleep, and works very long hours. Write a dialog between DR. NORMAL and MR. CALHOUN. The doctor wants to help MR. CALHOUN. MR. CALHOUN doesn't want to change. The doctor is telling MR. CALHOUN what he must do to lower his blood pressure and live longer. Use *have to, don't have to, must* and *mustn't.*

❑ Contrast your life in the United States with your life in your own country. You can use *have to, must, can,* and *could* and the negatives.

EXPRESSING YOUR IDEAS

1. Is the military budget high in your country? Does your country spend more on defense than on social programs? Do you agree with your country's policy on this? Why or why not?

2. Is your country in conflict with other countries? If so, which countries? Why do you think this conflict exists?

3. Describe the military in your country. About how many people are in it? Does it have modern weapons? Does it buy arms from other countries? How long do people have to serve in the military? What do you think about this?

4. What do you think about women in the military? Do women have to serve in your country?

5. What are some of the issues involved in voluntary versus compulsory military service? What are the arguments on both sides of the issue?

6. A conscientious objector is someone who refuses to join his or her country's army because he or she is opposed to war and killing for strong religious or moral reasons. Can a person in your country refuse to fight for these reasons? Do you think people have a right to refuse military service?

7. Do you think every country has to have an army? Why or why not?

8. Do you think there will ever be world peace? Why or why not?

9. In your opinion, what are some of the things that have to happen before there can be world peace?

10. Were you ever in the army in your country? Tell about your experience. What did you learn from your experience in the army?

11. What do you know about the problem of the homeless in the United States? Why are there so many homeless people here? Does your country have a large number of homeless people? If so, what are the causes of this? What do you think the government should do for homeless people?

Jack's fantasy.

Dialog

(MOLLY is in Vermont on a ski vacation. JACK did not go with her. He's talking to YOLANDA now.)

YOLANDA: Lucky Molly! She **must be having** a wonderful time up there in Vermont.

JACK: Yes, she **must be.** But why did she go alone? She didn't say much about that before she left.

YOLANDA: You know, I was a little surprised that she went alone too.

JACK: Why didn't she ask me to go with her? Something **must be** wrong.

YOLANDA: Why? Did you two have an argument about something?

JACK: No. I thought everything was fine. But now I'm beginning to wonder. **Could** she **be thinking** of breaking up[1] with me?

YOLANDA: Jack, she **couldn't be thinking** of that. Molly tells me almost everything.

JACK: She does?

YOLANDA: Stop worrying. She never said anything to me about breaking up with you.

JACK: I'm afraid she **might fall** in love with one of those handsome ski instructors. She **might forget** me. She **may not come** back. I **may** never **see** her again.

YOLANDA: Wow, Jack. You **must** really **be** in love.[2] Don't worry so much. Of course she'll come back.

JACK: I sure hope you're right.

YOLANDA: Look, Jack. You **could call** Molly. I have the telephone number of her hotel.

JACK: I thought of calling her last night, but then I changed my mind. Why hasn't she called me? She **must not be thinking** of me at all.

YOLANDA: Oh, come on. Why don't you give her a call? Who knows? She **might be missing** you very much.

JACK: Do you think so? Hey, I have an idea. I **could take** the bus up to Vermont tomorrow. I **could** really **surprise** her.

YOLANDA: But she'll be home in two days.

JACK: Oh, yeah. That's right. I guess I can wait.

---

[1]*To break up with someone* means "to end a relationship; to stop going out with someone."

[2]*To be in love* has a different meaning from *to love.* We can say, "I love my parents," but we can't say, "I am in love with my parents." For a relationship between a man and a woman, we can say both "Jack loves Molly" and "Jack is in love with Molly." *To be in love* has a romantic meaning.

Listening Comprehension Questions

1. Why does Jack think something must be wrong with his relationship with Molly?
2. Why is Yolanda so sure Molly could not be thinking of breaking up with Jack?
3. What is Jack afraid might happen while Molly is on her ski trip?
4. Did he call her last night?
5. When will Molly be back from her trip?

MAY AND *MIGHT*

Statements

May and *might* are used to talk about possibility when we are uncertain about something. *May* and *might* have the same meaning when we talk about possibility.

SIMPLE PRESENT AND FUTURE OF *MAY* AND *MIGHT*

Subject + { **may** **might** } (**not**) + base form

Molly may forget me. She might not come back.

Contractions: We don't usually use contractions with *may/might* + *not*.

Examples

Americans love to play games. After dinner people often spend an evening playing games with friends. One reason Americans love games **might be** because many Americans are very competitive. Yolanda has several games that are very popular. They are Scrabble,[3] Monopoly,[4] Nintendo,[5] and backgammon.[6]

[3]*Scrabble* is a word game.
[4]*Monopoly* is a game in which people try to buy imaginary property and try to accumulate paper money.
[5]*Nintendo* is a video game.
[6]*Backgammon* is a board game of chance and skill played with dice and markers.

> Tonight Yolanda and Arnold invited Jack over for dinner. They **might not go** out after dinner because it's very cold outside tonight. They **may stay** in and **play** games.

Questions and Short Answers

Look at this question: Might we play games after dinner? We rarely form questions with *might* in this way. This question sounds very unnatural. If we use *may* or *might* in a question, we usually follow this form.

(Do you think)	+	subject	+	{ **may** / **might** }	+	base form?

For example, Do you think we might play games after dinner? Another way to ask this question is to use the future tense: Are we going to play games after dinner?

We often respond to questions about possibility with a short answer using *may* or *might*.

> ### Example
>
> JACK: What are we going to do after dinner tonight? Are we going to play Monopoly?
>
> YOLANDA: We **might.** Would you like to?

We don't repeat the main verb in a short answer unless the main verb in the question is *be*.

> ### Example
>
> JACK: Yolanda, I know you have to work until 6:00. Is dinner going to be late?
>
> YOLANDA: It **might be.** We might not eat until 8:00. But why don't you come over around 7:30?

■ ACTIVITY 13A

☐ Talk about possible reasons for the following situations in class. Use *may* or *might* + base form.

1. Arnold never dances at parties. Why not?

   a. *He might not like to dance.* _____

   b. _____

   c. _____

2. Jack is planning to spend the whole day in bed. Why?

   a. _____

   b. _____

   c. _____

3. Jack is upset because Molly is away in Vermont. What do you think he's going to do to welcome her back home?

   a. _____

   b. _____

   c. _____

4. The rivers and oceans of the world are becoming polluted. Make predictions about what might happen to marine life and to people who depend on fish for food.

   a. _____

   b. _____

   c. _____

   d. _____

5. Some scientists feel pessimistic about our ability to produce enough food for the world's growing population. What do these scientists think may happen?

   a. _____

   b. _____

   c. _____

   d. _____

6. Other experts have a more optimistic view of the future and believe that technological advances may solve many of our present problems. What do they think may happen?

a. _____

b. _____

c. _____

d. _____

❑ Read the following paragraph. Notice that we don't use *may* or *might* in every sentence. We vary the style with *maybe* or *perhaps* and *will*.

Jack is planning to take a long trip this summer. He isn't sure where to go. He might take a trip around the United States. If he does, perhaps he will visit some of the beautiful national parks in the country. He might choose to travel by bicycle through the countryside of France. Maybe he will stay in youth hostels if he goes to France. Jack might choose to visit the Mayan ruins in the Yucatán Peninsula in Mexico. If he goes to Mexico, he will probably want to read some books about the Mayan Indians before he goes. He may also want to study some Spanish.

Choose one of the following topics and write a paragraph similar in form to the one that you have just read.

1. Write about some ideas you have about your own future.

2. Write about some world conflict and tell what you think might happen in the future.

3. Write about some problems in the United States or in your country and state how these problems might affect the future.

MUST

We use *must* to express what we think is a logical assumption or a deduction that is based on evidence that we have. It means that we have only one possibility in mind. We use *must* when we mean, "I'm almost sure." We use *may* or *might* when we mean, "I'm not sure, but it's possible." When we use *must* to make a deduction, we are usually talking about the present. Deductions with *must* about the future are not very common. To make a deduction about the future, we usually use *probably* and the future tense. Remember that *must* also has the meaning of obligation or necessity. (See Chapter 12.)

---

subject + **must (not)** + base form

Jack must be in love. He can't think of anyone but Molly.

Examples

(JACK is at YOLANDA's apartment now with ARNOLD.)

JACK: Look at all those games. You **must** really **enjoy** games, Yolanda.
ARNOLD: She does. And she enjoys winning too.
JACK: You **must be** a really good player then.
YOLANDA: I am.

Note: We don't often use *must* to form a question. When we use *must* in short answers, the rules are the same as for *may* and *might*.

■ ACTIVITY 13B

☐ Read the following short dialog and make logical deductions based on the information given. Use *must*.

1. ARNOLD: I stayed up playing at the nightclub until 3:00 A.M. last night, and I had to get up at 7:00 this morning.

   YOLANDA: You *must be very tired.*

2. YOLANDA: I just tried to phone Jack. There was no answer.

   ARNOLD: He _____ at home.
   (negative)

3. JACK: Who was the actress who played the role of Scarlett O'Hara in *Gone with the Wind?* I can't remember her name.

   YOLANDA: I can't remember either. Let's ask Arnold. He's an expert on old

   movies. He _____ the answer.

4. (ARNOLD is looking out the window. It is winter.)

YOLANDA: I wonder what the temperature is outside.

ARNOLD: It _____ really cold. The wind is blowing, and everybody is wearing a heavy coat.

☐ Here is some information about strange beings from an imaginary planet. Make deductions with *must* based on the information.

1. These strange beings have no ears, but they have long antennae that twitch when there is a noise.

   _____

2. They have eyes in the front, sides, and back of their heads.

   _____

3. They never wear clothes.

   _____

4. They can speak hundreds of different languages, they have a highly developed technology, and their doctors have found a cure for every disease.

   _____

5. There are no cemeteries on this planet.

   _____

6. These beings never carry weapons, and no one ever fights.

   _____

■ ACTIVITY 13C

Fill in each blank with *may/might* or *must* and the base form of any verb that you think is logical to complete the sentence. Use *must* if you have good reason to be almost sure of your deduction. Use *may/might* if you are thinking of only one of several possibilities.

1. JACK: Do you remember that friend of Arnold's that we met a few weeks ago at the nightclub?

   MOLLY: Do you mean Juan?

   JACK: Yes. What country does he come from? Do you remember?

MOLLY: I know he speaks Spanish. He *might come* from Spain, or

he *might come* from a country in South America.

JACK: Oh, wait a minute! I remember he told me that his parents live in Madrid.

MOLLY: Oh, he *must come* from Spain then.

2. ARNOLD: Molly, do you know where Yolanda is? I called her apartment, and there was no answer.

MOLLY: I don't know. She _____ at the office.

ARNOLD: Oh, yeah, now I remember. She has to work late tonight. She

_____ at the office.

3. ARNOLD: I don't feel well.

YOLANDA: What's wrong?

ARNOLD: I'm not sure. I _____ a simple cold, or I

_____ the flu.

YOLANDA: Let me feel your forehead. Hey, you're burning up.

ARNOLD: I _____ a fever.

4. ARNOLD: Look at that beautiful Rolls-Royce over there. I'd like to have a car like that, but I'll never be able to afford one.

JACK: The owner of that car _____ a lot of money.

5. (YOLANDA and ARNOLD are sitting in the park. They are watching a mother with four young children.)

YOLANDA: Look at that poor woman. I don't envy her. She looks so tired.

ARNOLD: She _____ a lot of patience to raise four children.

6. ARNOLD: What are your plans for the weekend?

JACK: I'm not sure yet. I _____ some museums on

Saturday, or I _____ home and study. What about you?

ARNOLD: I don't know either. Yolanda and I _____ a movie tomorrow.

PRESENT CONTINUOUS OF
MAY, MIGHT, AND *MUST*

---

subject + { **may** **might** **must** } (not) + **be** + base form + **-ing**

Molly must be having a wonderful time.

Examples

(JACK, ARNOLD, and YOLANDA are playing Monopoly.)

ARNOLD: What's the matter with you, Jack? You're losing very badly. You **must not be concentrating.**

JACK: No, I can't keep my mind on the game.

YOLANDA: You **must be thinking** of Molly.

JACK: I am. I keep wondering what she's doing now. Just think! She **may be sitting** in front of a beautiful fire. Or she **might be dancing** in the arms of one of those ski instructors.

YOLANDA: Oh, come on, Jack. Stop worrying. She's probably asleep now. It's late.

When we answer a question that is in the present continuous tense with a short answer using *may/might* or *must,* we use this form.

---

subject + { **may** **might** **must** } + **be**

> ### *Examples*
>
> (ARNOLD is looking out the window.)
>
> JACK: Hey, Arnold. Is it raining outside?
>
> ARNOLD: It **must be**. People are carrying umbrellas. But it must be raining very lightly. I can't see the rain very well.
>
> JACK: Where did Yolanda go?
>
> ARNOLD: She's in the kitchen.
>
> JACK: Is she serving the dessert now?
>
> ARNOLD: I think she **might be.**

■ ACTIVITY 13D

Read the description of each situation. Then make sentences using the present continuous tense of *may/might* or *must*.

1. Yolanda's grandmother is sitting at a window, and she's thinking about some of the happy moments in her life. What are some things that she might be thinking about?

   a. *She might be thinking about the birth of her first child.*

   b. _____

   _____

   c. _____

   _____

   d. _____

   _____

2. Jack and Molly are having a small argument. What do you think they are arguing about?

   a. _____

   _____

b. _____

_____

c. _____

_____

d. _____

_____

3. An old man is driving an old car up a very steep hill. There are a lot of cars behind him.

    a. He _____ very fast.
                             (negative, **drive**)

    b. The other drivers _____ angry.
                                   (**get**)

4. A man is standing in front of the teller's window in a bank. He's holding a gun and wearing a mask. What do you think he's doing?

_____

COULD—ALTERNATIVE SOLUTIONS, POSSIBILITY, AND IMPOSSIBILITY

Alternative Solutions—Future

When someone has a problem, we can suggest alternative solutions with *could*. This is a polite way to make a suggestion. We can also suggest solutions to ourselves; for example, in the dialog on page 208, Jack says, "I *could* take the bus up to Vermont tomorrow."

---

subject + **could** + base form

You could call Molly.

Examples

JACK: Arnold, I want to do something special for Molly when she gets back from skiing. I want to show her that I really missed her.

ARNOLD: You **could write** a poem for her.

JACK: Be serious!

YOLANDA: You **could get** tickets for that new show on Broadway. She really wants to see it.

ARNOLD: You **could meet** her at the airport with a dozen red roses.

JACK: Yeah. I **could do** that. That's a good idea.

Possibility—Present

Could has the same meaning as *may/might* when we use it in the present continuous tense.

subject + **could** + **be** + base form + **-ing**

Molly { could / may / might } be thinking of breaking up.

Examples

JACK: I keep wondering what Molly's doing now. Just think! She **could/may/might be sitting** in front of a beautiful fire. She **could/may/might be dancing** in the arms of one of those handsome ski instructors.

Could also has the same meaning as *may/might* with the verbs *be* and *have,* even when they are not in the continuous form.

Examples

(YOLANDA's telephone is ringing.)

YOLANDA: Who could that be? It's so late.
   JACK: It **could/may/might be** Molly.

(YOLANDA answers the phone.)

YOLANDA: Hi, Molly. How are you? Oh, no! Really? Your leg?
 ARNOLD: Uh oh. It sounds like Molly hurt herself.
   JACK: She **could/may/might have** a broken leg.
YOLANDA: Jack, come here and speak to Molly. It's nothing serious. She
           only sprained her ankle. She's coming home tomorrow.

We frequently use *could* in questions about possibility. It is not necessary to use "Do you think . . . ?" The rules for short answers are the same as those for *may/might* and *must*.

Examples

Could Jack **be** jealous?
 Yes, he **could be.** In fact, he probably is.

Could Jack **be losing** Molly?
 He's afraid that he **could be.**

Could Molly **be looking** for another man?
 She **could be,** but Yolanda doesn't think she is.

Impossibility—Present

When we are talking about possibility and use *could not* (*couldn't*), we mean that we think something is impossible. We also use *cannot* (*can't*) for this meaning.

Example

According to Yolanda, Molly **couldn't/can't be thinking** of breaking up with Jack. This is because Molly tells Yolanda everything, and she has never mentioned anything about that.

In affirmative sentences about the present moment, *may/might* and *could* have the same meaning. In negative sentences, the meaning of *could not* is different from the meaning of *may not* and *might not*.

Example

Molly telephoned and said she sprained her ankle very badly. Look at these two sentences.

1. Molly ~~might not~~ *be skiing* now.

2. Molly *couldn't be skiing* now.

Sentence 2 is logically correct in this situation. We know it is impossible for someone to ski with a badly sprained ankle.

■ **ACTIVITY 13E**

Read the descriptions of the following situations and offer several possible solutions using *could.*

1. Arnold is worried because he never has enough money. His only income is from playing in nightclubs three or four nights a week. What could he do about this problem?

   a. *He could get a part-time job as a waiter.*

   b. _____

   c. _____

   d. _____

2. Yolanda's colleague at the TV station lives in a very expensive apartment. She spends half her salary on her rent. She never has much money left for entertainment. What could she do about this problem?

   a. _____

   b. _____

   c. _____

   d. _____

3. Juan, one of Arnold's friends, is having trouble meeting Americans. What could he do to meet Americans?

a. _____

b. _____

c. _____

d. _____

4. What is a problem that your hometown or country faces? What are some things that the government could do to improve the situation?

a. _____

b. _____

c. _____

d. _____

■ ACTIVITY 13F

Think about members of your family or your close friends. What do you think they are doing at this moment? Use the present continuous tense of *could* for your sentences, but remember that *may* and *might* mean the same thing here.

1. _____

2. _____

3. _____

4. _____

5. _____

■ ACTIVITY 13G

Read the descriptions of the following situations and then write sentences with *couldn't* in the present continuous tense.

1. YOLANDA: Hi, Molly. Where's Jack? Is he studying at the library?

MOLLY: No, he *couldn't be studying* there because it closed half an hour ago.

2. Yolanda is lying on her bed. The radio is playing. Her windows are open. Children are screaming in the street below, and three garbage trucks are collecting trash just underneath her window. Is Yolanda sleeping?

_____ because there is so much noise.

3.   Jack: This is a great party. Do you think Molly is enjoying herself?

   Yolanda: She _____ herself. She's been talking to that boring man for more than an hour. She can't get away from him.

4.   Jack: Molly's phone has been busy for two hours. Who's she talking to?

   Arnold: Maybe she's talking to her mother.

    Jack: No, she _____ to her mother. Her mother went to Europe on vacation.

■ Activity 13H

Read the following sentences and then decide whether to use *may/might, could,* or their negatives. In each situation, remember to choose between the base form or the continuous form of the verb after *may/might* or *could.*

1. Yolanda is wearing a pretty dress and high heels. She's putting on her best jewelry.

She *may be going* to a party.
          (go)

(You would also be correct here if you chose to write, *She might be going* or *She could be going.*)

2.   Jack: Is Yolanda at home?

   Molly: No, she _____ at home because I just saw her on
               (negative, **be**)
the street.

3. Molly ate four hot dogs, two bags of popcorn, and some peanuts, and drank five sodas at a baseball game about an hour and a half ago. She

_____ very hungry right now.
  (negative, **be**)

4.   Molly: Are you going to the nightclub to hear Arnold play tonight?

   Yolanda: I'm not sure. I _____. But I _____
                  (go)   (negative)
because I have a lot of work.

5. ARNOLD: Look at those men over there. Why are they digging up the street again?

   YOLANDA: I don't know. I suppose they _____ in a new
   (put)

   water pipe.

6. JACK: What am I going to do? I have to hand in this paper tomorrow, and I can't type it myself by then. I type too slowly.

   YOLANDA: You _____ it to my friend Susan. She's a good
   (take)

   typist, and she doesn't charge very much.

7. ARNOLD: Jack, why don't we all take a drive to the country next weekend?

   JACK: That sounds like a great idea, but I _____ the car
   (negative, **have**)

   next weekend. I have to take it into the garage for some

   repairs. They _____ the repairs before Saturday.
   (negative, **finish**)

■ ACTIVITY 13I

Choose a classmate who comes from a city or country that you have never visited. Make speculations about what you think life might be like there. Talk about the climate, geography, political situation, food, transportation, industry, housing conditions, pace of life, or any other topic that interests you. Try to use *may, might, must,* or *could,* or their negative forms when you make your speculations. Your classmate will tell you if you are right or wrong.

EXPRESSING YOUR IDEAS

1. What are your favorite leisure-time activities? When you have free time on a weekend, what do you usually do? What do you think you might do this weekend?

2. When you take a vacation, what do you like to do? Where do you like to go? What do you think you might do on your next vacation?

These people are going to ask Ms. Know-It-All for advice.

Dialog

MOLLY: Yolanda, I'd like your advice about something. I think I **should move** out and **get** my own apartment.

YOLANDA: It's about time.[1] What finally made you decide?

MOLLY: I can't stand[2] living with my mother anymore. She wants me to do everything her way. I know I **should move out,** but I'm afraid of hurting her feelings. What **should** I **do?**

YOLANDA: Well, first of all, you **shouldn't feel** guilty about moving out. In my opinion, everybody has to leave home and become independent someday. Have you told your mother about your plans?

MOLLY: No, I've tried to tell her several times, but she always says, "I'**d rather not talk** about it now. Let's talk about it later."

YOLANDA: Your mother probably still thinks daughters **are supposed to live** at home until they get married.

MOLLY: She does. It's really going to blow her mind[3] when I tell her that I'm going to move out.

YOLANDA: You **ought to tell** her about it right away. You'**d better not keep** putting it off[4], or it will only get harder to tell her.

MOLLY: Okay, I'll tell her tonight. What do you think about this—**should** I **get** my own place or **should** I **find** a roommate?

YOLANDA: What **would** you **rather do,** live alone or with someone?

MOLLY: I think I'**d rather live** alone, but apartments are so expensive now.

YOLANDA: That's true. You'**d better make** a budget for yourself and see what you can afford. I'll help you with it and with anything else I can.

MOLLY: Thanks, Yolanda. I really appreciate it.

Listening Comprehension Questions

1. How does Molly feel about living with her mother?

2. In Yolanda's opinion, should Molly continue living with her mother or move into her own apartment?

3. What does Molly's mother say every time Molly tries to talk to her about getting her own apartment?

4. In Molly's mother's opinion, how long should a daughter continue living at home?

---

[1]*It's about time* means that Yolanda thinks Molly has already waited too long.
[2]*I can't stand* means "I really don't like."
[3]*Blow her mind* means "shock her." (slang)
[4]*To put something off* means "to postpone."

5. Why does Yolanda think Molly had better not put off telling her mother about her plans to move?
6. Would Molly rather live alone or with a roommate?

SHOULD

We use *should* when we want to offer advice or express a moral belief. It means, "In my opinion, it is good or advisable for you to do this."

To talk about the general present or future, we use this pattern.

---

subject   +   **should**   **(not)**   +   base form
                    (shouldn't)

Molly should move into her own apartment.

(Question word)   +   **should**   +   subject   +   base form   ?

Should Molly move out of her mother's apartment?

Yes, (subject)   should.
No, (subject)   shouldn't.

Examples

In many countries of the world, people think that young men and women **should live** with their parents until they get married. They believe that young women especially **should not live** alone.

Should young adults **live** with their parents until they get married?
  Yes, they **should.**
        or
No, they **shouldn't.**

When **should** young people **leave** home, in your opinion?

Note: *Should* can also be used to express a different meaning. Sometimes we use *should* to mean, "I have a good reason to expect, think, or assume that something is true."

Examples

MOLLY: How long do you think it will take me to find an apartment?

or

How long **should** it **take** me to find an apartment?

YOLANDA: It **shouldn't take** you more than about a week or two.

OUGHT TO

Ought to has the same meaning as *should,* but *should* is used more frequently. We use *ought to* in affirmative statements, but it is not very common in negative statements or in questions. In negative statements and questions, we usually change automatically to *should.*

---

subject + **ought to** + base form

Molly ought to get her own apartment.

Examples

Many young Americans place great value on independence. Many believe that young people **ought to leave** home after graduation from high school or college. They believe that they **ought to enjoy** a period of freedom and independence before getting married.

■ ACTIVITY 14A

In the United States, many newspapers have an advice column. The writer for the column (columnist) asks readers to send in letters explaining their problems and asking for advice. The columnist then publishes the letter in the newspaper and follows it with some advice.

Some typical problems that people write about when they ask columnists for advice are given below. Imagine that you are the columnist. Use modal auxiliary verbs to offer your opinions and advice. You can discuss each problem with your classmates first and then write a reply.

Use *should* and *shouldn't* to offer advice for this problem. Offer advice only about the future and general present, not about the past.

Dear Ms. Know-It-All,

I am twenty-four years old. I live with my mother, but I would like to move out and get my own apartment because my mother still treats me like a child. She complains if I stay out late with my friends. She tries to tell me how to spend my money and how to live my life. We argue all the time.

I love my mother very much, but I need to feel independent. I try to tell her that we will get along much better if we don't live together, but she doesn't want me to leave home. What should I do?

Molly

Dear Molly,

Your problem is very common nowadays. I'm sure our readers will be interested in reading about this. In my opinion, you should move into your own apartment.

(Now continue this answer and offer some specific advice.)

◼ ACTIVITY 14B

Use *should, ought to,* and *shouldn't* to answer these letters.

Dear Ms. Know-It-All,

My father-in-law died about two years ago. Of course my mother-in-law was very upset and lonely, so my husband invited her to live with us. I don't know what to do—I'm going crazy. My mother-in-law and I don't get along very well. She's a wonderful person and is very helpful to me in many ways, but she thinks she's the boss in our home. If I try to discipline the children and tell them that they can't do something, they go running to their grandmother, and she tells them they can do it! My husband and I have no privacy. What's worse is that she constantly criticizes me to my husband behind my back. I'm afraid this is going to break up our marriage. What should I do?

Jane

Dear Ms. Know-It-All,

Our daughter is twenty-one years old and is in her last year of college. She has been dating her boyfriend for about four months. The other day she told us that she moved into his apartment. When we asked her if they plan to get married, she said she doesn't want to get married yet because she is too young.

We are very upset about this because we believe it is wrong for young people to live together without being married. Our daughter tells us that we are old-fashioned and that all of her friends live with their boyfriends. Is she right? What should we do?

Mr. and Mrs. Old-Fashioned

■ ACTIVITY 14C

Imagine that a friend is coming to you with a problem and asking for your advice. With a classmate, act out and/or write a dialog between you and your friend, using questions with *should*. Answer with *should* or *ought to*. Include some *yes/no* questions and short answers. Also include some *wh-* questions (*what, when, who, why,* and *how*) with long answers.

1. Your friend comes to you with this story.

   We recently found some marijuana in our son's bedroom. He's fifteen years old. Last year he was an excellent student, but this year he hasn't been studying very much, and he's doing poorly.

2. Another friend comes to you with this story.

   Last night I was emptying the pockets of my husband's suit because I wanted to take it to the dry cleaner's and I found several pieces of paper with the names and telephone numbers of women. A few months ago I found papers like this too, but when I asked my husband about them, he got very angry and said I was acting ridiculous and childish. He told me that he loved me very much and that I had no reason to be jealous. Then he refused to talk about it anymore. I think he's seeing other women.

HAD BETTER

Had better has a similar meaning to *should*. We use it to offer advice. However, its meaning is usually stronger than the meaning of *should*. When we use *had better*, we usually mean, "If you don't do this, there will be a bad consequence or result." We often follow advice using *had better* with an *or* clause that explains the bad consequence.

We often use *had better* to give someone a warning. Because *had better* is stronger than *should*, don't use *had better* when you are talking to a person in a position of authority. It can be insulting.

GENERAL PRESENT AND FUTURE

Statements: subject + **had better** **(not)** + base form.

You had better make a budget.

Contractions: **I'd, you'd, he'd, she'd, we'd, they'd**
  (There is no possible contraction with **not** and **had better.**)

Questions: We don't use **had better** in questions very often.

Examples

(Yesterday MOLLY found an apartment that she likes. She's going to sign the lease later today. She and YOLANDA are talking about it.)

MOLLY: Here's the lease for my apartment. Would you read it with me?

YOLANDA: Okay. You**'d better not sign** it before we read it very carefully because it's a legal agreement. You**'d better be** sure that certain things are in the lease, or the landlord will never give them to you. For example, you want the landlord to paint before you move in.

MOLLY: Yes, and the landlord promised to give me a new refrigerator.

YOLANDA: Well, you**'d better ask** him to put it in writing, or he might forget his promise.

Note: When we speak informally, we sometimes don't pronounce *'d*. We often say, "You better ask him," instead of, "You'd better ask him."

■ ACTIVITY 14D

Use *had better* or *had better not*.

1.   MOLLY: How do you feel, Yolanda? Is your cold any better?

  YOLANDA: No, it's worse. I feel terrible.

MOLLY: You _____ to work tomorrow. You
   (negative, **go**)

_____ home and rest.
   (**stay**)

2. JACK: I need some cash. I have to go to the bank.

   ARNOLD: You _____, or you'll be too late. The bank is
      (**hurry**)

   going to close in about fifteen minutes.

3. MOLLY: I'm a little worried about Yolanda. She looks tired all the time.

   ARNOLD: Yes, she works too hard. She _____ some rest,
      (**get**)

   or she's going to make herself sick.

   MOLLY: Yes, she _____ working late so many nights.
      (**stop**)

4. MOLLY: Are we going to go out tonight, Jack?

   JACK: I don't know. I have a big exam tomorrow. I think I

   _____ tonight.
      (**study**)

   MOLLY: Yes, we _____ out, or you might be too tired
      (negative, **go**)

   tomorrow.

WOULD RATHER

Would rather means "prefer." *Would rather* is a way to compare two choices, so we use it when we make a choice between two or more alternatives. In the negative, *would rather not* is often a polite way to say, "I don't want to do that."

GENERAL PRESENT AND FUTURE

Statements: subject + **would rather** (**not**) + base form + (**than**) . . .

Molly would rather live alone.

Contractions: **I'd, you'd, he'd, she'd, we'd, they'd**
(There is no possible contraction with **not** and **would rather**.)

Questions:
(Question word) + **would** + subject + **rather** + base form ?

What would you rather do ?

Examples

In many countries, young married couples live with the husband's or wife's parents. In the United States, most young married couples **would rather move** into a tiny one-room apartment than live with their parents. They **would rather not depend** so much on their parents.

In your country, which **would** most young married couples **rather do**—live with their parents or live in their own home?

Would you **rather live** in your own home or live with your husband's or wife's parents?

Note: Sometimes we answer "Do you want to . . . ?" or "Would you like to . . . ?" questions with *would rather not.*

Examples

Does Molly want to live with a roommate?
She'**d rather not.** She'**d rather live** alone.

▮ ACTIVITY 14E

Use *would rather* or *would rather not* to fill in the blanks in the sentences that follow.

1. Read the first letter to Ms. Know-It-All (see page 229) about Molly, who lives with her mother.

   Would Molly rather live with her mother or in her own
   (live)
   apartment?

   She'd rather live in her own apartment.

2. Read the letter on page 229 about Jane and her problems with her mother-in-law.

_____ living with her mother-in-law or ask

(continue)

her mother-in-law to move out?

_____

Where _____ Jane's mother-in-law _____
with her son's family or in her own home?

_____

3. Read the letter on page 230 about the daughter who is living with her
boyfriend. Does the daughter want to marry her boyfriend now? (Give a
negative short answer using *would rather*.)

   No, _____

4. Read the problem on page 230 about the son who smokes marijuana.

   What _____—study or get high[5] on
marijuana?

5. Read the problem on page 230 about the wife who thinks her husband is
seeing other women. Does her husband want to talk to her about the
problem? (Give a negative short answer using *would rather*.)

   No, _____

■ Activity 14F

Sometimes people make choices, not because they want to, but because they
know it is better for them. Write a sentence with *would rather*. Then follow it
with a sentence with *had better*.

1. (Molly and Jack are going to a movie theater.)

   Molly: Which should we take—the subway or the bus?
   Jack: We don't have much time. The movie starts in only twenty

   minutes. *I'd rather take* the bus because it's quieter

   and cleaner than the subway. But we *had better take* the

   subway because it's faster, and we're a little late.

2. (Molly is trying to decide between two apartments that she looked at.
   One of them is big and in a very good location, but the rent is more

[5]*Get high* means "to feel intoxicated." Marijuana is a type of plant. When you smoke the
leaves, you have a reaction that is like getting drunk on alcohol.

than she can afford to pay. The other one is smaller, and the location is not as good, but the rent is reasonable. YOLANDA is giving her advice.)

YOLANDA: I know you _____ the big apartment, but

you _____ the small apartment, or you

won't have any money left for your other expenses.

3. (MOLLY wants to get a dog when she moves into her apartment. She likes big dogs better than small ones, but she knows that her apartment will be too small for a big dog.)

YOLANDA: What kind of dog are you going to get?

MOLLY: I _____ a big dog, but I

_____ because my apartment
      (negative)
is very small.

4. (YOLANDA's younger brother is going out the door now to meet some friends. He has a basketball in his hands. He hasn't been getting very good grades in school recently.)

YOLANDA'S MOTHER: I know that you _____ basketball

than study, but I think you _____ , or

you will fail your next test.

CONTINUOUS FORMS OF MODALS

When you want to use *should, had better,* or *would rather* to talk about the present moment (now), use this form.

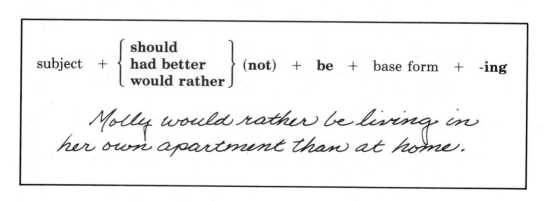

subject + { **should** / **had better** / **would rather** } (**not**) + **be** + base form + **-ing**

Molly would rather be living in her own apartment than at home.

> **Examples**
>
> Molly and Yolanda are walking from building to building looking at apartments for rent. Molly's feet hurt because she's wearing shoes with very high heels. She **shouldn't be wearing** high heels today because they aren't comfortable for walking. She **should be wearing** comfortable shoes with low heels.
>
> Molly and Yolanda are tired of looking at apartments. They **would rather be sitting** in a cafe and having a soda right now than walking around and looking at apartments.

■ ACTIVITY 14G

☐ Use the present continuous form of *should*. Choose carefully between affirmative and negative.

Arnold and Yolanda are walking in the park. Yolanda is wearing only a light sweater, so she's a little cold. She *shouldn't be wearing* such a light sweater. She _____ a jacket.

A teenager is carrying a big radio, which he is playing very loudly. The music is bothering people who came to the park for some peace and quiet. The boy _____ his radio so loudly.

There's some new grass with a big sign that says, "Please Don't Walk on the Grass." Some children are playing baseball on the grass. They

_____ there. They _____ in another place.

A child is picking some flowers next to a sign that says, "Please Don't Pick the Flowers." His mother isn't watching the child. The child

_____ the flowers. His mother _____ him.

☐ Write questions and answers. Use the present continuous form of *would rather*.

1. There is a basketball game on TV now, but Jack is studying for an exam, so he can't watch it.

   What ___*would Jack rather be doing*___ right now?

   ___*He'd rather be watching*___ the ball game on TV.

2. Yolanda's younger sister, Julia, is fifteen years old. It's Saturday night, and she's baby-sitting to earn money for college. Her friends are out dancing at a nightclub now.

   What _____?

   _____

3. Arnold's father wants to lose weight, so he's on a diet. He's eating half a grapefruit for dessert now, but he's thinking about a chocolate ice cream sundae.

   What _____?

   _____

BE + SUPPOSED TO

When we say that a person is *supposed to* do something, we mean that another person, the law, or the rules of society or good manners expect or require the person to do it.

GENERAL PRESENT, FUTURE, AND PAST

Statements:
subject + **be** { **am/is/are/ was/were** } (not) **supposed to** + base form

Daughters are supposed to live at home until they get married.

Questions:
(Question word) **be** + subject + **supposed to** + base form?

When is Molly supposed to come home?

Examples

In some countries, sons and daughters are expected to treat their parents with great respect. For example, children **are supposed to respect** their parents' opinions. They **aren't supposed to question** their parents' authority in any way. Also, when parents grow old, children **are supposed to take** care of them.

We often use *be supposed to* to mean that we expect or want a person to do something, but he or she isn't doing it.

Examples

(MOLLY's landlord promised to paint her apartment yesterday, but the painters didn't come. MOLLY is talking to the landlord.)

MOLLY: Mr. Jones, the painters **were supposed to come and paint** my apartment yesterday. They didn't come. What happened?

LANDLORD: I'm sorry. I thought you **weren't supposed to move** in until next week. We made a mistake. Don't worry. They'll be there tomorrow.

■ ACTIVITY 14H

❑ Jack's younger brother, Bob, is fourteen years old. Tomorrow night he is going to have his first date. He is asking Jack for advice about how to act on his date. Using *be supposed to,* complete the questions.

BOB: Jack, I don't know what to do tomorrow night. I don't know anything about girls or dating.

JACK: Don't worry. You'll be fine.

BOB: I have all these questions.

JACK: What's your first question?

BOB: Well, _____*am*_____ I *supposed to pick* her up, or
                                                 (pick)
    can we just meet someplace?

JACK: I think on a first date you should pick her up.

BOB: Should I help her with her coat and open doors for her and everything?

JACK: Yes, I think so.

Bob: And who _____?
(pay)

_____ for everything?
(pay)

Jack: In my opinion, the man should pay on the first date.

Bob: _____ her when I take her home?
(kiss)

Jack: I can't tell you everything. You decide.

☐ Imagine that a person who is a foreigner in your country is asking advice about good manners in your culture. What are or aren't you supposed to do at the dinner table? What aren't you supposed to talk about at the table? If someone invites you to his or her home for dinner, are you supposed to come on time or about half an hour late?

Example

In the United States, when you are invited for dinner, you're supposed to arrive on time. If you're going to be late, you're supposed to call. It's a nice idea to bring a small gift, such as a bottle of wine or some flowers. After dinner, you're supposed to compliment the host on the meal.

Now talk to your class or write about manners in your country.

☐ How was life different a hundred years ago for women? What did people believe that women were or weren't supposed to do? Write about some of the things women were or weren't supposed to do. For example, women weren't supposed to work outside the home. They were supposed to stay home and manage the household and take care of the children.

And what about men? What did people believe men were and weren't supposed to do a hundred years ago?

☐ We often use *was/were (not) supposed to* when we talk about a mistake that we made or about something another person expected us to do but that we didn't do. Use *was/were (not) supposed to* + base form in the following sentences.

1. Arnold: What happened last night, Yolanda? I didn't see you at the

   nightclub. You *were supposed to come* and hear my band play.

   Yolanda: I know. I'm sorry. I was exhausted last night.

2.   MOLLY: Can I borrow ten dollars, Jack? I_____ to

the bank at lunchtime, but I forgot. I didn't remember until

after 3:00, when the bank had already closed.

JACK: Sure. Is that all you need?

3.   JACK: Here's the red wine that you asked me to buy, Molly.

MOLLY: Oh, no! You _____ red wine. We're having
                          (negative)

fish tonight. You _____ white wine. But never

mind.

4. (MOLLY has just come home.)
MOLLY'S MOTHER: Molly, it's 2:00 A.M. You _____ home

by 12:00 P.M. I was really worried about you.

MOLLY: I'm sorry. But you really shouldn't worry about me.

■ ACTIVITY 14I

Remember that *have to/has to* means "It is necessary" and that *should* means "It is advisable or good in this situation." Choose which is better, *have to/has to* or *should*.

1.   MOLLY: You have a bad cold, Jack. I think you *should go* to bed early
                                                         (go)

tonight.

JACK: I know I *shouldn't stay* up late, but I
                   (negative, stay)

have to take an important exam in one of
      (take)

my classes tomorrow.

2.   ARNOLD: Look at this photograph of Los Angeles in the newspaper. You

can see the air pollution over the city.

YOLANDA: Everybody in Los Angeles drives. People never walk.

They _____ so much. They
        (negative, **drive**)

_____ public transportation, or
(use)

they _____.
(walk)

ARNOLD: Yes, but public transportation isn't very good in Los Angeles. It's

very difficult to get from one place to another without a car.

People in Los Angeles _____ a car to get to
(use)

many places.

3. Here is some information about renting apartments. Both the landlord

and the tenant have obligations:

By law, every landlord _____ a tenant a written lease, and the
(give)

tenant _____ it. It's a good idea to know exactly what is in a lease.
(sign)

The tenant _____ the lease very carefully before he or she signs it.
(read)

Almost all tenants _____ the landlord a security deposit, which is
(give)

usually one or two months' rent in advance. By law, if a tenant decides to

leave the apartment when the lease ends, he or she _____ the
(notify)

landlord thirty days before that date. If the tenant doesn't notify the

landlord, the landlord _____ the security deposit. Some
(negative, **return**)

cities have a law that says a landlord _____ an apartment every
(**repaint**)

three years.

Here are a few good rules for apartment hunters to follow.

a. You _____ more than about 33 percent of your
(negative, **spend**)

monthly paycheck for rent.

b. You _____ to find out about security and safety
(try)

in the building. You _____ to several of the tenants
(talk)

about service, maintenance, and safety in your building.

c. You _____ a walk around the neighborhood to see if
              (take)

you like it.

■ ACTIVITY 14J

❏ Read the following letter.

Dear Ms. Know-It-All,

    My wife is a businesswoman with a very successful career
as a young executive. She frequently comes home from work very
late because she has meetings or has to go out with the other
executives to talk business. Of course, most of the other
executives are men, and I am becoming very jealous. We never
have any time together, and I'm tired of making dinner all the time.

Jealous

Here is Ms. Know-It-All's answer to this man's letter. Fill in the blanks. Try to
use all of these modal auxiliaries: *should, ought to, had better, would rather, have
to/has to,* and the modal auxiliaries that we use to talk about possibilities or
alternatives (*may, might, could*) and logical deductions (*must*). In this exercise,
use *must* to talk about logical deductions. Use *have to/has to* to talk about
necessity.

Dear Jealous,

    You ___may feel___ very unhappy about this situation. You
           (feel)

are probably afraid that your wife is having an affair with one of her

coworkers. Perhaps you're afraid that your wife ___may be more comfortable___
                                     (be)

with her coworkers than with you. Have you talked with her about this

problem yet? If you haven't told her yet, she ___couldn't know___
                                 (negative, know)

how you feel. You ___had better talk___ about it, but you
                   (talk)

___haven't get___ angry or yell. Today, men ___should realized___
   (negative, get)   **(realize)**

that their wives' careers are important and that there are many times

when a woman ___must stay___ late at the office and can't be
                (stay)

home in time for dinner. Who knows? She ___may not enjoy___ these
                                 (negative, enjoy)

late meetings, but perhaps she has no choice.

However, it is important for couples to have time together. If a couple never spends time together, their marriage is in trouble and __should end__ in divorce. You __should try__ to
(end)   **(try)**
make your wife understand this. You __have to do__ something
(do)
about this problem soon, or it will only get worse.

(LISA is a friend of Yolanda's sister, SANDRA. She's only twenty-one years old. She has been dating John for about two months. John is forty-five years old.

LISA: Sandra, I need to talk to you. I didn't sleep at all last night. I was up all night thinking.

SANDRA: You __must be__ tired. What is it?
(be)

LISA: John asked me to marry him last night.

SANDRA: What? John __may be__ old enough to be your father.
(be)
How old is he?

LISA: Forty-five. But he's a wonderful man. I really love him, and I know he loves me. Age isn't everything. But I can't decide whether or not to say yes. Help me.

SANDRA: His age isn't so important now, but it __ought to become__
(become)
important later when you want to have children. You
__have to think__ about this very carefully. You
(think)
__can't make__ a decision too quickly. Also,
(negative, make)
ten years from now, you'll be thirty-one, and you
__may be__ a completely different person. You and
(be)
he __must not share__ the same interests then.
(negative, share)

LISA: That's true of any couple. I don't know. You're probably

right, but now I feel that I ___should *more* marry___ John than
                                        (marry)

any other man I've ever known. I love him.

SANDRA: Yes, but you've only been going out with him for two months.

You ___may not know___ him well enough to make this important
        (negative, **know**)

decision.

LISA: Maybe you're right. Thanks for your advice. I need to think

about my decision some more.

■ ACTIVITY 14K

Try to use the modals *may, might, could, must, should, ought to, had better, would rather,* and *be supposed to* in your answers to the questions below.

1. Look at Sandra's advice to her friend Lisa, who is thinking about marrying her forty-five-year-old boyfriend. Do you agree with Sandra's advice? Why or why not?

2. Think of a personal problem that you have or invent a humorous imaginary problem. Write a dialog between you and a friend in which you explain your problem and ask your friend for advice. Try to use all of the above modals and include some questions using them.

EXPRESSING YOUR IDEAS

1. In your country, when do young people move out of their parents' home and start living in their own place? Is it different for sons and daughters? How and why?

2. What are the advantages of living with parents? What are the disadvantages? What kinds of problems do young adults have when they live with their parents?

3. Should young adults live with their parents until they get married? Why or why not? When should they move out, in your opinion?

4. Are you living with your parents or relatives now? Would you rather be living in your own apartment? Why or why not?

5. In many countries, young married couples live with their in-laws after marriage. Is this good? Why or why not?

6. In the United States, many young people believe that a couple should live together for some time before they get married. What do you think about this? Why is it a good idea or a bad idea?

7. In many cities in the United States, the number of people who live alone is growing. Do many people in your country live alone? How do you feel about this? Would you rather live alone or with a roommate?

8. What problems occur when a person lives with a roommate? When a person lives alone?

9. Is it difficult to find an apartment in the city where you live now? Are apartments very expensive? Is it easier or more difficult to find a good apartment in your country than in the United States?

10. Name some of the ways in which people find apartments. What should you be sure of before you sign a lease for an apartment?

11. How did you find the place where you are living now? Was it difficult to find it? What did you have to do?

12. If you are a parent, do you want your children to continue living with you until they get married? When do you think your children should leave home?

15

TOO, ENOUGH, SO, AND *SUCH*

EXPLORATION AND ACHIEVEMENT

Dialog

(JACK, MOLLY, ARNOLD, and YOLANDA are going on a weekend camping trip to Mount Marcy, the highest mountain in New York State. Right now they are packing for the trip.)

JACK: You're going to love this trip. Mount Marcy is **so high that you can see for miles.**

YOLANDA: I'm really looking forward to this trip. I'm dying to get out of the city.[1]

ARNOLD: Yeah. It's a shame that we can't go camping for a whole week.

MOLLY: A weekend is **enough time for me to get all the fresh air I need for a lifetime.**

YOLANDA: Oh, Molly. Camping is **such fun that you won't want to come back.** You'll see.

MOLLY: Jack, where are we going to sleep? There isn't **enough space in that tent for all of us to fit.** Maybe I shouldn't go.

JACK: Don't worry. It'll probably be **warm enough to sleep out** under the stars.

MOLLY: Oh, no! There are **too many mosquitoes for us to sleep outdoors!**

YOLANDA: There aren't that many in September. Try your pack[2] on and see how it feels.

MOLLY: Okay, help me put it on. This pack is **too heavy for me to carry.** I can't walk!

ARNOLD: What do you have in there, Molly? Oh, no! There are **enough sandwiches here for a month.**

YOLANDA: And all these pots and pans! This is **too much equipment to take for such a short trip.** You can't take all these shoes and a pillow too!

MOLLY: But I have to take comfortable shoes.

ARNOLD: Okay, okay. But you'll sleep all right without a pillow. Think of the great explorers, Molly. They didn't take pillows. They had **so many hardships that it's a wonder they didn't give up.**

YOLANDA: That's right. And they ran into all kinds of wild animals.

JACK: I'll be surprised if we even see a rabbit.

MOLLY: That's good. And I don't want to get lost.

[1]*Dying to* means "want to do something a lot."
[2]*Pack* is the bag a camper carries equipment in. Usually the pack is carried on the back. It is also called a *backpack*.

ARNOLD: Jack's bringing **such good maps that we can't get lost.**

JACK: Look, let's get going. We have very few opportunities to get out of the city, and we're wasting time.

MOLLY: I've never climbed a real mountain. I'm afraid I'll get out of breath **so fast that I'll have to rest every five minutes.**

YOLANDA: You don't have to be the first to get to the top of the mountain. We aren't going to discover the mountain. We just want to climb it.

Listening Comprehension Questions

1. Arnold is disappointed that they only have a weekend for their camping trip. Does Molly feel the same way about it?
2. What's the weather going to be like this weekend? Will it be too cold to sleep outside the tent?
3. Why doesn't Molly want to sleep out under the stars?
4. Why is Molly's pack too heavy for her to carry?
5. In Arnold's opinion, is there any chance they can get lost?
6. Molly isn't looking forward to climbing the mountain. What does she fear will happen?

more than enough

TOO AND *VERY*

Very emphasizes or intensifies a quality. It makes the quality stronger. *Too* has an entirely different meaning from *very*. *Too* has the meaning of excess. Notice the difference in these two sentences:

This pack is *very* heavy, but I think I can carry it.

This pack is *too* heavy. I can't pick it up. No one can carry it.

TOO . . . TO
you need an explanation reason

Too with Adjectives and Adverbs

When we use *too* before an adjective or an adverb, we mean there is an excess of the quality. This is usually followed by an infinitive expressing result.

subject + verb + **too** + { adjective / adverb } + infinitive

This pack is too heavy to carry.

Examples

During the nineteenth century, people believed it was impossible to reach the North Pole. Even Greenland was **too far north to explore.** Robert Peary (1856–1920) was an admiral in the U.S. Navy. He led several expeditions to Greenland and the Arctic. He wasn't successful in reaching the North Pole, which was his main objective, until 1909. The Arctic Sea was **too icy to navigate** safely. The men on the expedition found the weather was **too harsh.** The explorers had to turn back several times. But Peary was **too adventurous to give up** for long.

Too with Quantifiers

subject + verb + **too** + $\left\{\begin{array}{l}\textbf{little}\\\textbf{much}\end{array}\right\}$ + mass noun + infinitive

This is too much equipment to take.

subject + verb + **too** + $\left\{\begin{array}{l}\textbf{many}\\\textbf{few}\end{array}\right\}$ + count noun + infinitive

There are too many mosquitoes to sleep outdoors.

Examples

In 1909, Robert Peary took an assistant and four Eskimos on the final expedition. They had **too much equipment to carry,** so they left a lot behind. They wanted to move very quickly. Peary said they traveled 134 miles in eight days and reached the North Pole on April 6, 1909.

Another explorer, Dr. Frederick Cook, claimed he had reached the North Pole in 1908. There was a bitter argument. Some people said they didn't believe Peary's claim of 134 miles. They said that was just **too many miles to cover** in eight days. There was **too little information to prove** absolutely which explorer got to the North Pole first. In 1911, the U.S. Congress decided to recognize Peary's claim. Cook died a bitter man.

Too with Adjective + *For* (Someone)

> subject + verb + **too** + $\left\{ \begin{array}{l} \text{adjective} \\ \text{adverb} \end{array} \right\}$ + **for** (object) + infinitive
>
> *This pack is too heavy for me to carry.*

Examples

Most people thought the expedition was **too dangerous for the explorers to bring** their wives.

Sometimes the infinitive is omitted.

The weather was **too cold for them** (to go).

■ ACTIVITY 15A

Some of the following sentences are incorrect in the use of *too* and *very*. Write *correct* below any sentence that is correct. Put an *X* next to any sentence that is incorrect. Then rewrite it correctly.

1. Many explorers in the nineteenth century were too courageous. They traveled to dangerous and remote parts of the globe.

   Many explorers in the nineteenth century were very courageous.

2. Their voyages were often too dangerous for their wives to travel with them.

   Correct

3. Often weather conditions at sea were ~~very~~ too severe for the ships to travel safely.

4. Sometimes there wasn't much food, and people became very hungry.

   correct

5. Sometimes the food was very spoiled to eat, so the men almost starved. (too)

6. A few explorers were too adventurous and traveled into places where no one had ever been before.

7. Some were too eager to discover new waterways for ships, so they looked for routes connecting different oceans.

8. Their days were often very full of excitement for them to sleep at night.

9. They were too brave. When they came home, they became too famous because they had accomplished great things for their country.

■ **ACTIVITY 15B**

Complete the unfinished sentences using this pattern.

$$\textbf{too} + \left\{ \begin{array}{l} \textbf{adjective} \\ \textbf{adverb} \end{array} \right\} + \textbf{to} \ \text{(or)} \ \textbf{too} \left\{ \begin{array}{l} \textbf{many} \\ \textbf{much} \\ \textbf{little} \end{array} \right\} + \textbf{noun} + \textbf{to}$$

Practice this activity orally in class before you write it.

1. Lewis and Clark were about to cross the Missouri River. There were a lot of rapids. It was very dangerous. They decided to look for another

   place to cross because the river was *too dangerous to*

   cross at that point.

2. The High Rockies are covered with snow all winter. Most of the snow melts by April. The explorers couldn't get across in January. There was

   to much snow in the mountains to get across in January

3. Some of the land was very difficult to travel over. There were areas

   that were very rocky and treacherous. Some places were *too difficult*

   to travel over

4. The explorers wanted to investigate many areas of the Far West, but they had little time before winter came. They couldn't investigate

   everything. They had ~~not~~ *too much time to do it*

   _____

5. They encountered many Indians. Many of them were hostile. The expedition could not travel safely in many areas. There were ___ *too*

   many Indians to travel safely

6. In the winter, there was a lot of extremely cold weather. They couldn't

   hunt in this cold weather for very long. There was ___ *too much*

   cold weather to hunt for very long

7. In winter, they couldn't cross the Rockies. They wanted to get back to St. Louis as soon as possible, but winter came very quickly. Winter came

   ___ *too quickly* ___ for them ___ *to* ___

   cross the Rockies

ENOUGH

Enough with Adjectives

> subject + verb (**not**) + $\left\{ \begin{array}{l} \text{adjective} \\ \text{adverb} \end{array} \right\}$ + **enough** + **for** (object)
>
> *It will be warm enough for us*
>
> + infinitive
>
> *to sleep outdoors.*

We use an adjective or adverb followed by *enough* to show that something is possible because there is a sufficient amount of the quality. This is usually followed by the infinitive form of the verb.

> ### *Examples*
>
> In 1803, much of the United States was still unexplored. President Thomas Jefferson was **perceptive enough to recognize** the importance of this unexplored territory. He appointed Meriwether Lewis and William Clark to head an expedition to the Far West and spoke **persuasively enough to convince** Congress to finance the entire project. Congress decided that the expedition was **important enough to support.**
>
> Lewis and Clark started to train the men in their party in 1803. The expedition was dangerous. They left from St. Louis in 1804.

Enough with Nouns

subject + verb (**not**) + **enough** + $\left\{ \begin{array}{l} \text{count noun} \\ \text{mass noun} \end{array} \right\}$ + **for** (object)

A weekend is enough time for me

+ infinitive

to get some fresh air.

Enough is used before a noun to show that there is a sufficient amount or number of something for something to happen or for someone to do something.

> ### *Examples*
>
> The Lewis and Clark expedition had a remarkable guide, the Indian woman Sacajawea. She gave members of the expedition **enough horses for them to continue** across the High Rockies. They crossed the Continental Divide and reached the Pacific Ocean. On the return trip, they did**n't** have **enough time to explore** everything, so they split into two groups. They traveled down two different rivers and met later on the Missouri River.

Sometimes we see this pattern. However, this pattern is less common, especially in spoken English.

---

subject + verb (**not**) + noun + **enough** + infinitive

A weekend is time enough to get some fresh air.

Ⓧ ■ **ACTIVITY 15C**

Combine each of the following pairs of sentences into one sentence, using *enough* + infinitive. Some sentences will be affirmative; others will be negative. In sentences 5 and 6, you need to add *for* + object.

Many Americans went out West to search for gold in the great Gold Rush of 1849.

1. Many people weren't very strong. They didn't survive the long and difficult journey west.

   Many people weren't strong enough to survive the long and difficult journey west.

2. The men who made it to California were very strong. They survived terrible hardships on the trip out.

   The men who made it to California were very strong enough to survived the terrible hardship on the trip out

3. A few found gold quickly. They were able to bring their families out West right away.

   A few found gold quickly enough to ~~be able~~ to bring their families out West right away

4. Others didn't have much money. They couldn't buy the equipment they needed.

   Other didn't have much money enough to buy the equipment they needed

5. There weren't many women out West. Not all of the miners could find wives.

   There weren't many women out West enough to find wives.

6. There wasn't a lot of gold. Not everybody became rich.

   There wasn't a lot of gold to became rid.
   enough

7. The miners had to buy a lot of supplies. The supplies had to last through a long, hard winter on the trip to California.

   The miners had to buy a lot of supplies enough to last through a long, hard winter on the trip to California

8. They had to take packhorses with them. The horses carried all their supplies and equipment.

   They had to take packhorses enough with them to carried all their supplies and equipment

9. There were very few lawmen. They couldn't protect everyone from outlaws.

   There were very few lawmen enough to protect everyone from outlaws

◼ ACTIVITY 15D

Make questions from the following sets of phrases. Then ask a classmate the questions and discuss your opinions. Use *enough* + infinitive or *too* + infinitive in both your questions and answers.

1. (a sixteen-year-old/   responsible/   have children)

   Is a sixteen-year old responsible enough to have children?

2. (a sixteen-year-old/   immature/   get married)

   Is a sixteen-year old too immature to get married?

3. (a sixteen-year-old/   old/   vote)

   _____?

4. (a fourteen-year-old/   mature/   drive a car)

   _____?

5. (a thirteen-year-old/   young/   smoke)

   _____?

6. (fifteen thousand dollars a year/   money/   live on in a big city)

_____?

7. (ten thousand dollars a year/   money/   support a family these days)

_____?

8. (five thousand dollars/   money/   make a down payment on a new house in your hometown)

_____?

9. (a person who has had three drinks/   drunk/   drive)

_____?

10. (a person who is sixty-five/   young/   retire)

_____?

SO ... THAT

So with Adjectives and Adverbs

Look at these two sentences.

Thomas Edison's family was very poor.

Edison had to work from the time he was a boy.

These sentences can be combined with *so* + adjective + *that*.

main clause   result clause

Edison's *family was so poor* that *he had to work from the time he was a boy.*

We use this pattern to show that the clause after *that* is the result of the main clause.

> subject + verb + **so** + $\left\{ \begin{array}{c} \text{adjective} \\ \text{adverb} \end{array} \right\}$ + **that**
>
> *Mt. Marcy is so high you can see for miles.*

Examples

Thomas Alva Edison (1857–1931) was a famous American inventor. His family was **so poor that** Edison had to work from the time he was quite young. He went to school for only three months in his entire life, but he was obviously very bright. Whenever he worked with any kind of machine, he immediately thought of ways to improve it. When he was working as a telegraph operator, he developed an automatic telegraph system. It was a great success. It worked **so efficiently that** it could send four messages simultaneously.

So . . . That with Quantifiers

So . . . that may also be used with quantifiers.

> subject + verb + **so** $\left\{ \begin{array}{c} \textbf{few} \\ \textbf{many} \end{array} \right\}$ + plural count noun
>
> *There are so many mosquitoes that Molly won't be able to sleep.*
>
> subject + verb + **so** $\left\{ \begin{array}{c} \textbf{little} \\ \textbf{much} \end{array} \right\}$ + mass noun
>
> *They'll have so much fun that they won't want to come back.*

Examples

Edison went to school for only three months in his entire life. He had **so little formal education that** he had to teach himself almost everything. Yet he invented **so many things that** he is considered to be one of the greatest inventors of all time. By his death he had 1,300 patents from his inventions. One of the most famous was the first electric light with a carbon filament. He did **so much work** in the field of electricity **that** his name is used by many utility companies today. He designed the first electric power plant in the world in 1881. **So few people** have accomplished as much as Edison did **that** it is truly appropriate to call him a genius.

So Much That

Look at these two sets of sentences.

Edison worked *a lot*. Sometimes he didn't get to bed until morning.

Edison worked **so much that** sometimes he didn't get to bed until morning.

People admired Edison's work *a lot*. They decided to preserve his laboratory intact.

People admired Edison's work **so much that** they decided to preserve his laboratory intact.

A lot is an adverb that tells how much Edison worked. If we want to add a result clause, we change *a lot* to *so much that*.

SUCH . . . THAT

We also make result clauses using nouns. Use these patterns.

such **a(n)** + adjective + singular count noun + **that**

Edison was such a brilliant inventor that he obtained 1,300 patents in his lifetime.

---

such (+ adjective) + $\left\{ \begin{array}{l} \text{mass noun} \\ \text{plural count noun} \end{array} \right\}$ + **that**

He achieved such fame that his laboratory is now a museum.

We do not always use an adjective before the noun.

Examples

Thomas Edison was **such a brilliant inventor that** he came up with new ideas almost every year. In 1877, he invented a telephone transmitter for Western Union Telegraph Company. In 1878, he designed the first successful phonograph. He was **such a genius that** he could imagine what was inconceivable to other people, and he had **such skill** as a craftsman **that** he could build the things he imagined. He designed **such wonderful inventions that** he changed the way people lived their daily lives.

■ **ACTIVITY 15E**

Combine the following pairs of sentences into sentences with *so . . . that.*

Helen Keller (1880–1968) was blind and deaf. She made a very important contribution by showing people that the handicapped are teachable and that they can be valuable members of society.

1. From the age of two, Helen Keller was badly handicapped.
   She couldn't see or hear anything.

   From the age of two, Helen Keller was so badly handicapped that she couldn't see or hear anything.

2. She was very isolated from other people.
   She became emotionally disturbed.

   She was so isolated from other people that she became emotionally disturbed

3. She became very wild.
   Her parents couldn't manage her.

   She became so wild that her parents couldn't manage her.

4. They thought Helen was very difficult to teach.
   Nobody could reach her.

   They thought that Helen was so difficult to teach that nobody could reach her.

5. At that time, there were very few people who knew how to teach the blind and the deaf.
   Helen's parents had no one to turn to for help with Helen.

   At that time there were so few people who knew how to teach the blind and the deaf that Helen's parents had no one to turn for help with Helen

6. They hired a special teacher for the blind.
   At first, she made very little progress with her student.
   Helen's parents became discouraged. (Combine only the second and third sentences.)

   At first she made so little progress with her student that Helen's parents became discouraged —

7. The teacher, Anne Sullivan, had a lot of faith in the human spirit.
   She refused to give up.

   The teacher, Anne Sullivan had so much faith in the human spirit that she refused to give up

8. Anne Sullivan had been blind herself.
   She had suffered a lot as a child.
   She understood how Helen felt. (Combine only the second and third sentences.)

   She had suffered so a child that she understood how Helen felt

cause
so ---- + hot
effect

9. Anne Sullivan was extremely patient, and she tried many different approaches.
Helen began to respond to her teaching.

Anne Sullivan was so patient, and she tried so many different ideas that Helen began to respond to her teaching

10. Helen wanted to learn very badly.
She mastered sign language very quickly.

Helen wanted to learn so badly that she mastered sign language very quickly

11. Helen loved Anne Sullivan a lot.
They remained close friends for the rest of their lives.

Helen loved Anne Sullivan so much that they remained close friend for the rest of their lives.

12. Helen Keller also learned how to talk.
She lectured in many places.
People all over the world were influenced by her. (Combine only the second and third sentences.)

She lecture in so many places that people all over the world were influenced by her.

13. She eventually learned to write beautifully.
Her autobiography and several other books became classics.

She eventually learned to write so beautifully that her autobiography and several other books became classics

14. She spent a lot of time and energy teaching people about the handicapped.
People all over the world were impressed by her dedication.

She spend so much time and energy teaching people about the handicap that people all over the word were impressed by her dedication

■ ACTIVITY 15F

❏ Combine the following pairs of sentences, using *such + that*.

Mount McKinley is the highest mountain on the North American continent. It is in Alaska. By 1905, no one had ever reached the top of Mount McKinley.

1. Frederick A. Cook was an ambitious man.
   He decided to lead an expedition to the top of Mount McKinley.

   Frederick A. Cook was such an ambitious man that he decided to lead an expedition to the top of Mount McKinley.

2. It was a very treacherous mountain to climb.
   The men in his party could not reach the summit.

   _____

   _____

3. There were terrible blizzards on the mountain.
   Most of the men suffered from frostbite.

   _____

   _____

4. The men had difficulty with the slippery rocks.
   Many of them wanted to turn back.

   _____

   _____

❏ Combine the following pairs of sentences. Choose between *so . . . that* and *such . . . that*.

1. Many people in Cook's party decided to leave.
   Cook was left with only one companion.

   _____

   _____

Later Cook claimed that he and his companion continued the climb. He said that they successfully reached the summit of Mount McKinley.

2. There was very little evidence.
   People did not believe Cook.

   _____

   _____

3. In 1907, Cook set out on a very long expedition to the Arctic.
   He didn't return for two years.

   _____

   _____

In 1909, both he and Peary claimed to be the first man to reach the North Pole.

4. They had a very bitter argument.
   It became the sensational story of the time.

   _____

   _____

5. Peary was very angry.
   He accused Cook of lying.

   _____

   _____

6. Later Cook got into a lot of trouble in an oil scheme.
   He went to jail for five years.

   _____

   _____

7. The public was very hostile to Cook.
   Hardly anyone believed his claim about Mount McKinley or about the North Pole.

   _____

   _____

8. Very few people believed Cook was the first man to reach the North Pole.
   He died a very disappointed man.

   _____

   _____

■ Activity 15G

Make sentences with *so . . . that* or *such . . . that*.

1. Muhammad Ali is very famous.

   Muhammad Ali is so famous that people all over the world know his name.

2. Sophia Loren is a very beautiful woman.

   _____

3. Aristotle Onassis was a very rich man.

   _____

4. Albert Einstein was a genius.

   _____

5. Alexander the Great was a great general.

   _____

6. Shakespeare was a great writer.

   _____

7. The families of Romeo and Juliet hated each other.

   _____

8. Don Juan was a great lover.

   _____

9. Joan of Arc was a brave woman.

   _____

10. Orpheus loved Eurydice.

_____

11. King Midas loved gold.

_____

12. Omar Khayyám wrote beautiful poetry.

_____

13. Caviar is very expensive.

_____

14. Learning English is very difficult.

_____

15. The Great Pyramids of Egypt are fascinating.

_____

16. The Soviet Union is a very big country.

_____

17. There are many different dialects of Chinese.

_____

■ ACTIVITY 15H

What complaints do people often have about large, overcrowded cities? Make sentences using the words below and this pattern.

$$So \quad \left\{ \begin{array}{l} Much \\ Many \\ Few \end{array} \right\} \quad + \quad Noun \quad + \quad That$$

crime   pollution   noise   parking spaces   people   garbage   strikes

1. *There's so much crime in many large cities that people are afraid to walk the streets at night.*

2. _____

_____

3. _____

_____

4. _____

_____

5. _____

_____

6. _____

_____

7. _____

_____

EXPRESSING YOUR IDEAS

Personal Questions

1. Talk about a time you succeeded in doing something that surprised other people or a success that was so unexpected that you even surprised yourself, for example, a time you won a special award or scholarship, a time you figured something out, or a time you overcame some obstacles and accomplished something that seemed remarkable to you.

2. What are some of the things that you are dissatisfied with? For example, what's wrong with your apartment, your school, your job, your family, or your country? Talk about what is lacking or what there is too much of.

3. Think about a time in your life when you weren't old enough to do the things you wanted to do. Talk about the things you wanted to do and what prevented you from doing them.

DISCUSSION QUESTIONS ON EXPLORATION AND ACHIEVEMENT

1. Why do people go exploring?

2. What do you know about the explorers of the eighteenth and nineteenth centuries? Why do you think governments supported their explorations? What was the importance of the discoveries the explorers made?

3. Some people explore new territories, and others explore new ideas in the field of science or engineering. For example, Thomas Edison and Alexander Graham Bell made discoveries that changed the course of history. Talk about a discovery or an invention that you think was important in changing history.

4. Who are some of the great explorers and inventors of your country? Tell what they did and the importance of each discovery and invention.

5. Talk about a famous person who had to overcome many obstacles to accomplish his or her goal. What things did this person lack? How did the person overcome these obstacles? For example, Columbus didn't have enough money to finance his trip by himself. He had to get money from the king and queen of Spain.

6. Do you think discoveries and inventions happen because of the particular needs of people at a particular time in history, or do you think they happen because of the genius of a particular person? Give reasons for your answer.

16

THE SIMPLE PERFECT TENSE

I now thee wed.

Dialog

(YOLANDA is talking with her younger sister, SANDRA.)

SANDRA: Guess what?[1] I have wonderful news. Jeff and I are engaged!

YOLANDA: What! You . . . engaged?

SANDRA: What's the matter? Aren't you happy for me?

YOLANDA: Of course I'm happy for you. I'm just . . . surprised.

SANDRA: I know this is all very sudden. I know you think we're very young, but we really love each other.

YOLANDA: Yes, I'm sure you do.

SANDRA: I **haven't told** anyone **yet. This is the first time I've spoken** about it. Will you come with me when I break the news[2] to Mom and Dad?

YOLANDA: Yes . . . but are you sure you know what you're doing? **I've never met** Jeff. Who is he?

SANDRA: **He's the most wonderful person I've ever known.**

YOLANDA: Where did you meet him?

SANDRA: I met him in biology class last semester.

YOLANDA: Oh, he's a student. **Has** he **finished** college **yet?**

SANDRA: He **hasn't graduated,** but he**'s already finished** most of his courses.

YOLANDA: How will you support yourselves?

SANDRA: We**'ve already discussed** that. I'm going to work until he finishes school.

YOLANDA: Sandra, you**'ve never been** on your own.[3] **Has** he? **Has** he **ever worked** before? **Has** he **ever lived** alone?

SANDRA: No, he **hasn't,** but that's not important. What matters is that we're in love.

YOLANDA: How do you know you're really in love? You **haven't had** much experience with men. How many guys **have** you **gone out**[4] with?

SANDRA: Well, not that many. **Jeff's the first one I've ever fallen in love with.** I feel as if I've **always known** him.

YOLANDA: I know, I know. Love makes the world go round. But **so far** you **haven't convinced** me that you know what you're doing. Why don't you wait for a while?

[1]*Guess what?*: People often say this when they have interesting news and want to get someone's attention.
[2]*To break the news* means "to tell someone something important that may be upsetting."
[3]*To be on your own* means "to be independent and totally responsible for yourself."
[4]*To go out* means "to date someone."

SANDRA: I thought about waiting. But I don't want to wait. I'm just too excited. They say sometimes you have to follow your heart.

YOLANDA: They also say, "Look before you leap."[5]

Listening Comprehension Questions

1. What is Sandra's wonderful news?
2. What does Yolanda think of her sister's announcement? Does she approve?
3. Has Sandra told their mother and father about her engagement yet?
4. Has Yolanda ever met Sandra's fiancé?
5. What does Jeff do for a living?
6. Have Sandra and Jeff discussed yet how they are going to support themselves?
7. How many men has Sandra gone out with?
8. Does Sandra plan to follow her older sister's advice and wait for a while before she gets married?

THE SIMPLE PRESENT PERFECT TENSE

The simple present perfect tense is formed in this way.

Statements

> I
> you
> we
> they } + **have (not)** + past participle
>
> he
> she
> it } + **has (not)** + past participle
>
> *Jeff hasn't graduated from college yet.*

[5]*Look before you leap* means, "Think before you act."

Questions

(Question word) + $\left\{ \begin{array}{l} \textbf{have} \\ \textbf{has} \end{array} \right\}$ + subject + past participle

Has Jeff ever lived alone?

This tense is called the simple present perfect tense because it expresses a connection between the present and the past. The word *perfect* here means "a completed action." The word *present* tells us that, in some sense, the action is not totally completed or that it was completed so recently that there is a clear connection to the present.

EVER, HOW MANY TIMES, ALWAYS, AND *NEVER*

Questions with *Ever* and *How Many Times*

When we want to ask if something has happened at any time between a time in the past and the present, we use the simple present perfect tense and *ever*. When we want to know the number of times something has happened, we use *how many times* with the present perfect tense. In addition to *how many times*, we also use *how many people, events, things,* and so on.

Examples

SANDRA: **Have** you **ever been** in love, Yolanda?

YOLANDA: Yes, I **have.**

SANDRA: When was the last time you were in love?

YOLANDA: I was really crazy about a guy from the station last year, but it didn't work out.

SANDRA: **Has** Arnold **ever mentioned** marriage to you?

YOLANDA: No, he **hasn't.** I only met him a few months ago.

SANDRA: **How many guys have** you **gone out** with, Yolanda?

YOLANDA: I've **gone out** with a lot.

SANDRA: Really, **how many times have** you **gotten** serious about a relationship?

YOLANDA: Only a couple of times up to now. My first love was my high-school sweetheart. That was a long time ago.

Did You Ever and *Have You Ever*

There is a difference between the questions *did you ever* and *have you ever*. If we are asking about a specific period of time in the past that is finished or completed, we must ask the question in the past tense (*Did you ever . . . ?*). If we are asking about an action that took place between some time in the past and now, we use the present perfect (*Have you ever . . . ?*).

Examples

SANDRA: When you were in high school, **did you ever think** about marrying the boy you loved?

YOLANDA: No, I **didn't.** I thought we were too young at the time.

SANDRA: **Have you ever wanted** to get married?

YOLANDA: No, I **haven't.** But who knows?

Always and *Never*

When we want to talk about something that began at a time in the past and has never stopped up to this moment, we use *always* with the simple present perfect tense. We use *never* with the simple present perfect tense to express the opposite meaning.

Examples

SANDRA: You and I are really very different people. A career **has always been** very important to you. **I've always wanted** to get married and have a family. **I've never been** very serious about a career.

YOLANDA: Marriage **has always frightened** me a little bit. **I've never thought** I could spend my life with one person.

■ ACTIVITY 16A

❏ Ask questions using the simple present perfect tense with *ever*. Use the words in parentheses as a guide for your questions. Ask a partner these questions.

1. (be in love)

   Have you ever been in love?

2. (be engaged)

_____ ?

3. (meet the person of your dreams)

_____ ?

4. (fall in love at first sight)

_____ ?

5. (read *Romeo and Juliet*)

_____ ?

☐ First ask a partner a question with *have you ever*. If the answer is yes, ask questions with *how many times* or *how many* (people, places, events) using the simple present perfect tense.

1. (be on a blind date)

   Have you ever been on a blind date?
   How many times have you been on a blind date.

2. (make a mistake in love)

_____ ?

_____ ?

3. (be proposed to)

_____ ?

_____ ?

4. (go to a fortune-teller)

_____ ?

_____ ?

5. (be serious about someone)

_____ ?

_____ ?

❑ Ask questions using the phrases in parentheses as guides. Ask the first question in the simple present perfect tense with *ever*. Then ask a question beginning with *when*. You must use the simple past tense with *when*.

1. (write a love letter)

Have you ever written a love letter?

When *did you last write a love letter?*

2. (buy flowers for someone you loved)

_____?

When _____?

3. (fight with your parents over the person you loved)

_____?

When _____?

4. (dream about a sweetheart)

_____?

When _____?

5. (promise to love someone forever)

_____?

When _____?

■ ACTIVITY 16B

❑ Here are some general statements about relationships between men and women that have been made over the centuries. Many people might say that these statements are stereotypes that have become outdated. Others may feel that the statements are simple truths. Read each statement. Then turn the statement into a yes/no question using *always* and/or *never* for a classmate to answer. The person who answers may want to explain why he or she feels the answer is yes or no.

1. Over the centuries, women have always had a greater desire to get married than men.

   Over the centuries, have women always had a greater desire to be married than men have?

2. Throughout history, women have always been more faithful than men.

   _____

   _____ ?

3. Over the centuries, the man has always been the chief provider[6] for his family.

   _____

   _____ ?

4. Men have never been content to have a relationship with only one woman.

   _____

   _____ ?

5. Throughout history, it has never been easy for couples to get divorced.

   _____

   _____ ?

☐ Now make statements in the simple present perfect tense with *always* or *never*.

1. (Throughout history, men . . . be as eager to get married as women.)

   _____

2. (Women . . . be the ones who stay home with the children.)

   _____

3. (Men . . . be the ones to go out and hunt or work.)

   _____

[6]*The chief provider* means "the one who earns money to buy food and clothing for the family."

4. (Society . . . reject marriage as an institution.)

_____

5. (From the beginning of time, . . . be a battle of the sexes.)

_____

6. (Over the centuries, love . . . be an inspiration to great writers.)

_____

7. (Marriage . . . necessary to preserve society.)

_____

❑ Can you think of any other stereotypes that people have always believed about men and women? Write them down. What is your opinion? Are these stereotypes disappearing now? Are men and women becoming more alike?

❑ Think of a person you know who has always had certain annoying characteristics. Describe the annoying characteristics. Has this person always annoyed you? What has he or she done that has bothered you? Tell about one specific time or incident to explain what this person is like.

UNSTATED PAST

Unstated Past with No Time Marker

Sometimes we talk about an event in the past but don't want to mention the definite time when the event took place or don't think the specific time is important. In this case, we use the simple present perfect tense.

> ### *Examples*
> Marriage patterns in the United States **have changed** a great deal. Sociologists **have studied** this change and **have found** that ninety-six percent of all Americans get married. More than forty percent of these couples get divorced. Many of these people get married again.

We cannot use the simple present perfect tense when we use a past tense time expression, such as *a week ago, yesterday, last year, in 1965*. We must use the simple past tense. We can't ask a *when* question about the past with the present perfect tense.

> ### *Examples*
>
> In 1968, the divorce laws **changed** radically in New York. It **was** very difficult to get a divorce before that time. Now it is much easier.

EXPRESSIONS THAT REQUIRE THE SIMPLE PRESENT PERFECT TENSE

In the $\begin{Bmatrix} last \\ past \end{Bmatrix}$ $\begin{Bmatrix} two \\ three \\ four \end{Bmatrix}$ $\begin{Bmatrix} days \\ weeks \\ months \\ years \end{Bmatrix}$ In recent $\begin{Bmatrix} years \\ weeks \\ months \end{Bmatrix}$

Recently

This is the $\begin{Bmatrix} first \\ second \\ third \end{Bmatrix}$ time that something has happened.

With the above expressions, you generally see the simple present perfect tense.

> ### *Example*
>
> **In the past forty years,** the American family **has changed** greatly. There are many possible reasons to explain this change. For example, **this is the first time in history** that so many women **have worked** outside the home.

■ ACTIVITY 16C

Fill in each blank with the correct form of the simple present perfect tense of the verb in parentheses.

The American family *has gone* through many changes in recent
    (go)

years. One of the reasons for this is the increase in divorce. The divorce

rate _____ to the point where one of every two marriages ends in
    (rise)

divorce. The increase in divorce _____ millions of families with
    (create)

only one parent.

Divorce is not the only reason that the family _____. Another
(change)

change in the family has to do with the fact that the number of working

mothers _____ sharply in the past decade. More than fifty percent
(increase)

of married women with school-age children _____ the work force.
(join)

More and more mothers need to work because the cost of raising a child

_____ up in recent years.
(go)

■ ACTIVITY 16D

❑ Fill in each blank with the correct tense of the verb in parentheses.
Choose between the simple present perfect tense and the simple past
tense.

One problem connected with divorce is the question of who will get

custody of the children. Up to now, mothers *have almost always kept* the
(almost always, keep)

children. At least up to now, most people, including judges, _____
(feel)

that mothers are closer to the children and are better able to raise them.

Because of this, traditionally judges _____ children to the mother
(give)

in most cases.

There _____ a famous case in custody rights in 1975. In this
(be)

case, Dr. Lee Salk, a famous child psychologist, _____ to keep his
(want)

children after he _____ a divorce. The mother also _____
(get)   (want)

them. The unusual part of this case _____ that the judge
(be)

_____ the children what they _____. In the end, the judge
(ask)   (want)

_____ the children to their father. He partly _____ his
(award)   (base)

decision on what the children _____.
(want)

This case marks a change in the way the legal profession is thinking

about custody cases nowadays. In the past few years, the courts

_____ to listen to the desires of children and fathers.
(start)

Judges explain that the father's role is changing in the family and that, in

some cases, he may be closer to the children and better able to care for them.

> ❑ Discuss or write about a recent change you have noticed in family life.
> Then give a specific example to support your notion.

■ ACTIVITY 16E

Fill in each blank with the correct tense of the verb given. Choose either the simple present perfect tense or the simple past tense.

Your instructor may use this as a listening comprehension activity first. Before you listen to your instructor read this to you, read the Listening Comprehension Questions at the end of this activity and keep them in mind. The first time that you listen, don't try to write anything. The second and third times that you listen, take notes to answer the questions and try to notice the verb tenses that are used.

There *has been* a major change in the American economy in
(be)

recent years. In the past five or six years, the number[7] of women who hold

professional jobs _____, so women now hold the overall
(increase)

majority of professional positions in the United States.

Of course, in the past, there _____ many more men who
(be)

_____ professional jobs than women. Men's traditional dominance
(hold)

continues today in some professions, such as medicine, law, and

engineering. But, in certain professions, companies _____ so
(hire)

many women recently that women are now in the majority. Today there

are more female psychologists, statisticians, editors, and reporters than

male, for example. Of course, women _____ dominant
(be, always)

in professions such as nursing and teaching, and their dominance in

these fields _____ in recent years.
(negative, change)

[7]*Number* is the subject of the verb here.

Even in the professions such as medicine, women

_____ progress. The percentage[8] of women
    (make)

doctors _____ by about three percent in the past
    (grow)

few years. In 1983, only fifteen percent of doctors _____
            (be)

women. Today about eighteen percent are women.

The statistics on men and women in higher education show significant

changes too. The percentage[9] of women who go to college _____
        (double)

in the past twenty years. In 1966, twenty-one percent of women _____
        (go)

to college. Today the percentage is around forty percent. In 1962, five

percent of medical, law, and architecture students _____ women.
      (be)

Recently the percentage _____ to close to thirty-five
    (grow)

percent.

Economists agree that the increase[10] in the number of women in

professional jobs _____ the service economy. In recent
    (affect)

years, the service economy _____, because, with more
    (expand)

women working, there is more need for day-care centers[11] and restaurants

for couples who don't have time to cook dinner.

Listening Comprehension Questions

1. What major change in the economy has there been in recent years?
2. Who now holds the majority of professional jobs in the United States—men or women?
3. Give some examples of fields in which men's traditional dominance continues.

[8]*Percentage* is the subject of the verb in this sentence.
[9]*Percentage* is the subject of the verb in this sentence.
[10]*Increase* is the subject of the verb in this sentence.
[11]*Day-care centers* are places where working mothers can leave their babies or children under the age of five while they are at their jobs.

4. Give some examples of fields in which women have recently become the majority.

5. What are some fields in which women have always been dominant?

6. What percentage of women were doctors in 1983? How has that percentage changed in recent years?

7. Give some statistics to show how the percentage of women who go to college has changed.

8. Which segment (part) of the economy has been affected by the increase of women in professional jobs? Give two examples.

■ ACTIVITY 16F

❑ Describe a situation in your own country. Use the expression *this is the first time in the history of my country.*

1. *This is the first time in the history of my country that there have been so many single-parent families.*

2. This is the first time in the history of my country _____

_____

3. _____

_____

4. _____

_____

❑ Now talk about how your country has changed or developed. Use the expression *in the last fifty years* or *in recent years.*

1. *The family has changed a great deal in the United States in the last fifty years.*

2. _____

_____

3. _____

_____

4. _____

_____

So Far, Up to Now, and *As of Now*

When we talk about actions between some nonspecific time in the past and the present moment and we want to show that related actions may still happen in the future, we use the simple present perfect tense with these expressions: *so far, up to now,* and *as of now.*

Examples

Statistics show that the American family is in trouble. Many sociologists have criticized the nuclear family,[12] but, **up to now**, most Americans haven't accepted other alternatives. The younger generation has experimented a great deal. **So far** they have tried many different family structures, such as communal living and open marriage.[13]

Already, Yet, and *Still*

ALREADY

When we want to emphasize that an action was completed at some unstated time before the present moment, we use *already* with the simple present perfect tense in affirmative statements. We usually place *already* between *has* or *have* and the past participle. It is also possible to place *already* at the end of the sentence.

Example

The way in which children are cared for is changing in many countries. In fact, it **has already changed** a great deal in countries such as the Soviet Union and Israel. For example, the governments of these countries have set up day-care centers run by the state.

YET AND *STILL*

We use *yet* and *still* in negative sentences with the simple present perfect tense when we want to emphasize that an action has not yet happened up to the present moment but that we expect the action to be completed at some time in

---

[12]*A nuclear family* consists of the mother, the father, and the children.
[13]*An open marriage* is one in which the husband and wife agree to date other people.

the future. We usually place *yet* at the end of the sentence. *Still* almost always comes after the subject of the sentence.

Examples

In the United States, many women's groups have asked the government to build more day-care centers for working mothers. The government **still hasn't done** much in this area. Some mothers support day-care programs, but other mothers **haven't accepted** this idea **yet.**

Questions

We use *already* and *yet* to find out if the action has happened before the present moment. *Yet* comes at the end of the question. *Already* comes after the subject or at the end of the question.

Examples

Have many European countries *built* day-care centers **yet?**
    Yes, Sweden and France have, for example.

How many communities in the United States *have* **already** *organized* an efficient day-care system?
    A few have.

■ Activity 16G

❑ The dialog between Yolanda and her sister continues. Use the simple present perfect tense whenever it is possible. Use the simple past tense only when it is not possible to use the present perfect tense. When you see *already, yet, so far,* or *still* at the end of a sentence, decide where to place these words in the sentence.

YOLANDA: Have you told Jeff's parents yet?

SANDRA: We *'ve already spoken* to his mother. (*already*) We

_____ her two days ago. We _____ his
    (**tell**)   (**negative, tell**)
father. (*yet*)

We know he'll be upset because Jeff _____
                                        (**negative, finish**)
school. (*still*)

YOLANDA: What _____ his mother _____ when you
_____ (say)
_____ her?
(tell)

SANDRA: She _____ very surprised. She thinks we
(be)
_____ enough about life. (*yet*)
(negative, **learn**)
She says Jeff _____ out on his own. (*yet*)
(negative, **be**)

YOLANDA: _____ you _____ on the date for the
(decide)
wedding? (*already*)

SANDRA: No, we _____. We _____ our minds a
(negative)   (change)
hundred times. (*already*)

☐ Continue the dialog by writing questions and answers with *already, yet, so far,* and *still.* Use these topics or add your own ideas to make questions.

find an apartment

have a blood test

get a marriage license

■ ACTIVITY 16H

☐ Fill in the blanks with the correct tense of the verb given. Choose between the simple present perfect tense and the simple past tense.

ARNOLD: What's the latest news on your sister? Is she still planning to
get married? _____ you _____ her yet that she
(convince)
is making a mistake?

YOLANDA: No, I _____. We _____ about it again the other
(negative)   (talk)
day. She's sure she's doing the right thing. I don't know though.
I just feel upset about it. My sister and I _____ very
(be, always)
close. She _____ this kind of snap decision[14] before. No
(make, never)
matter what I say, she just won't listen to me. When she

[14]*Snap decision* means "a decision made without careful thought."

_____ in high school, she _____ to me for advice.
ARNOLD: (be)   (come, always)

ARNOLD: _____ you _____ about why this makes you feel
                      (think, ever)
       so upset?

YOLANDA: Well, I don't know why... She's so young ...

ARNOLD: She's twenty years old. That's not so young.

YOLANDA: She _____ so level-headed.[15] She _____
            (be, always)   (be, never)
        impulsive before. Even when she _____ a little kid, she
                                      (be)
        _____ good judgment.
        (have)

ARNOLD: It's *her* life, Yolanda. You can't decide for her.

YOLANDA: I just don't understand it. Up to now, she _____ my
                                          (take, always)
        opinion very seriously.

ARNOLD: _____ you _____ you could be ... jealous?
                      (think, ever)

YOLANDA: Jealous!

ARNOLD: Just a little?

YOLANDA: I don't think so ... maybe ...

ARNOLD: Sometimes I think ... well, you know ... maybe we—you and I
        should try ... living together.

YOLANDA: Living together?

ARNOLD: Why not? We _____ to know a lot about each other over
                        (get)
        the past few months.

YOLANDA: I _____ like living with anyone before, but ...
         (feel, never)

ARNOLD: It could be really exciting.

☐ It is the next day. Yolanda and Arnold are talking about this again.
Write a continuation of the dialog above.

---

[15]*Level-headed* means "a very practical person who thinks about each decision very
carefully."

THE SIMPLE PRESENT PERFECT TENSE WITH THE SUPERLATIVE

We often use the simple present perfect tense with the frequency adverb *ever* in a clause that follows the superlative.

Examples

YOLANDA: Sandra, tell me more about Jeff.

SANDRA: Well, he's the most exciting guy that[16] **I've ever gone** out with.

YOLANDA: Really, and what does he look like?

SANDRA: Oh, he has the bluest eyes and the sexiest smile **I've ever seen.**

YOLANDA: I can't wait to meet him.

■ ACTIVITY 16I

In each sentence, fill in one blank with the superlative of the adjective in parentheses, and fill in the other blank with the verb in the present perfect tense.

(YOLANDA and ARNOLD are going to dinner and then to a nightclub tonight. They are both wearing new clothes, and they are very excited about the evening.)

ARNOLD: Yolanda, you look beautiful. That's *the sexiest dress*
(sexy dress)

that *you have ever worn* .
(ever, wear)

YOLANDA: Thanks. That's _____ that I
(nice thing)

_____ all day. You don't look too bad
(hear)

yourself.

ARNOLD: Okay. Let's go. We're _____ that New York City
(great couple)

_____ .
(ever, see)

---

[16]It is not necessary to use *that.*

(Later, YOLANDA and ARNOLD are at dinner.)

YOLANDA: Arnold, this is _____ that I
(good meal)

_____. This was really fun.
(ever, eat)

ARNOLD: Yes. Except for the music. It's _____ that I
(bad music)

_____.
(ever hear)

■ **ACTIVITY 16J**

☐ Get together with a partner. One of you can ask questions with the superlative and the present perfect tense. The other student should answer, using the same pattern. Later, switch roles.

1. (good movie ... ever see)

STUDENT A: What's the best movie that you've ever seen?

STUDENT B: *Casablanca* is the best move I've ever seen.

2. (high mountain ... climb)

3. (good restaurant ... eat in)

4. (beautiful place ... visit)

5. (interesting book ... read)

6. (good teacher ... had)

7. (cute man or woman ... kiss)

8. (dynamic person ... meet)

9. (famous leader of your country ... have)

10. (big lie ... tell)

11. (reckless thing ... do)

12. (embarrassing experience ... have)

13. (dumb thing ... do)

EXPRESSING YOUR IDEAS

1. Talk about love, courtship, and marriage in your country. What do you think is a good age to get married? How long do people date each other

before they get married? Do people get engaged? How long is the engagement period? Do people ever live together before they get married? Have attitudes toward living together changed in the past ten or fifteen years? What do you think about living together without getting married? What do couples have to do to get married? Is there a religious and a civil ceremony? Describe wedding customs in your country. If you are married, talk about your own courtship and wedding. Where do people go on a honeymoon in your country?

2. Has the structure of family life in your country changed in recent years? What changes have taken place? In your opinion, what is the most serious change that has taken place? For example:

   a. Have families gotten smaller? Why? Is it because more women have begun to work? If the family hasn't gotten smaller, has it stayed the same? Why?

   b. Have attitudes toward working mothers changed? Have men begun to take more responsibility for child care and housework? Have people's attitudes toward birth control changed in the past ten or twenty years? How?

3. In the United States, divorce has become more acceptable in recent years. Is this true for your country? Is it very difficult to get a divorce? Has the rate of divorce risen? Why? Do divorced people usually get married again? What are some of the emotional problems that divorced people face? When there is a divorce, who usually gets custody of the children? What are the problems that divorced parents face? Who do you think is better suited to raise the children—the mother or the father? Why?

17 THE PRESENT PERFECT CONTINUOUS AND THE SIMPLE PRESENT PERFECT TENSES

Making pottery.

Dialog

YOLANDA:	Oh, Jack! We're over here.
JACK:	I'm sorry I'm late. **How long have** you **been** here?
ARNOLD:	**We've been waiting for about thirty minutes.** We got here at 6:00. Where have you been?
JACK:	I was finishing a pot in my pottery class. It took me a really long time to clean up.
ARNOLD:	Your pottery class? **How long have** you **been taking** a class in pottery? You've never mentioned it before.
JACK:	I just registered for the class last week. I needed a break from all my science classes.
YOLANDA:	What a great idea!
JACK:	Yes, it is. **I've been having** a really good time. I've never tried to do anything creative before.
YOLANDA:	Hey, where's Molly? Isn't she coming?
JACK:	No, she's still working on that old oak table. **Since she got her own apartment,** she**'s been spending** all her free time fixing up the place.
YOLANDA:	Is she still working on that table? She**'s been trying** to get the paint off **since 8:00 this morning.** I know, because I called her then.
ARNOLD:	She's refinishing a table?
YOLANDA:	She just learned how. She's read several books on it.
JACK:	She**'s been running** around to antique stores and reading do-it-yourself books and not much else. She **hasn't been going out** much **recently**—at least not with me.
YOLANDA:	When the apartment's finished, things will get back to normal.
JACK:	I don't think she'll ever be finished.
YOLANDA:	I think she's much happier now than when she was living at home.
ARNOLD:	You can take some credit for that. You helped her make up her mind,[1] and she**'s been acting** like a new person **ever since.**

Listening Comprehension Questions

1. Why is Jack thirty minutes late?
2. How long has Jack been taking a class in pottery?
3. Why did he decide to take this class?

---

[1]*To make up (your) mind* means "to decide to do something."

4. Why isn't Molly joining them this evening?

5. What has she been doing since she got her own apartment?

6. Has she been going out with Jack much recently?

7. How has she been acting since she moved out of her mother's house?

THE PRESENT PERFECT CONTINUOUS TENSE

We use the present perfect continuous tense when we talk about an action that began in the past and is still going on in the present. This is not a completed activity but a continuing action. The present perfect continuous tense is formed in this way.

---

subject + $\left\{ \begin{array}{l} \textbf{has} \\ \textbf{have} \end{array} \right\}$ **(not)** + **been** + base form + **-ing**

Molly hasn't been going out much recently.

Examples

Molly **has been fixing up** her apartment for several days. She also **has been painting** the apartment herself.

In this example, notice that the sentences in the present perfect continuous tense show an unfinished and continuing action. When we talk about a physical action that began in the past and is still continuing (actions such as waiting for someone, talking on the phone, dancing, painting, and so on), we use the present perfect continuous.

Time Expressions

1. We often ask questions beginning with *how long* in the present perfect continuous tense. When we answer these questions, we use the following time expressions.

   for + a certain period of time: *for a few minutes, for two weeks, for several months since* + a specific date or time: *since 3:00, since yesterday, since 1977*

since + a clause: *since I left home, since I came here*

other time expressions: *all morning, all day, all week*

2. We often ask questions and make statements in the present perfect continuous tense by using the time expressions *lately* and *recently*.

Examples

YOLANDA: Molly, what are you doing? It's already 2:00. Aren't we going shopping?

MOLLY: I know it's 2:00. Everything takes twice as long to do as I expected.

YOLANDA: **How long** *have you been painting* those cabinets?

MOLLY: I started at 8:00 this morning.

YOLANDA: You mean you'*ve been painting* **for six hours!**

MOLLY: I really don't know what I'm doing. I've never painted before. Have you? Besides, nothing has gone right today. The man from the phone company still hasn't come. I'*ve been waiting for him* **all day.**

YOLANDA: What's that strange noise I hear?

MOLLY: Oh, that! That's the toilet. It'*s been running like that* **since last night.** Not only that, but the refrigerator *hasn't been working* properly **since I moved in.**

YOLANDA: Well, those things can be fixed. Just call the super[2].

MOLLY: I don't know. Maybe I've made a mistake. I'*ve been thinking* things over **lately.** Maybe I shouldn't have moved into this apartment. It needs too much work.

YOLANDA: It's not that bad. Your apartment will be great in another few days.

MOLLY: Maybe. All I know is that I moved in here last month, and I'*ve been having nothing* but headaches **ever since.**

YOLANDA: But don't forget that you've been having a lot of fun too.

Clauses with *Since* and *Ever Since*

We can use *since* clauses in two ways. This is the most common pattern.

Molly's been having a lot of problems **since** she moved into an apartment.

---

[2]*Super* is short for *superintendent.* It means the person in charge of an apartment building.

Here is a more emphatic way of expressing the same idea.

Molly moved away from home last month, and she's been having nothing but headaches **ever since.**

◼ ACTIVITY 17A

Here is some information about famous Americans who made important changes in their own lives, in the lives of others, or in their field of work. Your instructor may ask you to read the information, or he or she may choose to use it as a short listening comprehension passage. Form questions with *How long,* and answer the questions using *for* or *since.* Also be ready to tell some facts about the people and what they have done.

1. Mikhail Baryshnikov is a famous ballet dancer. He had already achieved fame in the Soviet Union, but he made the difficult decision to leave his motherland and find artistic freedom in the United States.

   How long ___*has he been living*___ in the United States?

   ___*He's been living here since*___ 1974.

2. George Lucas and Steven Spielberg are known for making films that revolutionized Hollywood. They each made these unique films when they were still young men. George Lucas's most famous films are *American Graffiti, Star Wars,* and *Raiders of the Lost Ark.* When George was in high school, he dreamed of being a racing car driver, but a serious car accident changed his mind. He began working in photography and then in film.

   How long ___*has he been working*___ films?

   ___*He has been working films since*___ he was a student in college. He made a short science-fiction film for his course at the University of Southern California and later made it into a full-length film for Warner Brothers.

3. Steven Spielberg worked with George Lucas on *Raiders of the Lost Ark.* His first big hit was *Jaws,* a film about a killer shark. Next came *Close Encounters of the Third Kind* and *E.T.,* two very popular films about visitors from outer space.

   How long ___*has he been working working with* G. Lucas___ films?

   ___*He has been working films since*___ high school. When he was just a teenager, he made many short films.

4. Sally Ride was the first American woman astronaut. She had been in the space program for five years before she was chosen for the seventh flight of the space shuttle. When she got off the space shuttle after it returned to earth, Americans greeted her with signs that said, "Ride, Sally, ride." This is a line from a popular rock 'n' roll song.

How long _____had_____ _____the___ women _____been_____ up into space on the shuttle flights?

Two _She had been going up_ _____since_____ Sally Ride's first ride in June 1983.

5. Paul Newman is one of the best-known American actors. His blue eyes are famous around the world. Some of his most famous films are *Cat on a Hot Tin Roof*; *The Hustler*; *Butch Cassidy and the Sundance Kid*; and his favorite, *Cool Hand Luke.*

How long _____has he been an actor_____?

He has been an actor since he graduated from college and joined a summer playhouse.

After many years as an actor, he decided to try something new. He became one of the best amateur racing car drivers in this country.

How long _____has he been a race driver_____?

_____He has been a race driver for_ more than fifteen years. He started when he was in his late forties.

6. Bill Cosby may be the comedian[3] that Americans love best. Cosby is a master of comedy who has earned millions of dollars from his popular TV situation comedy,[4] "The Cosby Show," his appearance in many commercials, and his comedy performances at the big hotels in such places as Las Vegas. In 1984, the situation comedy type of TV show was in trouble. Most shows were not funny, so the TV networks were losing viewers. "The Cosby Show," in which Cosby plays a black doctor and the father of five children, brought the American sit-com back to life.

How long _____has he been working_____ as a comedian?

_____He has been as a comedian since_ the fifth grade in elementary school. He performed a comedy act for his teachers and classmates that really made them laugh.

[3]*A comedian* is someone who tells jokes and acts in funny movies or TV shows.
[4]*A situation comedy* is a type of TV show in which the characters find themselves caught in a difficult but humorous situation; also called a sit-com.

7. Twyla Tharp is one of the most famous American dancers and choreographers. A choreographer creates dances for other artists to perform. Tharp studied both classical ballet and modern dance. Her work bridges the very different worlds of modern dance, pop, and ballet. She has created dances for such great classical dancers as Mikhail Baryshnikov, but she has also created highly unusual works, such as the dance that she asked the artists to perform on a basketball court.

   How long ___*has she been a dancer and choreographer*___?
   ___*She has been a dancer and choreographer since*___ the age of four, when her mother started to give her ballet and tap dancing lessons.

8. In 1957, Arthur Mitchell joined the New York City Ballet Company. The director, the world-famous choreographer George Balanchine, created a special solo role for Mitchell in one of the company's ballets. Mitchell became the first great black dancer in the world of classical ballet.

   How long ___*has he been a dancing of*___ classical ballet?
   ___*He has been a dancing dosered ballet since*___ he was a student at the High School of Performing Arts in New York City.

   Arthur Mitchell created the first black ballet company, the Dance Theater of Harlem. When it first opened, children only paid fifty cents a week for classes. Today the Dance Theater of Harlem performs all over the world.

   How long ___*has it been opened for interested in*___ ballet at the Dance Theater of Harlem?
   ___*It have been opened for*___ more than twenty years. It opened in 1969.

9. Henry Cisneros became the first Hispanic mayor of a large American city in 1979, when he won the election to head the government of San Antonio, Texas. He made a better future for the city by helping solve San Antonio's unemployment problem. He developed a plan to attract high-technology industries and provide job training for the city's mostly Mexican-American minority workers.

   How long ___*has he been*___ interested in city government?
   ___*He has been interested since*___ his graduation from college, when he took a job in the office of the city manager of San Antonio.

   has been + verb

■ ACTIVITY 17B

Finish these sentences. Use the present perfect continuous tense and put *ever since* at the end of each sentence.

1. Baryshnikov defected to the United States from the Soviet Union in

   1974, and he *has been living in the United*

   States ever since.

2. Steven Spielberg started making films when he was just a teenager, and

   he _____

3. Bill Cosby started making people laugh when he was in elementary

   school, and he _____

4. Paul Newman started racing cars when he was in his late forties, and he

   _____

5. Arthur Mitchell decided that black children should have the opportunity
   to study classical ballet. He opened the Dance Theater of Harlem in

   1969, and he _____

   _____

6. Twyla Tharp's mother gave her ballet and tap dancing lessons when she

   was four years old, and she _____

   _____

7. I got my driver's license when I was _____ , and I _____

   _____

8. I first became interested in _____ years ago,

   and I _____

9. I first started to _____ when I was _____ ,

   and I _____

CONTRAST OF THE SIMPLE PRESENT PERFECT TENSE AND THE PRESENT PERFECT CONTINUOUS TENSE

Cases in Which There Is a Change in Meaning

Examples

Molly has been doing a lot of work on her new apartment. So far she **has cleaned** the floors and the windows, but she **hasn't put up** curtains yet. As of now, **she's painted** the living room, but she **hasn't finished** the kitchen.

Notice that the sentences in the simple present perfect tense (*has cleaned, hasn't put up, hasn't finished*) do not refer to an action that is continuing now. When we use the simple present perfect tense here, it means that the action is completed. Note the difference in meaning in the following sentences.

Molly **has been cleaning** the floors.

Molly **has cleaned** the floors.

Cases in Which There Is Little Difference in Meaning

In the following type of sentence, we almost always use the present perfect continuous tense.

Molly **has been painting** her apartment since 8:00 this morning.

She started to paint at 8:00, and she is still painting at this moment. In this case, we don't usually say, "She has painted." However, when we talk about an action that has been continuing over a period of days, months, or years and that is not necessarily happening at the present moment (the moment of speaking) but is happening nowadays, we can use either the present perfect tense or the present perfect continuous tense without much change in meaning in many cases. When we use the present perfect continuous tense, we are emphasizing the continuous nature of the action.

Examples

In the 1950s, 1960s, and 1970s, young Americans generally tried to move out of their parents' homes as soon as they graduated from high school or college and had a job to support themselves. However, recently more and more young Americans **have been moving** back into their parents' homes after graduation from college. This is because rents for apartments and the cost of buying a home **have been rising** dramatically in recent years. Housing costs **have been increasing** so much that many young Americans can't afford to live apart from their parents.

All the verbs that are in the present prefect continuous tense in the example above can be written in the simple present perfect tense.

Here the idea of continuous action is not as strong.

Recently more and more young Americans **have moved** back into their parents' homes after graduation from college. This is because rents for apartments and the cost of buying a home **have risen** dramatically in recent years. Housing costs **have increased** so much that many young Americans can't afford to live apart from their parents.

SPECIAL VERBS THAT REQUIRE THE SIMPLE PRESENT PERFECT TENSE

We do not use the present perfect continuous tense with certain verbs when we want to express an action that began in the past and continues into the present. With these verbs, we have to use the simple present perfect tense. Here is a list of some common verbs that require the simple present perfect tense, not the present perfect continuous tense. Most of these verbs are on the list of stative verbs in Chapter 4.

be	belong	suppose	realize
know	own	believe	like
understand	possess	decide	dislike
owe	have[5]	conclude	hate
resemble	contain	prefer	love
tend	perceive	seem	want

[5]*Have* here means possession: I *have* a car.

> **Examples**
>
> Arnold **has known** Yolanda for nine months. They have been getting more serious about their relationship recently. Arnold **has loved** her since the day he met her.

Note: The correct form is *has known* and *has loved*, not *has been knowing* or *has been loving*.

ACTIVITY 17C

Choose the correct time expression for each of the following sentences. Choose among *for, since, ago, when, in,* and *ever since.* Finish the sentence, using the information in parentheses. *after, before, ever since*

1. Molly has lived in New York (1980)

   Molly has lived in New York since 1980.

2. Arnold wrote his first song (1982)

   Arnold wrote his first song in 1982. ✓

3. Arnold has been playing the guitar (1980)

   Arnold has been playing the guitar since 1980

4. Arnold played his first job in a nightclub (three years)

   Arnold played his first job in a night club 3 years ago

5. Yolanda has been living on her own (she got a job as a reporter) *since*

   Yolanda has been living on her own when she got a job as a reporter *since past the 1st part of the sentence*

6. Jack has been studying astronomy (three years)

   Jack has been studying astronomy for 3 years

7. Jack was accepted into graduate school (a year)

   Jack was accepted into graduated school a year ago.

8. Jack, Arnold, Yolanda, and Molly have been friends (quite a while)

   Jack, Arnold, Yolanda and Molly have been friends for quite a while.

9. Yolanda and Arnold have been going out (they met last autumn)

   <u>Yolanda and Arnold have been going out since they</u>
   <u>met last autumn</u>

10. Molly's been feeling better (she started to jog)

   <u>Molly's been feeling better since she started to</u>
   jog.

   (when)

   V.S.P.?

■ ACTIVITY 17D

Ask a partner information about himself or herself. Use the present perfect continuous tense whenever possible, but remember that some of the verbs can be used only in the simple present perfect tense.

1. Do you drive?

   How long <u>have you been driving</u>

   How long <u>have you owned</u> your car?
   (own)

2. Do you play an instrument?

   How long <u>have you been playing an instrument</u> ?

3. Do you have a hobby?

   How long <u>have you been had a car</u> ?

4. How long <u>have you known</u> your best friend?
   (know)

5. How long <u>have you been</u> interested in learning English?
   (be)

6. a. <u>How long have you been taking</u> care of yourself recently?
      (take)

   b. <u>How long have you been getting</u> enough sleep lately?
      (get)

   c. <u>How long have you been eating</u> the right food or
      (eat)
      <u>how long have you been eating</u> a lot of junk food?
      (eat)

   d. <u>How long have you been eating</u> too much?
      (eat)

   e. <u>How long have you been getting</u> enough exercise?
      (get)

   f. Do you smoke?

      How long <u>have you been smoking</u> ?

How much ___*have you been smoking*___ lately?

___*Have you been trying*___ to cut down recently?
(try)

7. What ___*have you been doing*___ since you graduated from
(do)

high school (college)?

___*How long have you been*___ came to the U.S.?

8. Are you married? If not, do you have a girlfriend or a boyfriend?

___*Have you loved*___ your wife/husband/girlfriend/boyfriend since
(love)

you first met him or her?

■ ACTIVITY 17E

Use only the present perfect and the present perfect continuous tenses to complete these sentences. Use the present perfect continuous tense wherever possible. Use the simple present perfect tense only when necessary.

MOLLY: Jack, I really like this pot you made. Maybe someday you'll be

good enough to sell your work.

JACK: Yeah, Lots of people turn their hobbies into professions. One of

my professors in art history left the university a few years ago and

moved to the country. He ___*has been making*___ jewelry there
(make)

ever since.

MOLLY: That's an interesting change. But can he make a living doing that?

How ___*has he been supporting*___ himself since he left his job at the
(support)

university?

JACK: He ___*has entered*___ several crafts fairs so far, and he
(enter)

___*has been trying*___ to get department stores to carry his
(try)

work. His shop is doing well too.

MOLLY: ___*Has he ever had*___ a show of his own?
(ever, have)

JACK: Yes, he __*has*__. He had a major show in New York just after he left the university.

MOLLY: How long __*has he been making*__ jewelry?
(make)

JACK: Since he took a night course in jewelry making about ten years ago.

MOLLY: __*Has*__ his family __*enjoy*__ their new life in the
(enjoy)
country since they moved?

JACK: Yes, so far they __*have*__. They __*hasn't become*__
(negative, **become**)
too bored yet. They all keep very busy. His wife

__*has been written*__ a book on changing careers.
(write)
She __*has written*__ most of the text, but she
(write)
__*hasn't written*__ a conclusion yet.
(negative, **write**)

■ ACTIVITY 17F

Fill in each blank with the correct tense of the verb in parentheses. Choose among the simple present, present continuous, simple past, simple present perfect, and present perfect continuous tenses.

(MRS. EMERSON lives across the hall from MOLLY. JACK and MOLLY have come to visit her.)

MOLLY: Hello, Mrs. Emerson. I hope we didn't interrupt you.

MRS. EMERSON: No, not at all. I __*am not doing*__ anything special
(negative, **do**)
right now. I just sat down to read.

MOLLY: What __*are you reading*__?
(read)

MRS. EMERSON: *War and Peace* by Tolstoy.

JACK: That's such a long book. How long __*have you been reading*__
(read)
it?

MRS. EMERSON: For about six months. It'll take me forever to finish it.

__*Have you ever read*__ *War and Peace?*
(ever, **read**)

JACK: Yes, I ___read___ it when I ___was___ in high school.
(read)   (be)

MRS. EMERSON: Don't tell me how it ends. I wish I had more time to

read, but I have so many things to do. Right now I

___am trying___ finish this patchwork quilt before
(try)

my grandchild is born. I ___have worked___
(work)

on it a lot recently.

MOLLY: It's exquisite. Where ___did___ you ___get___
(get)

the pieces of material to make it?

MRS. EMERSON: My daughter ___have been sending___ them to me regularly
(send)

for several years.

JACK: It really is beautiful. How long ___have you been making___
(make)

quilts?

MRS. EMERSON: I ___made___ my first one when I ___got___
(make)   (get)

married, and I ___have been making___ them ever since.
(make)

Each of my grandchildren ___have___ one.
(have)

MOLLY: How many ___did you make___ altogether over the
(make)

years?

MRS. EMERSON: I couldn't count them.

MOLLY: These quilts are lovely. You could sell them for a lot of money.

JACK: Yeah, you could. Prices ___went___ sky-high
(go)

in the past five or ten years.

MOLLY: Quilts are such an American art form. Women

___have made___ them since colonial times.
(make)

MRS. EMERSON: It's an art form I ___have always loved___
(always, love)

■ ACTIVITY 17G

A TV host is interviewing a famous woman author who is eighty-five years old. He is asking her about the changes she has seen in her lifetime. Fill in each blank with the correct form of the simple present, present continuous, simple past, simple present perfect, or present perfect continuous tenses.

HOST: I'd like to ask you some questions about changes you

__HAVE SEEN__ in your lifetime. What is the biggest change you
(see)

__HAVE NOTICED__ in your lifetime in the way people live?
(notice)

AUTHOR: That's a difficult question to answer. I guess it would be the

change in the younger generation. Young people __HAVE CHANGED__
(change)

a lot recently. In my day, young people __WERE__ very
(be)

different.

HOST: In what way __have they CHANGED__?
(change)

AUTHOR: To my way of thinking, they __HAVE been become__ *are becoming* too casual
(become)

and much too liberal in language, in dress, and in attitude in

general. I guess I'm just old-fashioned.

HOST: Would you give me an example of what you mean?

AUTHOR: Here's a small example. For the last fifteen years, since

my youngest granddaughter __left__ high school,
(leave)

students __have been wearing__ blue jeans and T-shirts to
(wear)

school. I understand that even some women teachers

__Have been wearing__ pants in the classroom recently.
(wear)

In my day, they __kicked__ you out of school
(kick)

when you __didn't dress__ properly.
(negative, **dress**)

HOST: What you're saying is true. Even professors at the universities

__lecture__ in blue jeans nowadays.
(lecture)

[handwritten margin notes: P.P.C / 1- PAST HABIT / 2- BEGAN PAST / CONTINUED / Present.]

AUTHOR: Of course, life-styles with the younger generation __is are__
(be)

completely different from what I __grew__ up with. It
(grow)

seems to me that for the last ten or fifteen years, young people

__have been tending__ to start dating at an earlier and earlier
(tend)

age. They start dating at thirteen, and, as you know, today many

couples __live__ together without being married. That
(live)

__was__ unthinkable in my day.
(be)

HOST: If it's not too personal, I'd like to ask another question. What is

the biggest change that you personally __experienced__?
(experience)

AUTHOR: That is another difficult question. I suppose I would say getting

married was the biggest change.

HOST: How long ago __did you get__ married?
(get)

AUTHOR: I __got__ married sixty years ago. My husband
(get)

and I __have been living__ happily together ever since.
(live)

HOST: Congratulations. It's nice to meet someone who __has been__
(be)

married for so long and __is__ still happy.
(be)

EXPRESSING YOUR IDEAS

1. Have you made any change in your life recently? What have you been
   doing since this change took place?

2. Choose a person that you know about whose life-style has changed.
   What change took place in the person's life? What was his or her life
   like before? What has he or she been doing since the change took place?

3. Do you have a particular hobby? Have you ever had one? How long have
   you been interested in this? How did you become interested in it? Why
   do you enjoy it? Why are hobbies important to people? What are some
   typical hobbies that people in your country enjoy?

4. Have people's eating habits been changing in recent years in your country? Has the quality of food changed in your lifetime? Has agriculture been mechanized? In recent years, have people been using processed food, such as canned food, frozen food, or specially prepared TV dinners? How do you feel about this change?

5. Have styles in fashion been changing much in recent years? Do people dress very differently nowadays from the way they did ten or fifteen years ago? How do you feel about this change?

6. How has the younger generation been changing in your country? Is the sense of morality with the younger generation different today from what it was twenty years ago? In what ways is it different? Why, in your opinion, has this change been taking place in your opinion?

7. Do people in your country return to college to take courses after they have retired or after they have been working for a number of years? Do they return to get a degree or just to take courses that are of special interest to them?

THE PAST PERFECT, THE PAST PERFECT CONTINUOUS, AND THE FUTURE PERFECT TENSES

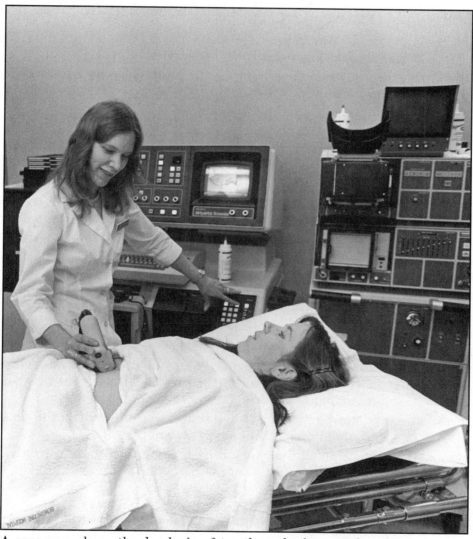

A sonogram shows the developing fetus through ultrasound waves.

Dialog

YOLANDA: You'll never believe this. You know my girlfriend Betty, the one who's expecting?[1] She just got her first baby picture.

ARNOLD: What do you mean, baby picture? She hasn't had the baby yet.

YOLANDA: I know. That's the exciting part. Doctors took a picture by ultrasound.[2] The ultrasound showed that Betty was expecting triplets! They were really surprised. **Up to that point,** they **hadn't suspected** anything unusual. *by the time*

ARNOLD: A picture by ultrasound! Modern medicine is really amazing. How did Betty take the news about triplets?

YOLANDA: She nearly passed out.[3] But **by the time she saw her husband,** she **had calmed down** enough to prepare him for the shock.

ARNOLD: What did he do when he found out?

YOLANDA: When Betty broke the news,[4] he nearly fainted. *des mo poder*

ARNOLD: She obviously **hadn't prepared** him enough.

YOLANDA: How could anyone be prepared for news like that? They **had** only **been thinking about** having a child for a couple of months **when Betty got pregnant.**

ARNOLD: Just think, **at this time last year,** they **hadn't** even **decided** to have children, and **by the end of this year,** their family **will have doubled** in size.

YOLANDA: More than doubled.

ARNOLD: At least they know ahead of time. Ten or fifteen years ago, no one **had heard** of ultrasound, and now it's commonplace.

YOLANDA: When our kids are ready to have children, I wonder what else doctors will be able to do?

ARNOLD: Who knows? **By that time,** maybe they**'ll have** already **developed** ways to correct almost all birth defects. I think they've already found a technique to correct a few of them before birth.

YOLANDA: Yes, and maybe they **will have found** a way to control the genetic makeup[5] of children. You know, "designer genes."

ARNOLD: If scientists do all that, they**'ll have gone** too far.[6] In my opinion, we should leave nature alone.

---

[1]*Expecting* means "awaiting the birth of a baby."
[2]*Ultrasound* is a device that can locate an object by means of sound waves.
[3]*Pass out* means "to faint."
[4]*Break the news* means "to tell someone something that will be surprising or shocking."
[5]*Genetic makeup* means "the composition of genes." Genes are parts of the body cells that decide what characteristics a person will inherit from his or her parents.
[6]*Go too far* means "to go beyond the limits of what is right."

Listening Comprehension Questions

1. What did Yolanda's friend Betty find out when her doctors did an ultrasound?

2. Had Betty suspected anything unusual about her pregnancy before the ultrasound was done?

3. How long had Betty and her husband been thinking about having children when she got pregnant?

4. Ultrasound is commonplace today. Had anyone heard of it fifteen years ago?

5. How does Arnold feel about the possibility that doctors will be able to control the genetic makeup of children?

THE SIMPLE PAST PERFECT TENSE AND THE PAST PERFECT CONTINUOUS TENSE

The Simple Past Perfect Tense   *shows that happen in the past*

We use the past perfect tense to talk about an action that took place before another action in the past. These two past events should be clearly mentioned or implied. If we are talking about only one event in the past, we use the simple past tense. Don't make the mistake of using the past perfect tense in this case. The past perfect tense is only used *in relation to* another past time. We form the past perfect tense in this way.

---

subject + **had** **(not)** + past participle

Betty's doctor hadn't suspected anything unusual before he did an ultrasound.

Here are some cases in which the past perfect tense is usually required.

BY ... /BY THE TIME ...

When we use a phrase with *by* or a clause with *by the time* in a sentence about the past, we usually use the past perfect tense in the main clause. In this case, *by* and *by the time* mean "before."

Examples

Louise Brown is one of the most famous babies in history. In fact, *by the time she was born in 1978*, she **had** already **become** the subject of intense interest. Newspapers called her the world's first test-tube baby. *By the time of her birth*, one London newspaper **had paid** thousands of dollars for the rights to her story and pictures.

By the end of 1979, a woman in India **had given** birth to a test-tube baby.

WHEN CLAUSES

There are two different kinds of *when* clauses about the past. We often use the simple past tense in the main clause and in the *when* clause about an event in the past. In this case, we mean the action in the main clause happened after the action in the *when* clause. *When* means "after."

				main clause	
when (after)	+	subject	+	simple past, (first action in time)	subject + simple past (second action in time)

Examples

When Mr. and Mrs. Brown **discovered** they couldn't have children, they **went** to Dr. Patrick Steptoe of Oldham Hospital in London. Dr. Steptoe and his associate, Mr. Robert Edwards, promised to try to help.

Very often we use the past perfect tense when we use a *when* clause in a sentence about the past. When we do this, we mean the action in the main clause (in the past perfect) happened before the action in the *when* clause (in the past tense). *When* means "before" in this case.

				main clause	
when	+	subject	+	simple past, (second action in time)	subject + past perfect (first or previous action in time)

> ### *Examples*
> When the Browns **came** to Oldham Hospital, Steptoe and Edwards **had had** some success in placing embryos in the bodies of women. However, none of these embryos **had lived** for a long time.

PAST PERFECT TENSE WITH CERTAIN ADVERBS

Many uses of the past perfect tense are parallel to those of the present perfect tense. The following expressions usually require the past perfect tense when we are talking about an action that took place before another action in the past.

still	*earlier*	*from the time that*
already	*up to* + specific past time	*That was the first time*
yet	*for* + period of time	*that I* _____ .
before	*since* + specific past time	

> ### *Examples*
> Mr. and Mrs. Brown were eager to accept the help of Steptoe and Edwards. They **had tried** to adopt a child for two years *before* with no success. They felt that was their last chance. In a complex process, Steptoe and Edwards placed an egg cell from the mother and sperm cells from the father in a glass container. Life began. Later the embryo was taken out of the glass container and was put into Mrs. Brown's womb. The fetus then grew until baby Louise was ready to be born. *This was not the first time human life* **had begun** outside a woman's body. Seventeen years earlier, an Italian scientist **had performed** the same experiment. *Up to 1978*, however, no test-tube embryo **had developed** into a full-grown baby.

```
  subject   +   had        (not)  +  past participle
               ↑        ↑                         ↑
            (still)  (already)                  (yet
                                                before
                                                earlier)
```

Note: *Still* and *yet* are used only in negative sentences in the perfect tenses. *Yet* is also used in questions.

The Past Perfect Continuous Tense

We use this tense when we mean that an action continued over a period of time up to a certain time in the past. It is often used to express the amount of time (how long) an action continued before a time in the past.

---

subject + **had (not)** + **been** + base form + **-ing**

The Browns had been trying to have a baby for years before they went to Steptoe and Edwards.

Examples

Steptoe and Edwards **had been experimenting** for a number of years when the Browns came to them. They **had been working** together since the 1960s.

Questions for the Simple Past Perfect and Past Perfect Continuous Tenses

---

Past Perfect: **Had (not)** + subject + adverb + past participle
            (ever, already)

Past Perfect
Continuous: **Had (not)** + subject + **been** + base form + **-ing**

Examples

YOLANDA: Arnold, isn't the story of baby Louise just amazing?

ARNOLD: Yeah, it is. It's medical history. **Had** doctors ever **tried** anything like that before Steptoe succeeded?

> YOLANDA: No, they hadn't—not really. They had succeeded with animals. But Louise is one of the first attempts with human life, as far as I know.
>
> ARNOLD: It's fascinating. How long **had** Steptoe **been trying** to do this before Louise?
>
> YOLANDA: I don't know, but he'd been interested in that area of medicine since the 1960s, I think. **Had** you ever **heard** of him before?
>
> ARNOLD: No, I never had.

■ ACTIVITY 18A

☐ Fill in the blanks with the past perfect tense. Use the verb in parentheses.

1. Before the mid-nineteenth century, no dentist *had ever used*
   (ever, use)
   anesthesia.

2. Before 1893, no doctor ___HAD EVER OPERATED___ on the heart.
   (ever, operate)

3. Before the 1930s, no doctor ___HAD EVER OPERATED___ on the brain.
   (ever, operate)

4. Before the 1960s, no one ___HAD EVER TAKEN___ a picture of an unborn
   (ever, take)
   child inside the mother's body.

5. As of 1961, doctors ___HADN'T SUCCEDED___ in starting human life outside
   (negative, succeed)
   the mother's body.

6. Before 1964, doctors ___HAD NEVER ATTEMPTED___ to perform an animal-to-
   (never, attempt)
   human transplant. In that year, a doctor implanted[7] a chimpanzee heart
   into a sixty-eight-year-old man.

7. The year 1967 was an important year in medicine. That was the first
   time a doctor ___HAD EVER PERFORMED___ a human heart transplant.
   (ever, perform)

[7]*Implant* means "to put something into living tissue."

8. The Baby Fae operation was a major milestone[8] in this area of medicine too. A doctor transplanted a baboon heart into a fourteen-day-old baby girl. The baby survived for twenty days. That

   was the first time that a patient __HAD SURVIVED__ so long
   (survive)

   with an animal heart.

9. Bioengineering is a fairly new field in medicine that combines medicine and physics. In the 1960s, the field of bioengineering was almost unknown. But by the early 1970s, a number of medical schools

   __HAD OPENED__ departments of bioengineering.
   (open)

10. In the late 1970s, doctors made great progress in the technique of microsurgery. With this technique, doctors use microscopes to magnify tiny nerves and blood vessels. If someone loses a finger or a hand, for example, doctors can often reattach it. Up to the late 1970s, doctors

    __HADN'T HAD__ much success in doing this.
    (negative, have)

11. The year 1974 was an important year for research in helping blind

    people. A thirty-three-year-old man __had lost__ his eyesight
    (lose)

    ten years earlier in a shooting accident. He __HADN'T BEEN ABLE__ to
    (negative, be able)

    see anything since then. Doctors implanted electrodes[9] in the man's brain. Then they connected a TV to his brain. He was able to see white horizontal and vertical lines on a dark background. This was the first

    time that doctors __HAD USED__ electronic impulses[10] to help a
    (use)

    blind person see.

Write four more sentences of your own if you know of other medical or scientific advances.

12. Before __1980s__, __no doctor had ever made ecagrophies__

13. Before __1800s__, __no doctor had use laser in surgery of eys.__

14. As of _____, _____

---

[8]*Milestone* means "an important event in life."
[9]*An electrode* is the terminal of a conductor of electricity.
[10]*Electronic impulse* means "an electrical force or push acting suddenly."

15. The year __1885__ was an important year. That was the first time that   *the sa…*

_____had_____ ever ____DEFEATED__ a *virus*

☐ Describe one medical discovery that you know about. Tell what had not been possible previous to this discovery.

Activity 18B

Answer the following questions about yourself, using the past perfect tense and the past tense.

1. a. What time did you get home last night?

   I got home at 10:45.

   b. What had you accomplished by the time you got home? (Write at least two sentences and include *by the time* in each sentence.)

   By the time I got home, I had finished my homework. By the time I got home arrived in Elm, I had read the newspaper

2. a. Where did you go on your last vacation?

   I went to Disney

   b. Had you ever been there before, or was that the first time that you had been there? _No, I had never been there before I went on vacation._

   c. Did you do anything that you had never done before? (Answer using the pattern below.)

   I had never gone surfing before. I went surfing for the first time on this trip. I had never gone to Berlin before I went to Berlin for the first time last weekend.

d. Did you see anything that you had never seen before?

Yes, I saw the fish I had never seen them before

3. Which of the following things had you done by your sixteenth birthday? (The verbs are given in the base form. Use the past perfect tense to answer.)

smoke a cigarette	learn how to support myself
learn to drive	live apart from my parents
go on my first date	learn everything there is to know about life
get drunk	be on an airplane
study calculus	learn to speak another language well
study physics	get a job
fall in love	decide what I wanted to do for a living
have my first kiss	

By my sixteenth birthday, I had smoked cigarettes and had decided that I was never going to smoke again.

By my sixteen birthday I had learned to drive and had decided that I was never going to drive again

Now practice asking a classmate questions.

By your sixteenth birthday, had you smoked cigarettes?

By your sixteenth birthday, had you got drunk?

By your sixteenth birthday, had you fallen in love?

By your sixteenth birthday, had you got a job?

■ ACTIVITY 18C

☐ Choose between the simple past tense and the past perfect tense. Use the verb in parentheses.

Albert Schweitzer is one of the most famous names in the history of medicine. He *decided* to become a doctor when he *was*
(decide)   (be)

thirty years old. By this time, he *had established* himself in two
(establish)

other careers, music and theology. In fact, he ___had already published___ two
(already, publish)

books—one on the life of Jesus and the other on the works of Bach. Even

though he ___BECAME___ famous in these fields, he ___had given GAVE___
(become)   (give)

them up in order to become a doctor and help the sick of Africa. It

___TOOK___ him seven years to complete his medical studies. So, at the
(take)

age of thirty-seven, he ___ARRIVED___ in Equatorial Africa to begin his
(arrive)

service. When he ___ARRIVED___, no one ___had built___ a hospital yet, so he
(arrive)   (build)

___RECEIVED___ his first patients in a house where chickens ___had lived___
(receive)   (live)

before. Conditions did not remain so difficult, however. Schweitzer

___had USED___ his own money, which he ___had EARNED___ in Europe from
(use)   (earn)

organ recitals and lectures, to build a hospital. His success in Africa

was so impressive that he ___received___ the Nobel Peace Prize in 1952. In
(receive)

his acceptance speech, he ___TALKED___ about the problems of peace
(talk)

in the world. Peace and respect for life ___had been___ concerns of his
(be)

from the time he was a young boy. His philosophy is sometimes simply

called "reverence for life." By the time he ___died___ in 1965, he
(die)

___had spent___ over fifty years of his life treating the sick of Africa. After
(spend)

his death, his daughter ___remained___ at the Schweitzer Hospital to carry
(remain)

on his work.

Although he is regarded as an authority in many fields, his greatest contribution is perhaps his life itself, an example of devotion to the sick and poor. When Larimer Mellon, a member of a very wealthy American family, _____heared_____ about Schweitzer, he _____deaded_____ to follow his
(hear)   (decide)
example. He _____had recevd_____ his medical degree when he _____WAS_____ in
(receive)   (be)
his forties. Then he _____WENT_____ with his wife to Haiti, where he
(go)
_____found_____ the Albert Schweitzer Hospital.
(found)

❑ Talk about a famous person or someone you know about who is no longer living. Tell about this person's life. Try to use *by the time* and *when* clauses.

❑ Describe an event in your past that changed your way of living or thinking. What had your life been like before this event? What was it like afterwards?

◼ Activity 18D

Read the following sentences about Marie Curie. They are in chronological order.

1. Marie Curie was born in Warsaw in 1867.

2. She went to Paris in 1891 to study at the Sorbonne. She met her husband, Pierre Curie, there.

3. She married Pierre Curie in 1895.

4. They started to work together in 1897.

5. They discovered radium in 1898.

6. Marie and Pierre shared the Nobel prize in physics with another French scientist in 1903.

7. Pierre died in an accident in 1906.

8. Marie took over his teaching position at the Sorbonne a few years later.

9. She was the first woman professor there.

10. In 1910, she isolated pure radium.

11. She received the Nobel prize for chemistry in 1911.

12. In 1921, she began to have trouble with her eyesight. She had trouble reading her lecture notes and the numbers on her test tubes.

13. In 1923, she decided to allow doctors to operate on her eyes because she had almost gone blind. The operations were successful.

14. In the early 1920s, doctors began to document[11] cancer deaths among people who worked with radium (X-ray technicians, research scientists, and factory workers who painted the dials on watches with radium paint). Marie admitted that radium was a dangerous substance.

15. In 1932, Marie became so ill that she had to stop working.

16. Marie Curie died in 1934 from leukemia, an illness almost certainly caused by radiation from her experiments.

❏ Complete these questions about the life of Marie Curie. Each question begins with a *when* clause. In your questions, use the past perfect tense. Answer the questions.

1. When Marie married Pierre, how long *had she been in Paris?*

   She'd been there for four years.

2. When Marie and Pierre received the Nobel prize in 1903, how long *had they been* _____ together?

   They had been together for twelve years.

3. When Pierre died in 1906, ~~how long had they been~~ married very long?

   No, they hadn't been married for a very long time. They had been married for eleven years.

4. When she won the Nobel prize for chemistry in 1911, how long *had she taken his teaching position* at the Sorbonne?

   She had taken his teaching position few years later he had

5. When she decided to allow doctors to operate on her eyes, *had she gone almost* blind yet?

   Yes, she had. She had almost blind for two years

6. When she became ill, *had she been with* the dangers of radium for very long? *Yes, she had been with the danger of radium for a long time*

[11]*Document* means "to keep an official record so something can be proven."

7. When she died, how long _had she been_ ill?
She had been ill for two years

☐ Write sentences using *when* clauses about Madame Curie's life. Use the simple past tense in the *when* clause. In the main clause, use either the simple past tense or the past perfect tense.

1. _When Madame Curie left Warsaw, she went to Paris to study._

2. _When Marie and Pierre started to work together, they had been married for a year._

3. _When Madame Curie discovered the radis, she had been married for three years_

4. _When Madame Curie share the Novel Price, she had worked with her husband for 3 years._

5. _When Madame Curie went to Paris, she meet her husssand_

6. _When M C decided to operted her eyes, she had been almost blind for 2 years_

7. _When M.C. became ill, the doctor had written a document about x-ray tecnique_

8. _When M C died, she had been ill for 2 years_

THE FUTURE PERFECT TENSE

We use the future perfect tense to talk about an action that will be completed before another action in the future. This tense is used only in relation to another time in the future.

subject + **will** + **have** + past participle

Researchers will have discovered many cures by the year 2000.

Here are some cases in which the future perfect tense is usually required.

By . . . /By the Time . . .

By and *by the time* mean "before" in these cases.

Examples

Many experts in the medical field predict vast changes in medicine, even in a simple doctor's visit. By 2000, some doctors **will have turned over** most of their work to machines. In the future, people will be examined painlessly by many different machines, and the results will be sent to a central computer. By the time the patient is dressed again, the computer will have analyzed all the tests and **will have sent** its suggested treatments to the doctor.

When Clauses

Examples

No one knows where scientific research will lead. One thing seems certain. (1) Whenever doctors make a discovery in medicine, they **will want** to put this discovery into practice. This alarms some people, who make terrible predictions about what the future holds for us. (2) They say, for example, when today's children are ready to have children, maybe researchers **will have developed** ways to "grow" children in a laboratory. They hope that before research goes this far, the government **will have stepped in** to stop it.

In sentence 1 we mean that *after* doctors make a discovery, they will want to put it into practice. In sentence 2 we mean that scientists will develop ways to "grow" children in a laboratory *before* our children are ready to have families.

The Future Perfect Tense with Certain Adverbs

When we use adverbs such as *before, still, yet, already, earlier,* and *previously* to talk about an action that will take place before another action in the future, we usually use the future perfect tense.

Examples

Some people see the year 2000 as a turning point. Certainly by that time scientists **will have already perfected** many artificial organs. For example, they **will probably have discovered** how to perform artificial eye transplants by then. When a person loses the use of an eye or another organ of the body, a doctor will be able to replace it with an artificial one. It is possible that doctors **still won't have conquered** heart disease, but everyone hopes that they **will have come closer** to finding a cure for it.

---

subject + **will (not)** + **have** + past participle

(still)   **(already)**   **(yet, before, earlier, previously)**

Note: *Still* and *yet* are used only in negative sentences in perfect tenses. Notice their different positions in the sentence.

Questions

Will + subject + **have** + past participle?

Will researchers have discovered a cure for cancer by the turn of the century?

> ### Examples
> ARNOLD: You know, with all the warnings about the danger of heart disease, I should really watch my diet more closely.
>
> YOLANDA: Yes, you eat too much junk food. It's high in cholesterol. If you continue like this, you'll be a perfect candidate for heart trouble when you're fifty.
>
> ARNOLD: That's true, and a little scary. But anyway, that's a long way off.
>
> YOLANDA: But be realistic. Don't wait until you're fifty to do something. Medicine can't cure everything. **Will** doctors **have discovered** a way to cure heart disease by then? **Will** they **have perfected** an artificial heart by that time? An ounce of prevention is worth a pound of cure.[12]

■ ACTIVITY 18E

❑ Fill in each blank with the future perfect tense. Use the verb in parentheses.

1. By the year 2000, perhaps scientists *will have found* a cure for cancer.
   (find)

2. By this time, maybe they _____ how life begins.
   (discover)

3. By the time our grandchildren are born, maybe researchers

   _____ many strange new forms of life.
   (develop)

4. By the time our grandchildren are born, maybe scientists

   _____ how to clone[13] people.
   (learn)

5. By this time, scientists _____ many revolutionary
   (certainly, make)

   discoveries.

❑ Write some predictions of your own, using the sentences above as models.

1. Have scientists discovered how to help the deaf hear and the blind see? Not exactly. They've made some important progress in this area.

   Perhaps by the year 2000, _____

---

[12]*An ounce of prevention is worth a pound of cure* means, "It's easier to prevent an illness by taking care of yourself than it is to cure the illness later."

[13]*Clone* means "to grow an exact copy of an organism (an animal or person) from a single cell."

2. Have doctors found a way to keep a person alive for several years with an artificial heart?

No, but perhaps by the year 2000, _____

3. By the year _____, _____

4. By the time _____, _____

5. By the time _____, _____

☐ By the time your grandchildren are grown, what changes do you think will have taken place in your family, in your hometown, and in your country?

■ **ACTIVITY 18F**

Fill in each blank with the correct tense, using the verb in parentheses. Choose among the present perfect, past, past perfect, present, future, and future perfect tenses.

DOCTOR: _*Have*_ you _*ever had*_ a complete physical
                         (ever, have)

examination before?

ARNOLD: No, I _____. This is the first time I
              (negative)

_____ so many tests.
        (take)

DOCTOR: Of course, I think everyone should have a complete checkup once

a year. Now I need some information about your medical history.

Which childhood diseases _____ you _____?
                                         (have)

ARNOLD: Oh, I _____ all of them. In fact, by the time I
              (have)

_____ eight years old, I _____ measles, mumps,
    (be)   **(have)**

and chicken pox.

DOCTOR: How old _____ you when you _____ down with
                 (be)   **(come)**

the measles?

ARNOLD: Five. I remember because it was just before I _____
                                                    (start)

school. I _____ from the chicken pox when I
      (just, recover)

_____ measles. I _____ the first two weeks of
(catch)   (miss)

school.

DOCTOR: I see. And when _____ you _____ the mumps?
(get)

ARNOLD: Oh, that _____ just before the second grade. I
(be)

_____ them first, and then I _____ them to my
(get)   (give)

sister. She _____ sick for a month.
(be)

DOCTOR: I notice that you wear contact lenses. How long _____
(wear)

you _____ them?

ARNOLD: I _____ them for the past two years. When I
(wear)

_____ them, I _____ glasses for ten years.
(get)   (wear)

DOCTOR: Do you smoke?

ARNOLD: I'm afraid so. About a pack a day.

DOCTOR: How long _____ you _____ so much?
(smoke)

ARNOLD: Since high school. When I _____ from high school, I
(graduate)

_____ a cigarette, even though most of my
(never, touch)

friends at that time _____. But I _____ a lot
(smoke)   (smoke)

since I _____ to perform.
(start)

DOCTOR: You know how dangerous it is. All I can do is recommend that

you stop or at least cut down.

ARNOLD: I _____ to cut down before, but I can't. I promise I
(try)

_____ to stop.
(try)

DOCTOR: You seem to be in relatively good health. I _____ only
(find)

one thing wrong so far. Your cholesterol level is too high. I want

you to follow the diet that the nurse _____ you when you
(give)

_____.
(leave)

ARNOLD: Diet? I _____ on a diet before. _____ I
                (never, be)

        _____ change my eating habits from now on? I play rock
        (have to)

        music. I don't have time to eat right.

DOCTOR: If you _____ to take care of yourself, you _____
                (want)   **(have to)**

        change. This diet is very detailed. It tells you what you can eat

        and what you absolutely cannot eat. It doesn't tell you how much.

        That's up to you. Now, by the time I _____ you next, I
                            (see)

        hope that your cholesterol level _____ down.
                                (go)

ARNOLD: See you again? When _____ that _____?
                                  (be)

DOCTOR: Four weeks from now.

ARNOLD: All right. I _____. Maybe by this time next month, I
                 (try)

        _____ my taste for junk food, and maybe I
        (lose)

        _____ smoking altogether.
        (stop)

EXPRESSING YOUR IDEAS

1. Talk about the system of medical care in your country. Is there a
   government-sponsored health care system? Who pays for major medical
   expense—the government, the employer, or the individual? Is everyone
   entitled to the same benefits? What is the major problem that the
   health care system faces?

2. What is the status of doctors in your country? Do they enjoy a high
   standard of living? Do you think that doctors charge too much for their
   services?

3. Researchers are currently working on methods of altering or
   determining the genetic makeup of human beings. In the future, they
   may be able to determine the sex, intelligence, and appearance of
   people. Should they be allowed to continue this research? Who should
   control this research
   —the government, private industry (pharmaceutical companies, chemical
   companies), citizens' committees, or anyone at all? If researchers ever
   succeed in this area, what might some of the problems be?

4. With modern medical technology, it is possible for doctors to freeze a person's body just before death. After doctors have found new medical cures and can extend the life span, the frozen body would be brought back to life. What is your opinion of this process? Would you do this if you had the opportunity? How do you think you would feel when you woke up?

5. Some people have agreed to donate certain organs of their body to medical science after they die. How do you feel about these organ banks? Would you leave your eyes, heart, or kidneys for use by someone else after your death? Why or why not?

6. Louise Brown was the world's first test-tube baby. What do you think of this new technique? Do you think it is ethical or not? Explain. If you couldn't have children any other way, would you use this method? If it were possible to "grow" a baby in the laboratory for nine months, would this be ethical? What questions would this raise for society?

7. In the United States today, men can donate or sell their sperm to a sperm bank. When a couple can't have children because the husband is infertile, they can use the services of a sperm bank. What do you think of this? Has science gone too far or not?

8. In California, there is now a special bank that accepts only the sperm of Nobel prize winners. Only women of very high intelligence can use their sperm bank. What do you think is the purpose behind this kind of sperm bank? How do you feel about this? Why?

19 MODAL PERFECTS

Dialog

(JACK just got off the telephone.)

MOLLY: Who were you just talking to?

JACK: That was my friend Johnny. You'll never believe what happened to him.

MOLLY: Is that the friend who's been taking skydiving lessons?

JACK: You mean the one who *was* taking. He'll never take another skydiving lesson again. He made his first and last jump yesterday.

YOLANDA: He **must have been** terrified.

JACK: He was. He looked so terrified that the instructor told him he didn't have to jump. He **could have waited** for two or three more lessons.

YOLANDA: Why didn't he?

JACK: I don't know. He **might not have wanted** to look like a coward. So he jumped.

YOLANDA: What happened?

JACK: Everything went wrong. His parachute **should have opened** automatically at 2,500 feet, but it didn't.

MOLLY: What did he do?

JACK: He didn't do anything. He **should have pulled** the cord and **opened** the parachute manually, but he was too scared to remember where the cord was. He panicked when he realized he was all alone, 2,000 feet above the earth . . . falling.

MOLLY: Then what happened?

JACK: Well, the second parachute **should have opened** when the first one didn't, but something was wrong with it. Johnny didn't pull the cord for another 200 feet. Finally it opened automatically.

YOLANDA: He **must have been** out of his mind with fear[1] until the parachute opened!

MOLLY: He's lucky the second parachute opened.

YOLANDA: I don't understand how anybody could jump out of a plane. He **could have killed** himself.

MOLLY: He **must have been praying** all the way down.

JACK: Wait till you hear the rest of the story. He saw himself floating toward some treetops. He doesn't remember how he did it, but he **must have done** something to change his direction. He landed in a swimming pool on a country estate, in the middle of a big party.

MOLLY: Boy, they **must have gotten** the surprise of their lives.

---

[1]*Out of his mind with fear* means "crazy with terror."

YOLANDA: Were they angry that he crashed[2] their party?

JACK: Well, they **couldn't have been** too angry because they invited him to stay for dinner.

Listening Comprehension Questions

1. What kind of lessons has Johnny been taking recently?
2. Did Johnny have to jump, or could he have waited until the next lesson to jump?
3. What should Johnny have done when his parachute failed to open automatically? Why didn't he do it?
4. What saved Johnny?
5. What does Molly think Johnny must have been doing while he was falling?
6. Where did Johnny land?
7. Were the people angry with him?

MODAL PERFECTS

Here is how to form a modal perfect.

subject + { **may** **might** **must** (of deduction) **should** **ought to** **could** } **(not)** + **have** + past participle

Johnny's parachute should have opened automatically, but it didn't.

MAY/MIGHT/MUST + *HAVE* + PAST PARTICIPLE

When we use *may* and *might*, we have several possibilities in mind. There is no difference between *may* and *might*. When we use *must*, we usually have only one possibility in mind. In negative statements *may*, *might*, and *must* usually do not form a contraction with *not*.

[2]*Crashed* means "went to a party uninvited." In this case "crashed" is a pun: he literally landed with a crash.

Examples

Amelia Earhart was a famous American pilot. She was the first woman to cross the Atlantic, and she was the first person to fly alone from Honolulu to California. These flights were in the 1930s. She **must have been** very brave to make these flights alone in those early planes. In 1937, she set off with a copilot on a trip around the world. After they left New Guinea, they were never heard from again. The world was saddened at this, and people developed many theories to explain what happened to them. For example, their plane **may have run** out of gas, or they **might have lost** control of the plane in a storm. Some say they **might have landed** on an island and that they **might not have died.** No evidence of a crash was ever found.

SHOULD/OUGHT TO + HAVE + PAST PARTICIPLE

We use this pattern when we want to say that something was a good idea or advisable in the past but that this action was not done. If we tell someone that he or she shouldn't have done something, we mean that he or she did something, and we think it was a bad idea. Notice that we can contract *should* with *not* (*shouldn't*); we rarely use *ought to* in the negative.

Examples

The *Titanic* was a magnificent ocean liner that sank on its maiden voyage[3] from England to the United States. Many important and famous passengers who were on board wanted to see icebergs close up, so the captain changed course and went father north. He **shouldn't have listened** to their request. He **should have followed** the course he had already set, and he **should have paid** closer attention to the warnings about icebergs in that area of the North Atlantic.

COULD + HAVE + PAST PARTICIPLE

When we use the modal perfect of *could* in affirmative statements, we believe that something was possible in the past but that it wasn't done for some reason. When we say that someone couldn't have done something, we make a strong logical deduction based on what we know about the situation. We believe it was impossible for something to have happened.

[3]*Maiden voyage* means "first voyage."

Examples

On the night of April 14, 1912, the *Titanic* struck an iceberg and began to sink. There was a ship fewer than ten miles away that **could have reached** the *Titanic* in time. Unfortunately, the ship's radio operator was asleep and never heard the SOS from the *Titanic*. The crew on the *Titanic* also set off distress flares. However, people from other ships thought these flares **couldn't have been** a call for help. They believed that the *Titanic* was unsinkable, so they thought the flares were just a fireworks display.

QUESTIONS AND SHORT ANSWERS

We can ask questions by using a modal perfect in this pattern.

(Question word) + modal **(not)** + subject + **have** + past participle?

Should Johnny have jumped out of the plane?

Short Answer:
subject + modal **(not)** + **have**

No, he shouldn't have.

If the main verb is **be,** the short answer is:
subject + modal + **have** + **been.**

Examples

Could more people **have survived** the disaster?
  Yes, they **could have.** Some of the lifeboats were less than half full.

Was there a lot of confusion after the ship struck the iceberg?
  There **must have been.** People probably didn't know exactly what had happened.

Were there enough lifeboats for the passengers of the *Titanic?*
  No, there weren't, unfortunately, but there **should have been.**

MODAL PERFECT CONTINUOUS TENSE

We use the continuous form of modal perfects in sentences where we would use a continuous tense about the past.

---

subject + modal (**not**) + **have** + **been** + base form + **-ing**

Jack's friend must have been praying all the way down.

Example

The captain didn't slow the *Titanic* down even after he had warnings of icebergs. In fact, the ship **must have been going** very fast when it struck the iceberg because four out of five compartments of the engine room were ripped open.

■ ACTIVITY 19A

In the late nineteenth century, Cuba was a Spanish colony. For a long time, the Cubans had been unhappy under Spanish rule. They began to rebel against Spain in the 1890s. The United States did not want the Spanish to control the island of Cuba. They did not want powerful European countries to control territories so near to the United States.

In January 1898, the United States sent a battleship called the *Maine* to Cuba. On February 15, 1898, an explosion in Havana harbor killed 260 men on the *Maine* and sank the battleship. The incident helped to start the Spanish-American War in April 1898.

Most Americans blamed the Spanish for the disaster. There were investigations. Although the U.S. Navy reported that a submarine mine caused the explosion, no one could say exactly who was responsible.

The Spanish blamed the disaster on an explosion that took place inside the *Maine*. They said it had been an accident.

The cause of the accident was never satisfactorily explained.

People had many theories about what happened to the *Maine*. Complete the following sentences, considering some of the possibilities. Use *may have* or *might have* + past participle.

1. An accident?

    a. The explosion *might have been* _____ an accident.
                                  (be)

    b. What _____ the accident?
                        (cause)

    c. A submarine _____ a mine in the harbor.
                        (leave)

    d. The battleship _____ the mine by accident.
                        (strike)

    e. Did a terrorist leave the mine close to the battleship deliberately?

       He _____. (short response)

2. The Spanish?

    a. The Spanish _____ the *Maine*.
                       (blow up)

    b. The Spanish _____ a bomb on board the *Maine*.
                    (put)

    c. They _____ the Americans to go home.
                 (want)

    d. They _____ the battleship was
                    (think)
    going to attack them.

3. The Cubans?

    a. The Cubans _____ the *Maine*.
                     (destroy)

    b. They _____ to start a war between the Americans
               (want)
    and the Spanish.

    c. They _____ the Americans to fight the Spanish
               (want)
    for them.

    d. Did they think a war would help them win their independence from

       Spain? They _____. (short response)

4. The Americans?

    a. The Americans _____ the bomb on their own
                    (plant)
    battleship.

    b. They _____ an excuse to begin the fighting.
                 (need)

c. They _____ this was a means of getting
                  (believe)

   Spain out of Cuba.

d. Did the people who planted the bomb know there were so many

   sailors aboard the *Maine?*

   They _____. (short response)
         (negative)

■ Activity 19B

There is an area of the West Atlantic Ocean between Miami, Bermuda, and San Juan, Puerto Rico, known as the Bermuda Triangle. More than a hundred planes, ships, and small boats have come into this area and disappeared without a trace. More than a thousand people have been lost here in the last thirty-six years. There has been almost no sign of a plane crash or of a wreck. Most planes disappeared in perfectly calm weather. Often they radioed that all was well just before they went out of radio contact. There are many theories about what happened to these lost ships and planes.

   Imagine what happened to the missing people, planes, and ships. Use *may* and *might + have +* past participle if you are not sure of what happened. Use *must + have +* past participle if you are almost sure of what happened.

1. During the nineteenth century, many ships disappeared in the area known as the Bermuda Triangle. In 1945, the first planes disappeared. Six navy bombers took off at 2:00 P.M. on December 5, 1945, for routine training exercises. Their commander was Lieutenant Charles Taylor, who had 2,500 hours of flying time. All the pilots and crewmen were experienced fliers. They completed their training exercise and were returning to the base. Everything had gone well.

   They *mustn't have been expecting* trouble.
           (negative, expect)

2. The temperature was 65°F, and the sun was shining. There was a slight breeze and only a few clouds in the sky.

   It _____ good flying weather.
         (be)

3. At 3:15 P.M., when the bombers were returning to the base, the flight tower received this radio message from Lieutenant Taylor: "This is an emergency. We seem to be off course. We cannot see land. . . . Repeat . . . we cannot see land."

   They expected to be over land, so they _____ lost.
                              (get)

4. A little later, they radioed again. They said their compasses were "going crazy." Although the planes were all flying in the same direction, their compasses each showed a different reading. Why did this happen? There are several possibilities.

    a. The compasses _____ defective.
    (be)

    b. A magnetic field _____ the compass needles.
    (affect)

5. The bombers could not hear the radio tower, but the radio tower could hear them. There was a lot of static. Why was there so much static? (Use the continuous form.)

    a. Enemy forces of the United States _____ to destroy
    (try)

    the bombers.

    b. Flying saucers (UFOs) from outer space _____
    (cause)

    this static.

6. A radio message from the bombers said that winds were as high as seventy-five miles per hour. The weather had been fine a little earlier. No high winds had been reported until that time. Why did they report such high winds?

    a. Their instruments _____ properly.
    (negative, **work**)

    b. Some supernatural force _____ nearby.
    (be)

7. At 4:00 P.M., Lieutenant Taylor turned the control of the planes over to a new pilot. Why do you think he did this?

    _____

8. A great search began. More than 300 planes, submarines, and destroyers searched 380,000 square miles for the 6 missing planes. They found no sign of a wreck. What do you think happened to the 6 planes?

    _____

9. People learned that before the flight one of the instructors suddenly said he did not want to go. Why do you think he didn't want to go?

    He _____ a premonition.[4]

_____

[4]*To have a premonition* means "to have a feeling that something is going to happen."

■ ACTIVITY 19C

Review the information about the *Titanic* on pages 331–332. Then read the following information and use the cue words in parentheses to make a sentence with *should have* + past participle.

1. The engineers who designed the *Titanic* were very proud of their new, ultramodern ocean liner. In fact, they were overconfident; they thought that they had constructed a perfect ship that could never sink. They didn't put enough lifeboats on the *Titanic* to accommodate all the passengers because they were so sure that the ship was unsinkable. As a result, 1,500 passengers died in the tragedy.

   a. (*overconfident*)

   The engineers shouldn't have been so overconfident.

   b. (*more lifeboats*)

   _____

2. The passengers who asked the captain of the *Titanic* to approach the iceberg were partying and drinking on the night of the accident. They were probably drunk and didn't even think about the danger.

   (*ask the captain*)

   _____

3. On the night of the accident, it was foggy, but the captain didn't slow the ship down much as he approached the iceberg because he didn't want to lose time.

   (*go so fast*)

   _____

4. A ship that was about ten miles away never received the SOS from the *Titanic* because the radio operator was asleep.

   a. (*sleep on the job*)

   _____

   b. (*a cup of coffee*)

   _____

5. When the people on another ship saw the *Titanic*'s distress flares,[5] they thought the flares were a fireworks display for the celebration of the *Titanic*'s maiden voyage. The ship could have rescued many of the *Titanic*'s passengers, but it never even tried to approach the *Titanic*.

(*make sure*)

_____

6. Until 1985, no one knew the exact location of the wreck of the *Titanic*. Then it was found in 12,500 feet of water 350 miles southeast of Newfoundland by an American and French expedition. The French members of the expedition decided to dive down and remove objects such as coffeepots, jewelry boxes, and plates from the wreck to put them in museums for everyone to see. The American members of the expedition disagreed with this decision.

(*leave*) They thought that the divers _____ the objects on the *Titanic* as a memorial to the people who died in the tragedy.

■ ACTIVITY 19D

(Jack's mother visited MOLLY last night. MOLLY was very nervous and did everything wrong. Today she feels terrible. She is talking to YOLANDA on the telephone.) Complete the sentences with *should have* + past participle. Make up the sentence that best supplies the meaning.

MOLLY: I didn't get home until late. I wanted to clean the whole house

before she got there. When she rang the bell, I was still vacuuming.

I should have vacuumed the day before.

YOLANDA: I'm sure she didn't mind. She knows you have a lot to do.

MOLLY: Then I asked her to come in, and I forgot to take her coat.

I _____

YOLANDA: That's not so bad.

MOLLY: I didn't tell her about the broken couch. She sat down, and the

seat collapsed.

I _____

_____

[5]*Distress flares* are small rockets that a crew can send up that light up the sky and signal for help when a ship is in trouble.

YOLANDA: She probably thought it was funny.

MOLLY: I don't think so. Then I offered her a cup of tea, but she wanted coffee. I didn't have any in the house.

I _____

in the afternoon. Then she asked me about my life. I didn't know what to say. I just kept talking on and on. I never asked her about herself.

I _____
(short form)

YOLANDA: She probably knew you were nervous. Don't worry.

MOLLY: And then I was trying to carry everything at once—the teapot, the cups and saucers, the sugar, and the cream. I dropped the tray because I was trying to balance everything.

I _____ at once.
(negative)

YOLANDA: What a day! What happened then?

MOLLY: She was really very nice. She helped me pick everything up. But I kept apologizing over and over again.

YOLANDA: Oh, you _____
(negative)
She sounds like a nice woman. I bet she understood.

■ ACTIVITY 19E

Shakespeare's famous tragedy *Othello* is a story of love and death. Desdemona was a beautiful Italian girl who fell in love with an exotic Moor named Othello. She loved to listen to his stories of faraway places. She didn't know him very well, but she decided to marry him against the advice of her father and others. After the marriage, they were only happy for a short time because Iago, an evil man who was Othello's servant, decided to ruin Othello's life. Iago knew that Othello was very jealous, so he made a plan to convince Othello that his loving wife, Desdemona, was unfaithful to him. Othello had given Desdemona a handkerchief that had belonged to his mother. Iago told his wife, Emilia, who was Desdemona's servant, to steal the handkerchief. Emilia knew nothing of her husband's evil plan, so she did as he had told her and took the handkerchief. Iago then told Othello that Desdemona had a lover and that she had given this handkerchief to that lover. When Othello asked Desdemona to show him the handkerchief, she couldn't find it, and Othello was convinced that Iago's story was true. Othello became wildly jealous and strangled his wife. Later, when he discovered Iago's evil lie, Othello killed himself too.

Read the following sentences about Othello and Desdemona. Then write a sentence with *could have* when you want to say that something was possible but was not done and with *could not have* when you want to say that something was impossible. Use the verbs in parentheses in your sentences.

1. Desdemona was a beautiful young woman from a wealthy family. Many young men from good families wanted to marry her. She didn't have to marry Othello.

   She ___*could have married*___ anyone she wanted to.
                (marry)

2. Othello made many mistakes. The tragedy didn't have to happen.

   a. He _____ to listen to Iago.
                (refuse)

   b. He _____ himself why Iago was
                (ask)
   telling him these terrible things about his wife.

   c. He _____ to Desdemona. He
                (talk)

   _____ her if what Iago had said was true.
           (ask)

   d. _____

3. Desdemona never overheard the conversations between Othello and Iago. Do you think she understood why her husband turned against her?

   _____
              (negative, understand)

4. Iago never told his wife, Emilia, why he wanted her to take the handkerchief from Desdemona. Emilia was a loyal servant and a good

   woman. She _____ that Iago planned to
              (negative, know)
   use the handkerchief to destroy Othello.

■ ACTIVITY 19F

Two thousand years ago 20,000 people lived in Pompeii, a city in southern Italy off the Bay of Naples. Pompeii was built at the foot of Vesuvius, a volcano 4,000 feet high.

Select the correct modal perfect form to write each missing sentence. Use *may, might, should, must,* and *could.*

1. Pompeii had a lot of ships in its harbor. Many wealthy Romans came to stay in its resorts. Statues and mosaics decorated many of its buildings. What kind of a city was Pompeii?

   Pompeii must have been a rich Roman seaport.

2. For four days before the volcano Vesuvius erupted on August 24, A.D. 79, there were tremors and vibrations under the ground. The volcano was smoking, and no one could get water from the wells. How do you think people in Pompeii felt?

   _____

3. Less than twenty years before, there had been a serious earthquake in Pompeii. Some people who felt the earth trembling on August 20, A.D. 79, decided to leave Pompeii right away. Why did they decide to leave?

   _____

4. Many people laughed at those who left. They didn't believe that there was any reason to be afraid. This mistake cost many of them their lives.

   They _____

5. When the volcano erupted, it forced a lot of rocks and lava to shoot upward. There was also a huge flame that flew up into the sky, and there was a great crash. The earth shook. What do you suppose happened in Pompeii?

   Buildings _____

   People _____

6. People saw a great black cloud in the sky. It was like night even though it was daytime. Then the cloud started raining poisonous material. It rained on the nearby towns. Some people made the mistake of going down into their cellars rather than trying to escape by sea. They got trapped in their cellars.

   _____

7. Some time passed between the eruption of the volcano and the rain of poisonous material. Not everyone who died had to die. There was some time to escape.

   More people _____,

   but they panicked and made foolish mistakes.

8. Pliny the Elder, a famous Roman writer, was across the bay when the volcano erupted. So was his nephew, Pliny the Younger. Pliny the Elder received a note from someone across the bay. It was a call for help from a close friend. Pliny decided to go across the bay to help people there. His nephew did not go with him. Why not? Give two possibilities.

   He _____

   He _____

9. Pliny the Elder took his ship and crew and sailed across the bay. He sailed exactly toward the place of greatest danger. Everyone else was going in the opposite direction. The people warned Pliny to turn his ship around, but he refused.

   Pliny _____,
   _____**(turn around)**_____

   but he didn't. He went on shore to look for his friend. Later he died on the beach.

10. The city was rediscovered in 1847. At first people were amazed by the gold and treasures of the city. They didn't try to keep everything exactly as it was. They were more interested in stealing the treasures.

    They _____
    _____(negative, **steal**)_____

    It wasn't until the nineteenth century that the city was excavated by responsible archeologists. Now it is preserved almost exactly as it was on the day the volcano erupted in A.D. 79.

■ ACTIVITY 19G

Divide the class into groups composed of two storytellers and two listeners. The storytellers must think of a major mistake that they made in life. Here are some ideas:

1. a time you did something and lost a friend

2. a time you didn't say something you should have said

3. a time you didn't study for an important exam

4. a time you didn't make an application for something you really wanted

5. a time you wanted to meet someone but didn't

6. something you tried to cook that turned out wrong

7. an accident that was your fault

What prevented you from doing what you should have done?

The listeners' task is to suggest alternative actions using *could have* or give advice with *should have*. After the group has finished, one listener from each group can retell the story for the whole class (that is, if the storyteller is not too embarrassed), and the whole class can offer suggestions with *should have* and *could have*.

EXPRESSING YOUR IDEAS

1. Have you ever done anything you consider dangerous? For example, have you ever participated in skydiving, scuba diving, car racing, or some other sport that wasn't very safe? Why did you do it? Was it more exciting because it was dangerous? Why do people do dangerous things? Have you ever made a dangerous mistake? What was it? What happened?

2. People sometimes live in dangerous places—for example, in an area where there are a lot of earthquakes, near an active volcano, or underneath a dam that could burst. Why do you think people live in these areas? How does it influence their lives? Have you ever lived in a place you considered dangerous? Why did you leave or remain there?

3. Many people put their lives in danger for different reasons. For some, danger is connected to a sport. Others risk their lives to help people. Many scientists and explorers have done this. Tell about some famous person or someone you know who has done this. Can you imagine yourself risking your life for others?

4. Have you ever done anything foolish or dangerous because you didn't want to look like a coward or because you were afraid of what other people would think? Tell about it.

5. Write about a time when you almost got married, but you didn't. Should you have? Why or why not?

6. Discuss an accident that happened to you or someone you know—a time you were in a car crash or a plane crash, or a time you were in a boat that capsized. What could have prevented these accidents? Should you have done something you didn't do? Should someone else have done something he or she didn't do?

7. Write about a famous mistake in your country's history. What should have happened that didn't happen, or what shouldn't have happened that did? Describe the causes of the mistake. If you don't know, guess about the causes.

8. Write about a famous court case or a famous trial in which some mistake was made. Tell who was tried, whether the person was condemned or freed, and what you think should have happened.

9. A serious accident occurred near Harrisburg, Pennsylvania, on March 28, 1979, at the Three Mile Island nuclear power plant. A lot of radiation was released into the environment. Many people left the area to avoid the radiation. A lot of people stayed. Many mistakes were made. What could the government and the nuclear industry have done to prevent this accident? What do you think people from Harrisburg should and shouldn't have done at the time? Do you know about any other nuclear accidents around the world?

20 THE SIMPLE PASSIVE VOICE—PRESENT, PAST, AND FUTURE

The Capitol Building, Washington, D.C., with the Washington Monument in the background.

Dialog

YOLANDA: What's wrong, Jack? You look ill.

JACK: You know I **was hired** part-time at the observatory[1] this semester. I just got my first paycheck.

YOLANDA: So why are you so down?[2] You should be happy.

JACK: I was ... before. But when I looked at my paycheck and saw how much money **was taken** out in taxes, I couldn't believe it.

YOLANDA: I feel the same way. Taxes are already high, and the governor[3] wants to raise state taxes next year.

JACK: What! If taxes **are raised** any more, I won't have any salary left. Is he kidding?

YOLANDA: No. I guess the governor hopes that a lot of problems **will be solved** by increasing taxes.

JACK: Great, but how do I make ends meet?[4] I can't live on my income now. The cost of living is just too high. Why **isn't** something **done** about it? If my rent **is raised** again this year, **I'll be forced** to move.

YOLANDA: Everyone has the same problem. We **are** all **going to be asked** to sacrifice a little with this new tax increase.

JACK: What's it like for you? When **were** you last **given** a raise? **Are** your raises **determined** by the cost of living?

YOLANDA: No, I don't think so. I guess our raises **are based** on merit. If the boss likes your work, you**'re given** a raise. And speaking of work, I need to finish this story I'm working on, or **I'll be fired.** See you later, Jack. Cheer up.

JACK: See you.

Listening Comprehension Questions

1. Why does Jack look ill?
2. How does he feel about the possibility that taxes will be raised next year?
3. Is Jack having trouble making ends meet?
4. What will happen if his rent is raised again this year?

[1]An *observatory* is a special building where astronomers can observe the stars.
[2]*Down* means "unhappy, depressed (colloquial)."
[3]The *governor* is the head of a U.S. state.
[4]*Make ends meet* means "have enough money to pay all your bills."

5. At the television station where Yolanda is a reporter, are raises determined by the cost of living?

6. What does Yolanda say will happen to her if she doesn't finish the story she's working on?

THE PASSIVE VOICE

Active Voice

Up to now we have studied verb tenses only in the *active* voice. The active voice means that the subject of the sentence performs the action of the verb in that sentence.

> ### Examples
>
> 1. In the United States, citizens **elect** the president.
>
> 2. The media **announce** the results the day after the election.

Passive Voice

In the passive voice, the subject of the sentence does not perform the action of the verb.

> ### Examples
>
> 1. In the United States, the president **is elected** (by the citizens).
>
> 2. The results of the election **are announced** the day after (by the media).

We use the passive voice when we want to put more emphasis on the person or thing that receives the action than on the person or thing that does the action. In the sentence *In the United States, the president is elected* (by the citizens), the word *citizens* is called the agent. The agent is the person or thing that performs the action of a verb in the passive voice. (The citizens elect the president.)

The passive form of any tense contains two things: the verb *to be* and the past participle.

Past: subject + { **was** / **were** } (**not**) + past participle

Jack was hired at the observatory.

Present: subject + { **is** / **are** } (**not**) + past participle

Our raises are based on merit.

Future: subject + { **am** / **is** / **are** / **will** } (**not**) + **going to be** + past participle
                                              be   + past participle

A lot of problems will be solved by raising taxes.

USE OF THE PASSIVE VOICE

We use the passive voice for different reasons.

Agent Is Known

Sometimes we know who did something, and we want to talk about who received an action instead. In the sentence *The president is elected,* we know he is elected by the people. If the agent is common knowledge, we don't use it. Look at the following examples for this use of the passive voice.

Examples

Past

George Washington, the first president of the United States, **was elected** in 1789. He served eight years, or two terms, as president. Then he decided not to run again. The custom **was established** at that time for a president to serve no more than two terms. It was not until Franklin D. Roosevelt **was elected** to a third and fourth term that this custom **was broken.**

Present

Elections **are followed** with great interest in the United States. The president is the head of the political system, and presidential elections

are held every four years. Many people work under the president. Many of them **are not elected** though. Members of his cabinet **are appointed.**

Future

Presidents have usually been men who are white, Protestant, and married with families. John F. Kennedy broke one of these traditions. He was a Catholic. But the traditions of race and sex **aren't going to be broken** very easily. Some people are trying to change these traditions though. Jesse Jackson, a black man, ran for president in 1988 but was defeated. Some people hope a black or a woman **will be elected** president of the United States someday. However, it seems likely that a black or a woman **will not be elected** president in the very near future.

Agent Is Unimportant

The following paragraph is about Mount Vernon, the house George Washington lived in. In this paragraph, we want to concentrate on Mount Vernon and its history, not on the Washington family. Therefore *Mount Vernon, the furniture,* and *a writing desk* become the subjects of sentences, and the verbs are usually in the passive voice. Sometimes we add the agent (*by the family*) to give additional information.

Examples

Mount Vernon is the name of the estate where George Washington lived. The house **was built** not far from Washington, D.C., on the Potomac River. It is a beautiful house and interesting to visit. No one knows exactly when the main part **was constructed,** but we know that it **was owned** for many generations by *the Washington family* before George inherited it. More sections **were planned** and **added** later *by George Washington* when he lived there. Some of the furniture in the house is original. Upstairs in the "blue bedroom" is a writing desk that **was imported** from France *by Washington's wife, Martha.* The kitchen contains some original utensils that **were used** by *slaves* to prepare the meals.

Agent Is Unknown

Often we use the passive voice when we want to describe a process or how something is done. In this case, the agent may be completely unknown or not very important.

Examples

One of the duties of government is to mint money. Most coins **are made** in Philadelphia, but some **are also minted** in Denver. Minerals such as copper, zinc, and silver **are delivered** to these mints and **are used** to make coins. Pennies **are made** mostly of copper. Dimes and quarters have no silver, but half-dollars contain forty percent silver. The mottoes In God We Trust, E Pluribus Unum, and Liberty **are placed** on all coins. The date **is also stamped** on each coin. Gold **isn't used** in coins anymore. Gold that **is owned** by the government **is stored** in Fort Knox.

Questions

Past: (Question word) + { **was** / **were** } + subject + past participle?

Was Jack hired full-time?

Present: (Question word) + { **am/is** / **are** } + subject + past participle?

How are Yolanda's wages determined?

Future: (Question word) + **will** + subject + **be** + past participle?

When will the president be reelected?

(Question word) + { **am/is** / **are** } + subject + **going to be** + past participle?

When are taxes going to be raised?

Examples

ARNOLD: Boy, money isn't worth much anymore, is it?

YOLANDA: I know silver dollars aren't made with silver anymore. The price of silver is too high.

ARNOLD: How about pennies? **Are** they still **made** of copper?

> YOLANDA: I don't think so. Going back to[5] silver dollars, what ever happened to that Susan B. Anthony coin? **Was** it **taken** out of circulation?
>
> ARNOLD: Yes, it sure was. No one liked it. It was too easy to confuse with a quarter. Hey, why **was** Susan B. Anthony **chosen** for that coin?
>
> YOLANDA: She was a famous suffragette. She worked hard to get the vote for women.
>
> ARNOLD: Paper dollars wear out really fast. **Is** a new silver dollar **going to be minted** soon?
>
> YOLANDA: I don't know. It takes a long time to design a coin.

■ ACTIVITY 20A

Fill in each blank with the correct form of the passive voice. Use the past or present passive tense with the verb in parentheses.

Monticello is the name of a famous American home. It *is located*
(locate)
near Charlottesville, Virginia, and looks out over the beautiful hills and

mountains of Virginia. The house _was built_ in the 1770s by Thomas
(build)

Jefferson, the third president of the United States. It _was made_ of red
(make)

brick and wood, and the construction of the house _was carried out_
(carry out)

by the slaves of Thomas Jefferson. Most of the materials, such as bricks

and nails, _were produced_ on the plantation. The house
(produce)

was designed by Jefferson himself. It is a beautiful example
(design)

of classical revival architecture. The inside of the house was also beautiful

and very different from other houses of the period. For example, Jefferson

loved space, so he built the beds into the walls. Storage space

was built under the beds. Jefferson's bed
(build)

was placed between his bedroom and his study. When
(place)

the bed wasn't in use, it _was raised_ by ropes. This home has
(raise)

many interesting inventions of Jefferson's.

[5]*Going back to* means "I want to return to the subject (of silver dollars)."

Monticello is open to the public and ___is visited___ by a great many

tourists each summer. The house and the grounds ___are maintained___ by a
      (visit)

group of interested citizens. A small fee ___is charged___ to help with the
                              (maintain)

upkeep. Monticello is well worth a visit.
        (charge)

☐ Choose a famous building that is important in the history of your
   country. Tell when, how, where, and why it was built. Give a little of its
   history.

■ ACTIVITY 20B

☐ Make questions using the passive voice. The subject and verb that you
   must use are given. The question word is given in parentheses. Form the
   questions in the passive voice first. Then write the answers in complete
   sentences. Work in groups to make the questions, and then see if any of
   your classmates know the answers. If no one knows the answer, look on
   page 355.

1. Past

   a. (Where)   the first battles of the Revolutionary War   fight

      Where were the first battles of the Revolutionary War fought? They were fought in Lexington and Concord in Massachusetts.

   b. (When)   the Constitution   write

      _____

      _____

   c. (How many)   amendments   add at that time

      _____

      _____

   d. (What)   these amendments   call

      _____

      _____

e. (When)   the South   defeat

_____

_____

f. (Where)   Abraham Lincoln   assassinate

_____

_____

g. (How many times)   Franklin D. Roosevelt   elect

_____

_____

2. Present

   a. (How)   a presidential candidate   choose

   _____

   _____

   b. (?)   the presidential finances   make public

   _____

   _____

   c. (How)   the votes   count

   _____

   _____

   d. (How many)   representatives   elect from each state

   _____

   _____

   e. (How many)   senators   elect from each state

   _____

   _____

f. (How)   federal judges   choose

_____

_____

g. (How long)   Supreme Court judges   permit to stay in their job

_____

_____

Future

❑ Form questions about the future. These are questions that many people in the United States are asked nowadays.

1. (a woman ... elect president)

   Will a woman ever be elected president?

2. (new political parties ... form)

   _____?

3. (the voting age ... lower from eighteen to sixteen)

   _____?

(Today election campaigns are primarily financed by private donations.)

4. (presidential election campaigns ... finance by the government)

   _____?

5. (taxes ... raise)

   _____?

6. (social programs such as socialized medicine ... enact by Congress)

   _____?

7. (a world government ... form)

   _____?

❑ Ask more questions about U.S. history. Use either the active or the passive voice.

❑ Interview a classmate. Find out about how his or her country was founded. Were battles fought? Was a revolution fought? Was his or her country liberated by a famous person? Was it colonized by another country?

ANSWERS

1. a. Lexington and Concord in Massachusetts
   b. 1789
   c. ten
   d. Bill of Rights
   e. 1865
   f. in Ford's Theater in Washington, D.C.
   g. four

2. a. at national conventions
   b. yes
   c. usually by machine
   d. it depends on the population
   e. two
   f. by appointment
   g. for life

◼ ACTIVITY 20C

❑ Fill in each blank with the correct verb form. Use the verb in parentheses. Decide between the active and the passive voice. The passage describes a process and is written mostly in the present tense.

Everyone who works in the United States ___*pays*___ an income tax.
                                              (pay)
Every month taxes *are taken out* of an employee's paycheck. First, the
                    (take out)
federal tax _____ from the total amount of the check. Some states
             (subtract)
_____ an income tax, so the state income tax _____ too. In
  (have)   (take out)
addition, if you live in New York City, a city income tax _____. Of
                                                            (take out)
course, a large amount _____ of everyone's salary for Social
                        (take out)
Security. This means that when a person _____, a certain amount
                                          (retire)
of money _____ to him or her every month by the federal government.
          (pay)

Every January tax forms _____ to every worker by the federal
(send out)
government. These forms _____ and _____ before April 15.
(fill out)   (return)
If a person has paid too much money to the government, this extra money

_____. However, if the taxpayer still _____ money to the
(refund)   (owe)
government, a check for the difference _____ with the tax forms. If
(include)
the forms _____ to the Internal Revenue Service by midnight of
(negative, **mail**)
April 15, a penalty _____.
(add)

There are more taxes, of course. People in the United States also

_____ taxes if they _____ property. These property taxes
(pay)   (have)
_____ by the city government. They _____ for public
(collect)   (use)
schools, local roads, public hospitals, and many public services, such as

police and fire departments. Finally, almost every time an American

_____ something, he or she _____ a sales tax, which can
(buy)   (pay)
be anywhere from two to eight percent, depending on the state. No wonder

people say there is no end to taxes.

❑ Describe how citizens are taxed in your country.

■ ACTIVITY 20D

Look at the following paragraphs. All the sentences are in the active voice.
Rewrite the paragraph, and, in every sentence where it is possible, change the
main verb to the passive voice. Decide when it makes sense to add the agent.

Before a presidential election in the United States, candidates campaign
very hard. They begin their campaigns as much as one year before the election.
Candidates spend a great deal of money. They do this in a number of different
ways. For example, the government allows taxpayers to donate $1 of their taxes
to presidential campaigns. In addition, business corporations and labor unions
contribute heavily. They make these contributions public, of course. Finally,
private citizens may contribute. Candidates give special fund-raising dinners;
at these dinners, people sometimes pay $250 a plate. The government limits
the amount anyone can contribute.

One reason campaigns are so expensive is that candidates often advertise on TV, and TV time is expensive. Television is a new element in American political life. Some say political "spots"[6] are like commercials. Because spots are short—usually about thirty seconds—candidates don't discuss the issues. Often cameramen film them with their families or in a local neighborhood talking to voters. Critics of TV spots ask these questions: Is a candidate's image becoming more important than the issues? Do the American voters become familiar with the issues?

Before a presidential election in the United States, candidates campaign very hard. Their campaigns are begun as much as one year before the election.

■ ACTIVITY 20E

Fill in each blank with the correct verb tense. Choose between the active and the passive voice.

Within the next two weeks, a congressman is going to introduce a bill to lower taxes. This bill will begin in the House of Representatives because all tax bills must start there. In order for this bill to become a law, it must go through many steps. Here are the steps that this bill will follow.

First this bill <u>will be sent</u> to a committee in the House, where it
           (send)

_____. Experts _____ to testify about the advantages and
  (debate)   (ask)

disadvantages of this bill. After the bill _____, it _____ on.
                     (discuss)   (vote)

If it _____ a majority vote, it _____ to the floor of the
    (receive)   (go)

House. If it _____ a majority vote, it _____. On the floor
     (negative, **receive**)   (die)

[6]*Spot* means "a short television or radio commercial, usually lasting fifteen or thirty seconds."

of the House, it _____ again. If it _____ a majority vote,
(discuss and vote on)   (receive)

it _____ to a committee in the Senate. Here it _____, and
(send)   (debate)

experts _____ again. Once more, if it _____ a majority
(testify)   (negative, receive)

vote, it _____. If it _____ by this committee, it
(die)   (pass)

_____ to the floor of the Senate. After the bill _____ the
(go)   (reach)

floor, it _____ the same process again. If the bill _____ by
(follow)   (pass)

the Senate, it _____ to the president. If he _____ it, it
(send)   (sign)

_____ a law. If he _____ it, it _____ to the House
(become)   (veto)   (return)

and the Senate. If it _____ a two-thirds majority vote, it
(receive)

_____ a law without the president's signature.
(become)

■ ACTIVITY 20F

People in the United States are naturally mistrustful of government power.
They watch as government grows in size and are afraid of the consequences.
They fear that their lives will be controlled by "Big Brother"[7] and that they will
lose their individuality. Here are some fears and predictions about the future.
Read the following predictions and discuss in groups or with a classmate
whether or not it is possible for any of these things to happen. Give reasons for
your opinions.

1. People's lives will be controlled by the government in the future.

2. People will be told what to study.

3. People will be told what career to enter.

4. People will be told when they can get married.

5. The number of children people can have will be regulated.

6. Only the most intelligent and attractive people will be allowed to have
    children.

7. Gender, I.Q., and athletic ability will be decided on before birth.

8. The gender of children will be determined by the government.

9. Antisocial people will be reeducated. Prisons will be a thing of the past.

10. People's moods and personalities will be regulated by drugs.

[7]*Big Brother* means "a government that controls all aspects of our lives."

Make some predictions of your own about future developments in government or science.

■ ACTIVITY 20G

Look at the following topics. Choose one of them and make a report to your class on the topic. Remember to include some examples of the passive voice.

1. Choose a product (food products such as cheese or beer, clothing, movies, or any product that your country is famous for or you know about) and describe the process by which it is made.
2. Tell how a government official (for example, the president or prime minister) is elected in your country.
3. Describe how many branches or divisions of government there are in your country. Tell what the functions of each are.
4. Choose a famous person. Tell when he or she was born, where he or she was brought up and educated, and what he or she achieved.

EXPRESSING YOUR IDEAS

1. Are people taxed at a high rate in your country?
2. Are taxes based on how much a person earns? What do you think of this?
3. Do you agree with how the money is spent in your country? In the United States?
4. Can you think of any programs in which the tax money was misspent?
5. Do people receive good services for their taxes in your country? In the United States?
6. Are taxes taken out of your paycheck, or do you pay them at the end of the year?
7. Do people pay sales taxes and property taxes in your country? Are they high?
8. Name several items that are taxed in your country and several that are tax-free. In the United States, for example, cigarettes are heavily taxed, but most food isn't taxed. What items do you think should be tax-free? Shouldn't be tax-free? Explain why.
9. Are most people honest when they pay their taxes?
10. People in the United States are beginning to protest against the high rate of taxation and are voting for tax reductions. Is this happening in your country?

21

PERFECT PASSIVES, CONTINUOUS PASSIVES, AND MODAL PASSIVES

UCLA graduation.

Dialog

MOLLY: Yolanda, I have big news to tell you. I've made a very big decision.

YOLANDA: Well, come on. What is it?

MOLLY: I'm going to apply to engineering school!

YOLANDA: You're what? I thought you were almost finished with your degree in history.

MOLLY: Not exactly. I still have a way to go, and anyway, I can transfer a lot of my credits.

YOLANDA: But why switch now? I thought you didn't like math or chemistry so much.

MOLLY: That's true, but I've been doing a lot of thinking lately. Several articles about starting salaries **have been published** recently, and I've been reading them carefully. Do you know that now recent graduates with a degree in chemical engineering **are being paid** about thirty percent more a year than those with other types of degrees?

YOLANDA: Hmmm. That is a significant difference.

MOLLY: I've really been having second thoughts[1] about teaching history in high school. Dozens of articles **must have been written** about the low salaries and low status of teachers, and I'll bet that I've read them all. I'm getting discouraged about teaching.

YOLANDA: I guess I can understand that. Teachers certainly **should be paid** more. But **aren't** efforts **being made** to increase teachers' salaries?

MOLLY: Yes, but not enough **has been done** so far. Teachers still **aren't being paid** enough.

YOLANDA: Okay, but money isn't everything. You know my cousin John. His parents pushed him really hard to study engineering, and he's miserable now. He studies constantly, and he just doesn't enjoy his courses. He **should have been allowed** to study liberal arts.[2]

MOLLY: Look, I love history, but I also love the idea of supporting myself well when I get out of school. I'm tired of being poor.

YOLANDA: I guess I can understand that. I just want you to be sure that you're making the right decision.

MOLLY: Thanks for your concern, but I think I am.

---

[1]*To have second thoughts* means "to have doubts; to think about changing one's mind."
[2]*Liberal arts* means "courses in the humanities—literature, history, philosophy, and the fine arts."

Listening Comprehension Questions

1. What decision has Molly made recently?

2. Why is Yolanda surprised to hear this news?

3. How much more a year are graduates with a degree in chemical engineering being paid than those with other types of degrees?

4. Molly mentions that dozens of articles have been written about the salaries and status of teachers. How have these articles helped to change her mind about teaching?

5. Does Yolanda think that teachers should be paid more?

6. Why did Yolanda's cousin decide to study engineering?

7. How does he feel about his choice now?

8. What does Yolanda think that he should have been allowed to study?

9. Molly says that she loves history, but she also loves something else. What is that?

THE PASSIVE VOICE OF THE PERFECT TENSES

The Passive Voice of the Simple Present Perfect Tense

Review the uses of the present perfect tense in Chapters 16 and 17. Do not try to use the passive voice with the present perfect continuous tense. We almost never use it. Use the active voice or the simple present perfect passive.

Statements: subject + { **have (not) been** / **has** } + past participle

Many articles about teachers have been written recently.

Questions: (Question word) + { **have** / **has** } + subject + **been** + past participle?

Has Molly's decision been affected by these articles?

Examples

Some professors think that in recent years too much pressure **has been put** on students to make very early decisions about graduate school and careers. Some students start worrying about it even in their freshman[3] year. They are choosing majors that will look good to graduate school admissions officers and to industry recruiters who come to college campuses looking for graduates to hire. More signs of stress **have been observed** in undergraduate students in recent years.

Which majors **have been chosen** more often in recent years?
Practical majors such as marketing, business administration, and engineering are the ones that **have been chosen.**

Has some of this pressure **been put** on students by parents because college tuition **has been raised** so much in the past five years?
Yes, the large increase in tuition has to be part of the reason.

■ ACTIVITY 21A

Read the examples above before you do this exercise. Fill in the blanks with the passive voice of the present perfect tense.

Your instructor may choose to use this activity for listening comprehension first. If so, look at the Listening Comprehension Questions at the end of the activity first and keep them in mind as you listen. The first time that you listen, just try to understand the information. The second or third time that you listen, take notes to answer the questions (don't try to write complete sentences) and listen for examples of the present perfect passive.

In recent years, special advertising and recruiting[4] efforts

<u>*have been made*</u> by many American colleges to make sure
(make)

that they will have full classrooms. The advertising campaigns have been

successful for the fifty to one hundred top colleges. An increase in the

number of applications _____ by the top schools. It seems
(report)

that seventy-five percent of the high-school graduates are applying to

twenty-five percent of the schools. Because private colleges now charge

---

[3]*Freshman year* means "the first year of college or high school."
[4]*Recruiting* means "trying to attract applicants to your school."

more than $15,000 per year,[5] parents and students want to make sure that

they will get a return on this huge investment[6] when they graduate. A

degree from a top school will help get them a better job with a higher salary.

However, in recent years, a big effort _____ by
                                              (make)

many colleges to attract students from outside the white middle class.

Schools want more diversity[7]—diversity in racial, ethnic, and economic

backgrounds. White middle-class students _____ by this
                                              (affect)

change. The competition to get into the top schools has become very stiff.[8]

To increase their chances of admission, many students have started

their own personal advertising campaigns. Over the last several years,

hundreds of videotapes _____ by college admissions
                            (receive)

offices along with the applications. In these videotapes, applicants[9] show

off their special talents: karate, music, tap dancing, and so on. They hope

that this will make them seem different from the hundreds of other

applicants and help the admissions officers remember them.

Of course, students have tried other things beside videotapes to

help them get into the top schools. Ever since the early 1980s, when

competition to get into the top schools began to get stiff, big profits

_____ by the owners of special schools that offer cram
     (earn)

courses[10] for the SAT[11] tests. American students take these tests for

---

[5]This figure is for 1989.

[6]*Return on an investment* means "the profit or value received in exchange for money spent."

[7]*Diversity* means "variety; difference."

[8]*Stiff* means "very hard."

[9]*Applicants* means "people who apply for admission."

[10]*Cram courses* are courses that try to teach you a lot in a very short time; they are designed to prepare you for a test.

[11]*SAT tests* are the Scholastic Aptitude Tests. The test score is one factor that college admissions officers consider when a student applies.

admission to college. The courses cost $800 or more. Also, many

independent education consultants _____ by nervous

(hire)

parents. These consultants charge $2,000 (sometimes less, sometimes

more) to look at a student's strengths and weaknesses, make a list of

recommended schools, and help the student practice going through an

imaginary interview with a college admissions officer.

The cost of applying to college _____ a great deal

(raise)

by these extras. As a result, a question _____ by

(raise)

lower-middle-class parents who just can't afford the extras. Is this fair?

They are afraid their children will be at a disadvantage if they don't have

the extras.

Listening Comprehension Questions

1. Today there are fewer students of college age than in the 1950s and 1960s. Why has an increase in the number of applications been reported by the top colleges?

2. Sending a child to a private college is a major investment for parents. How does this help explain the increase in the number of applications to the top colleges?

3. In recent years, a big effort has been made by many colleges to attract students from diverse racial, ethnic, and economic backgrounds. How have white middle-class students been affected by this?

4. Explain why many videotapes have been received by college admissions officers over the last several years.

5. What kind of special schools have earned big profits in recent years?

6. *True or false*: Many independent education consultants have been hired in the past few years to help get students into the top colleges.

7. How much do these consultants charge?

8. What question has been raised by lower-middle-class parents about the cost of cram courses for the SAT tests and private consultants?

▮ ACTIVITY 21B

Write questions using the passive voice of the present perfect tense.

American high-school students must take a standardized test in mathematics and verbal ability called a Scholastic Aptitude Test (SAT) before they can apply to college. The score on the test is a major factor in a college's decision to accept or reject an applicant. The College Entrance Examination Board has been using this test for many years.

1. How long *has this test been used* by the College Entrance
                      (use)
   Examination Board?

   Since 1947, when the Educational Testing Service of Princeton, New

   Jersey, began making such tests.

2. How many students _____ to take this test since 1947?
                             (require)
   Millions. About 1.2 million high-school seniors take the test each year.

3. _____ the questions from one year's test ever

   _____ on another test?
          (use)
   Yes, they have been. In the past, all questions and answers were kept secret.

4. _____ this system of testing ever _____ or
                                     (criticize)

   _____ ?
      (question)
   Yes, in New York State, a "truth in testing" law was passed in 1979. This

   law requires manufacturers of standardized tests to publish the

   questions and to let students see their answer sheets.

5. For what other reasons _____ this test _____?
                                                   (criticize)
   Some people say that there are too many possibilities for error in

   scoring the test. Also, some people argue that the test does not measure

   imagination, creativity, or motivation—qualities that are also necessary

   in college work. Others say that the test is culturally biased.

■ ACTIVITY 21C

Interview a classmate who comes from another country about higher education in his or her country. You can use the following questions and any others you want to add.

1. At what age and after how many years of high school can someone enter a college or university?

2. How hard is it to enter a university? Can almost anyone who graduates from high school attend, or is it extremely difficult to be accepted? What kind of tests does one have to take to be admitted to college? Have fewer students been admitted to colleges in recent years, or has enrollment increased? Have entrance requirements been raised or lowered? (Has it become more difficult or easier to enter a university?)

3. Is there a shortage of colleges and universities in your country? Do many students go to the United States to study for this reason? Have many new universities been built in recent years?

4. Are there certain degrees, such as a Master of Business Administration (MBA) or a Ph.D. in education that are difficult to get in your country because very few schools offer them?

5. If you are accepted at a good university, do you have to study very hard to stay there, or do students have to work harder in high school than they do at the university?

6. Do you already have a college degree? If so, what do you think of the education you received? Were the courses valuable?

7. If you do not have a college degree, do you plan to go to college? Why or why not? Do you think it's necessary to have a college degree?

■ ACTIVITY 21D

Prepare a brief talk for your class on these subjects.

1. What changes have taken place in your country's economy, society, or government in recent years? For example, has production of a particular product been increased or decreased or promoted recently? Has more of a particular product been exported or imported recently? Have taxes been increased? Have new programs been started to help poor people? Have demonstrations or protests been made against the government? Has a new leader recently been elected?

2. Have your country's society and culture been changed by outside influences in the past five or ten years? Has the structure of the family been influenced or weakened by some changes? Have women been influenced by the women's liberation movement? Have divorce laws been liberalized? How has the family been affected by this? Have new programs that affect the family (such as birth control programs) been started by the government?

THE PASSIVE VOICE OF
THE SIMPLE PAST PERFECT TENSE

Review the uses of the past perfect tense in Chapter 18. Do not try to use the passive voice with the past perfect continuous tense. Use the active voice or the simple past perfect passive.

Statements: subject + **had (not)** + **been** + past participle

John's major had been decided for him before he started college.

Questions: (question word) + **had** + subject + **been** + past participle?

Had John's major been decided for him?

Examples

The United States has a system of free public education. Thomas Jefferson was president from 1801 to 1809. He was one of the first Americans who believed in free public education, and he fought long and hard for this system. Many other people took up the fight after he died. However, public education did not develop quickly. Between 1800 and 1870, only about fifty percent of school-age children attended school. People who believed in the importance of education for all continued to push for public education, and by 1918 compulsory school attendance laws **had been passed** in all states. Before 1918, the decision to send children to school or keep them at home **had been left** to the parents.

Other changes in education occurred during the nineteenth century. New subjects such as history, English grammar, and music were added. What subjects **had** children **been taught** before? In most cases, they had been taught only reading, writing, and arithmetic.

Special schools for teachers were opened beginning in 1820. How much education **had** teachers **been required** to have before this time? Most had been required to have only an elementary-school education.

■ ACTIVITY 21E

Fill in each blank, using the passive voice of the past perfect tense. Use the verb in parentheses.

Horace Mann is one of the most famous educators in American history.

He brought about many changes in the field of education. He became the

secretary of the new Massachusetts State Board of Education in 1837, a

time when the public-school system was in very bad condition. Mann

fought long and hard to change it. By the end of his twelve-year period

of service, public interest in the improvement of public education

had been awakened. School problems _____ to
(awaken)   (bring)

light and _____. A movement for better teaching and
          (discuss)

better pay for teachers _____, and training schools
                        (start)

for teachers _____. The curricula of the schools
             (establish)

_____ to include history and geography.
(expand)

In Horace Mann's time, most colleges for men and women were

separate. Mann was a strong believer in coeducation.[12] In 1853, he became

the first president of Antioch College, one of the first coeducational

schools. By the end of Mann's term in office, the practicality of

coeducation _____ and the academic standards of
            (demonstrate)

the college _____.
            (raise)

THE PASSIVE VOICE
OF THE CONTINUOUS TENSES

The only tenses in which we use the continuous passive are the present
continuous and the past continuous. See Chapters 1 and 9 for the uses of these
tenses.

---

[12]*Coeducation* means "men and women attending the same school."

Statements: subject + $\left\{\begin{array}{l}\textbf{am}\\\textbf{is}\\\textbf{are}\\\textbf{was}\\\textbf{were}\end{array}\right\}$ **(not)** + **being** + past participle

Efforts are being made to improve teachers' salaries.

Questions: (question + word) $\left\{\begin{array}{l}\textbf{am}\\\textbf{is}\\\textbf{are}\\\textbf{was}\\\textbf{were}\end{array}\right\}$ + subject + **being** + past participle?

Are teachers being paid enough?

Examples

Present Continuous

Many changes are happening in U.S. education today. Developments in technology **are being used** in the classroom. Children **are being taught** mathematics with calculators. Television **is being used** to teach basic reading and mathematics.

Are computers **being experimented** with in the classroom?
  Yes, they are.

What subjects **are** they **being used to teach?**
  In many schools where they teach English to speakers of other languages, computers **are being used** to help teach English. In many elementary schools, children **are being taught** how to read and write on computers.

Past Continuous

Not all of these new methods are successful. A number of years ago, universities experimented with television in college lectures. Professors recorded their lectures on videotapes, which were later played in class. The professors were not present in the classroom. This new method **was being used** when studies came out showing that students were not learning. One professor received an unpleasant surprise when he entered his classroom. His lecture **was being shown** on the TV, but no students were in the room.

■ ACTIVITY 21F

❑ Fill in the blanks, using the passive voice of the present continuous tense. Use the verbs in parentheses. We can use the simple present passive in several sentences here, but the present continuous passive emphasizes that these changes are happening nowadays.

Here is one of the changes that is happening in education today. In the traditional classroom, the teacher is in complete control. The teacher decides when the class will study which subject, and all students must work on the same subject at the same time. In some schools, a new method called "the open classroom" *is being used* these days. More and
(use)
more students _____ to choose for themselves which
(permit)
subject they want to work on and for how long. Students can work by themselves or in groups. Children are usually enthusiastic about this new method, but some parents are beginning to have doubts. According to these concerned parents, the children _____ too much freedom
(give)
nowadays, not enough time _____ on real work, and the
(spend)
children _____ the subjects that are most important. In
(negative, teach)
some schools that have experimented with the open classroom in the past, the traditional methods of teaching _____.
(reinstate)

❑ Prepare a brief talk on the subject of modern education. What new methods and theories are being used in the field of education in your country today? What about public schools and private schools? Are taxes being increased to build more public schools?

❑ JACK is talking to ARNOLD on the phone.

JACK: I'm going crazy. I'm trying to type my job resume and send out

applications for jobs, and my apartment is a mess right now. Can

I spend the next day or two at your place?

ARNOLD: Sure, but what's happening in your apartment?

JACK: It's <u>*being painted*</u>. All my furniture is in the middle
               (paint)

of the room. And that's not all. The landlord decided to

make several other repairs at the same time. A new shower

_____, and a new floor _____
      (install)   (put)

down in the kitchen.

ARNOLD: _____ anything _____ about that
                                (do)

prehistoric stove you have?

JACK: Yes, it _____ too.
                 (replace)

ARNOLD: I suppose that means that your rent _____ too.
                                        (raise)

JACK: Yeah. It's going up fifty dollars a month.

THE PASSIVE VOICE OF MODALS

Modal Passives—Present and Future

STATEMENTS

subject +
can
should
may
might
could   **(not)** + **be** + past participle
have/has to*
must (necessity)
would rather
had better

College teachers should be paid more.

*In American English, the negative form is { **don't** / **doesn't** } **have to.**

QUESTIONS

(Question word) + $\left\{\begin{array}{l}\textbf{can}\\\textbf{should}\\\textbf{could}\end{array}\right\}$ + subject + **be** + past participle?

Should teachers be paid more?

or

(Question word) + $\left\{\begin{array}{l}\textbf{do}\\\textbf{does}\end{array}\right\}$ + subject + **have to** + **be** + past participle?

Do children have to be given shots before they start public school?

or

(Question word) + **would** + subject + **rather** + **be** + past participle?

Would you rather be sent to a private school or a public school?

Examples

Integration of black and white students in schools is still a major issue in American education today. American law says that all children **must be given** an equal opportunity to get a good education. Before 1954, in many states black children weren't permitted to attend white schools. In 1954, the Supreme Court decided that segregated schools were unconstitutional. The law now says that black children **can't be segregated** in separate schools. It has been difficult to desegregate schools in some areas because black people and white people frequently live in different neighborhoods. Since children usually go to the school closest to their homes, this creates a different form of segregation.

How **can** this problem **be solved?** In some communities, the law says that some children from white neighborhoods **have to be taken** by bus to schools in black neighborhoods, and some black children **must be bused** to schools in white neighborhoods. Many parents feel that busing **shouldn't be used** as a solution to the problem. Where **should** children **be sent** to school in these parents' opinion? They believe that their children **should be sent** to school in their own neighborhood.

■ ACTIVITY 21G

☐ Write questions using the passive voice of the verb in parentheses. If you have an opinion, answer them. Try to use the passive form of a modal auxiliary in your answer.

1. Some people believe that schools have to be integrated for children to receive an equal education. What's your opinion?

   Do *schools have to be integrated* for children to
   (integrate)
   receive an equal education?

   Answer: _____

2. Some schools have only white children or only black children because the neighborhood is all white or all black. Many people believe the problem should be solved by busing children. What's your opinion?

   How _____?
   (solve)
   Answer: _____

3. Many parents feel busing should not be used as a solution. What do you think?

   Should _____?
   (used)
   Answer: _____

☐ Fill in the blanks with the passive voice.

The United States has always been a country of immigrants. In the

big cities, there are thousands of children in the public schools who speak

little or no English. Many teachers and parents feel that these students

cannot *be put* in the same class with native speakers for many
(put)
reasons. They might _____ by the other students. They might
(ridicule)
_____ by their inability to do the schoolwork and develop a bad
(discourage)
attitude toward school. Also, the other students might _____ back
(hold)
by students who can't speak English. Many parents and teachers believe

that these children shouldn't _____ in regular classes, but they
(place)

don't think they should _____ in classes for slow learners either.
(place)

Massachusetts was the first state to pass a bilingual education law to try to
solve this problem. The law says that in schools that have a large number
of students who speak the same language but who can't speak English,
these students must _____ all their subjects in their own native
(teach)

language. They also have to _____ classes in English as a second
(give)

language so that after they learn enough English, they can _____
(place)

in regular classes. Other states have since passed such laws.

What's your opinion about this law? What do you think should be done
when a school has a large number of students who can't speak the language
of that country?

Modal Passives—Past

MODAL PERFECTS

subject + { may might could must should would rather }	+ (not) have + been +	past participle

More children should have been given an opportunity for education in the nineteenth century.

Past Tense of *Can*

subject + **could (not)** + **be** + past participle

Many children couldn't be sent to school because they lived on isolated farms far from any school.

Past Tense of *Have to*

subject + { **had to** / **didn't have to** } + **be** + past participle

Several colleges had to be closed in the 1970 s because they ran out of money.

Examples

YOLANDA: There really aren't many women doctors, are there?

MOLLY: No, I've been reading about that. And do you know that there weren't any women doctors in the United States until 1847? Elizabeth Blackwell was the first woman doctor. She was turned down by twenty-eight medical schools before she was finally admitted.

YOLANDA: People **must have been shocked** by the idea of a woman doctor in those days.

MOLLY: They were. Her friends and relatives thought she was crazy when she told them that she wanted to be a doctor, but she **couldn't be persuaded** to change her mind. Also, her male classmates thought she **should not have been admitted** to the medical college. They treated her coldly at first, but finally she **had to be accepted** as an equal because she had the highest marks in the school.

■ ACTIVITY 21H

Fill in each blank, using the past form of the modal auxiliary and verb below the blank in the passive voice. The dialog continues.

YOLANDA: Any other woman _*might have been discouraged*_
(might/discourage)

by so much opposition.

MOLLY: Well, her father gave his daughters the same education that he

gave his sons. Everyone thought he was making a mistake.

When Elizabeth announced her decision to become a doctor,

they said, "She _____ all that geometry,
(negative, **should, teach**)

Latin, and history. She _____ only how to sew,
(**should, teach**)

cook, and sign her name. That's all a woman needs to know."

Also, she had a lot of responsibility when she was young.

Her father died when she was just eighteen. Something

_____ to support the family, so Elizabeth
(**have to, do**)

and her sisters started a school in their home.

YOLANDA: Where did she get the idea to become a doctor?

MOLLY: She had a friend who was dying of cancer. While Elizabeth

was nursing her, the friend said that Elizabeth should become

a doctor. At first Elizabeth thought that the suggestion

was ridiculous, because in those days only men

_____ to medical school, but she
(**can, admit**)

_____ by the suggestion, because she
(**must, influence**)

later made the decision to study medicine.

YOLANDA: What did she do after she graduated from medical college?

MOLLY: She went to Paris to study surgery, but this dream

_____ because she caught an eye infection
(negative, can, fulfill)

from a sick patient and lost the sight of one eye.

YOLANDA: She _____ by that.
(must, discourage)

MOLLY: I suppose so, but when she went back to New York, she started

a hospital for nurses in the United States and later a medical

school for women. When she died in 1910, there were 8,000

women doctors.

■ ACTIVITY 21I

☐ Fill in each blank with the correct tense of the verb below the blank.
Most of the verbs are in the passive voice, but some are in active voice.
When you see *modal + verb*, choose the correct modal auxiliary verb,
tense, and voice.

In the United States today, there are many difficult problems in the field of
education. However, people from all over the world come here to study because
the United States has one of the best educational systems in the world.
American education is particularly excellent in the field of science. In 1979,
Americans won many of the Nobel prizes for science. There were three prizes in
physics; Americans won two of them. There were two prizes for medicine,
chemistry, and economics; Americans won one in each category.

In this dialog, JACK and ARNOLD are discussing the reasons for this.

ARNOLD: Hey, Jack. Why wasn't your name on the list of Nobel Prize

winners in the newspaper today?

JACK: Don't worry. My turn will come. Do you know that since 1946

more than half the science prizes *have been won* by
(win)

Americans?

ARNOLD: That's fantastic! I guess the sciences _____
(teach)

really well in this country. Also, American scientists

_____ more support from the government than
(give)

scientists in other countries.

JACK: That's true. I was reading an article about that in a magazine. The government and the scientific community _____ (become) partners during World War II, and that special partnership _____ and _____ by the government (continue) (encourage) since then. Millions of dollars _____ to science (give) since the war. Also, the situation in America is different from that in many other countries because American scientists _____ a great deal of freedom in their research. (always, give)

ARNOLD: Many scientists from other countries _____ to (modal + **attract**) this country by this freedom.

JACK: Yes. Arno Penzias _____ here from Nazi Germany. He (come) _____ the Nobel prize for physics. And Einstein came (win) here too, but he had won his Nobel prize before that. I think the government _____ all scientists freedom, (modal + **give**) or they will never discover anything really revolutionary. In some countries, scientific research _____ by a central (direct) agency. Scientists who _____ to the agency (belong) _____, and promotions _____ on (negative, modal + **fire**) (base) seniority instead of achievement.

ARNOLD: That's not good for research. If you want good scientists, promotions _____ on the quality of their research. (modal + **base**)

JACK: What do you think about the future? Do you think the United States will continue to do so well in science?

ARNOLD: Well, the situation might change, because a lot of people in this country think less money _____ on science and (modal + **spend**)

more money _____ on helping the poor. If the
                    (modal + **spend**)

government _____ back on money for scientific research,
            (**cut**)

who knows what will happen?

❏ Arnold says that he guesses that the sciences are taught really well in the United States. What is your impression? Do you think U.S. high-school students are taught science and mathematics better than students in your country, or is it the other way around? Do you know anything about test scores that compare the scores of U.S. high-school students in math and science with the scores of their peers in some other countries?

EXPRESSING YOUR IDEAS

1. Are colleges and universities having financial problems in your country now? Why or why not? What is the government doing about the problem? Do the colleges get money from the government, from private sources, or from both?

2. If you have a bachelor's degree (four years of college or university) in your country, does it guarantee that you will find a job? If you have a master's degree (usually about two more years after the bachelor's degree), are your chances better? Are they better with a Ph.D.?

3. Which fields are the best to study if you want to be sure of finding a job? Do many professional people with master's degrees and Ph.D.s have trouble finding jobs in your country? Do many professionals leave your country to find better jobs in other countries?

4. Is teaching a respected profession in your country? Is it difficult for teachers to find jobs? Are teachers well paid? Would you like to be a teacher? Why or why not? In your country, how much education do you need to become an elementary-school teacher? A high-school teacher? A university professor?

5. Are boys and girls educated in the same way in your country? Are schools coeducational? Do girls have the same opportunity as boys to go to college or to professional and technical schools?

6. Many people choose not to go to college. Are there good technical or vocational schools in your country?

7. How do you feel about your education? Are you satisfied with your educational experiences so far?

8. Describe the different levels of education in your country. At what age does one start school? After how many years does one move on to the next stage of education, the next, and the next? Compare this with the

American system of preschool (nursery school), kindergarten, elementary school, high school, college (undergraduate), and graduate school (M.A., Ph.D.).

9. How do you feel about the TOEFL test (Test of English as a Foreign Language) that students from other countries have to take if they want to study at a college in the United States? Have you taken it yet? Are you planning to take it? Do you think it's an accurate and fair way to judge someone's English ability? Can you suggest a better way for a school to decide whether a student's level of English is good enough to permit him or her to study college courses in the United States? How did you prepare (or how are you preparing) for the TOEFL test?

Automobile welding at Marysville, Ohio, the first Honda plant in the United States.

Dialog

(ARNOLD is visiting his father, MR. CALHOUN. They are sitting together watching the evening news. MR. CALHOUN is upset about the economic problems in the United States. One of the problems is the budget deficit. A budget is a plan for spending money—the government decides how much money to spend on military defense, how much on education, how much on health care, and so on. When the government spends more money than it can collect in taxes or from other sources, there is a budget deficit. The United States has had a budget deficit for many years. Another problem of the U.S. economy is the trade deficit. This means that the United States imports more products than it exports to other countries.)

MR. CALHOUN: Well, I've had enough of the news tonight. I'm going to turn it off. I just get depressed when I watch the news.

ARNOLD: Yeah, you don't see too much on the news to make you feel good. Problems, problems, and more problems! Homeless people, drugs . . . I **wish** the news **were** a little more cheerful.

MR. CALHOUN: What's this country coming to?[1] America is going down the drain.[2] **If** those politicians in Washington **had** some brains, maybe this country **wouldn't be** in such a big mess.

ARNOLD: Aw, come on, Dad. It's not that bad. I **wish** you **would calm** down. You know what the doctor said about your high blood pressure.

MR. CALHOUN: Not that bad! This country is turning into a third-rate power.[3] What about the balance of trade? **Would** all those foreign countries **be buying** up our real estate **if** we **didn't have** such a big trade deficit? If we don't watch out, those other countries are going to own the United States. I hope we wake up before it's too late.

ARNOLD: Hey, don't forget that this country needs foreign investments. We benefit from the situation too. And what about all the property that the United States owns in other countries?

MR. CALHOUN: And speaking of deficits, what about the budget deficit? **If** these leaders of ours **weren't** so afraid of losing votes, they

[1]*What's this country coming to?* means "What's happening to this country?" This question implies that the speaker thinks something bad is happening to this country.
[2]*Going down the drain* means "falling apart."
[3]*A third rate power* means "a country that is in third position in terms of power in the world."

might stop spending so much. I **wish** I **could sit** down and **work** on that budget. I'd balance it in no time.[4]

ARNOLD: I'm sure you would, Dad. But, I'll tell you, I sure **wouldn't want** the president's job.[5] It must be the toughest job in the world. I **wouldn't take** it even **if** they **offered** me $1 million.

Listening Comprehension Questions

1. Why does Arnold's father want to turn off the news before it's over?
2. What does Arnold wish about the news?
3. What does Arnold's father think of the politicians in Washington, D.C.?
4. Arnold's father is getting upset during this discussion. Why does Arnold wish he would calm down?
5. In Arnold's father's opinion, why are foreign countries buying up U.S. real estate?
6. Why does he say, "I hope we wake up before it's too late"? What is his prediction?
7. What does Arnold think about foreign investment in the United States? Does he agree with his father?
8. What does his father think would happen if U.S. leaders weren't so afraid of losing votes?
9. If he had a chance to work on the budget, what would Arnold's father do?
10. Would Arnold like to be president of the United States?

WISH CLAUSES—PRESENT

Complete Statements

When we talk about something that we want but that we don't think is possible to have, we often use a *wish* clause followed by another clause.

---

subject + **wish** + **(that)** + subject + past tense

I wish that the news were more cheerful.

---

[4] and [5]Notice that in these sentences it is not necessary to have an *if* clause. We understand that Arnold's father means, "If I had the chance, I'd balance it in no time." We understand that Arnold means, "I sure wouldn't want the president's job, even if someone offered it to me."

Note:

1. It's correct but not necessary to use *that*.

2. With the verb *be*, the correct form is *were* with both singular and plural subjects.

> ### *Examples*
>
> People in the United States *wish* that the budget deficit **weren't** so big.
>
> They *wish* economists **knew** how to solve all their economic problems.
>
> They *wish* they **didn't have** to pay so much for the basic necessities.

Short Responses

We often ask questions in the present tense that can be answered with a *wish* clause. Notice that the short answer form is *did(n't)*, *were(n't)*, or *could(n't)* after the *wish* clause.

> ### *Examples*
>
> Do economists have any real solutions to the deficit problem?
>   No, they don't, but **Americans wish they did.**
>
> Can young Americans afford new houses?
>   Many say they can't, but **they wish they could.**
>
> Is there an easy way for the average person to beat the high cost of living?
>   There isn't really, but **we all wish there were.**

X ■ **ACTIVITY 22A**

   ❑ Using *wish* clauses, make statements about the following situations.

1. Nobody likes to pay taxes, but nothing is sure in life except death and taxes.

   We all wish _____*there weren't any*_____ taxes.

2. One reason that the budget deficit is so high in the United States is that this country spends billions of dollars on military defense. There's not much peace in our world today.

   We all wish _____there were more_____ peace in our world.

3. The United States and the Soviet Union have had several summit meetings in recent years to try to stop the nuclear arms race, but there is no perfect solution to the problem.

Many people wish _____*there weren't any*_____ nuclear arms.

4. Some Americans think that the United States spends too much money on defending other countries and that many countries don't contribute enough money for their own defense.

These Americans wish some countries _____*contributed*_____ more for their own defense.

5. Another big part of the budget in the United States goes to special programs to help poor people. There doesn't seem to be an easy cure for poverty.

Americans wish _____*there were*_____ an easy cure for poverty.

6. There's a lot of disagreement in the United States about the amount of money this country spends on welfare programs for the poor. Some Americans believe that the government gives too much help and makes people lazy.

These Americans wish the government _____*didn't spend*_____ so much on welfare programs. Others feel that the government doesn't give enough help to poor people.

They wish the government _____*spent*_____ more on welfare programs.

☒ Respond to each of these questions with a short answer, followed by a *wish* clause.

1. Molly is a student now, so she's on a very tight budget. Can she afford a great apartment?

   _____*No, she can't, but she wishes she could.*_____

2. Molly has some problems with her new apartment.
   Does Molly have a large enough kitchen?

   No, she _____*doesn't*_____, but she _____*wishes she did*_____

3. She enjoys entertaining her friends.
   Can she give large dinner parties?

   _____*No, she can't, but she wishes she would*_____

4. Molly's apartment is very dark.
   Is there enough light to grow plants?

   No, there isn't but she wishes there were

5. Her neighbor is a musician.
   Does he practice late at night?

   No he doesn't but she wish he did.

6. Is the superintendent ever in the building when Molly needs him?

   No, he _____, but Molly _____

   ☐ Write five sentences about things that are wrong with your home or apartment. After each sentence, write what you wish.

1. *My apartment doesn't have a view.*
   I wish it did.

2. _____

   _____

3. _____

   _____

4. _____

   _____

5. _____

   _____

6. _____

   _____

PRESENT UNREAL CONDITIONALS— *IF* CLAUSES

Statements

We use an unreal conditional pattern when we want to talk about situations that are contrary to existing facts or reality.

> If + subject + past tense . . . , subject + $\begin{Bmatrix} \textbf{would} \\ \textbf{could} \\ \textbf{might} \end{Bmatrix}$ + base form
>
> *If Arnold's father were president, he would balance the budget.*

Americans worry a great deal about the budget deficit. **If we had a balanced budget, the economy would be a lot stronger.** But nobody wants to make sacrifices. For example, parents of school-age children don't want the government to make cuts in the funds for education. Many Americans don't want any cuts in military spending. **We could solve the budget deficit if everybody were willing to make some sacrifices.**

The easiest way to solve the problem is by raising taxes. Of course, no one wants to pay higher taxes. Some voters refuse to vote for a politician who is in favor of raising taxes. **If politicians weren't afraid of losing votes, they might not be so afraid to raise taxes** to help solve the budget deficit.

Note:

1. Notice that the *if* clause can come at the beginning or end of the sentence. When the sentence begins with an *if* clause, a comma separates it from the main clause.

2. We often use a contraction with *would* in spoken English. The contraction is formed with *'d* (*I'd, you'd, she'd, he'd, they'd*).

Questions and Short Answers

1. What **would** Arnold's father **do** if he were president?
   He**'d solve** the budget deficit.

2. **Would** he **raise** taxes if he were president?
   He probably **wouldn't.** He**'d cut** government spending instead.

Continuous Form

We often use the continuous form in the *if* clause or in the main clause.

Examples

The United States economy is not expanding as fast as the economies of other countries, such as Taiwan and Korea. If the U.S. economy **were expanding** more rapidly, Americans **wouldn't be worrying** so much about the position of the United States in the world today.

■ ACTIVITY 22B

Fill in the blanks with the correct form of the <u>unreal</u> conditional, using the verb in parentheses.

1. Some people say that this country has too many people who depend on government welfare payments. Some say that the reason for this is that the system of public education doesn't prepare people well enough

   for jobs. If the public schools ___*did*___ a better job of preparing
   (do)

   people for jobs, this country ___*wouldn't have*___ so many
   (negative, **have**)

   people on welfare.

2. Because the U.S. government doesn't take in enough money in taxes to meet all the expenses in the budget, it has to borrow money. When you borrow money, you have to pay interest on the loan. If the U.S.

   government ___didn't have to___ pay such a large amount
   (negative, **have to**)

   of interest, it ___would have___ more money to spend on
   (have)

   education.

3. Some people think the government should raise taxes on tobacco and alcohol even higher than they are now. They say smoking and drinking cause illness and add to the health care costs in this nation. If there

   ___were___ a higher tax on cigarettes and liquor, this money
   (be)

   ___would help___ pay the high cost of health care.
   (help)

4. When people speak of economic problems in this country, they generally speak of the budget deficit and the trade deficit. The economists don't all agree, but some say that the budget deficit and the trade deficit are connected. They say that the United States

_____wouldn't have to_____ a trade deficit if it _____didn't + have_____
   (negative, **have**)   (negative, **have**)

such a big budget deficit.

5. Other countries' economies are growing rapidly because the United States imports so many of their products. If the United States

_____didn't import_____ so much, the economies of these other
   (negative, **import**)

countries ___could be___ hurt.
         (**be**)

6. Over the years, the United States has lent large sums of money to

Third World countries. These countries _____wouldn't earn_____
                                          (negative, **earn**)

dollars to pay off the debt if the United States _____didn't import_____
                                                   (negative, **import**)

their products. Because of this, it is difficult for the United States to cut back on imports to help solve the trade deficit.

7. The United States would like other countries with strong economies, such as Japan and West Germany, to import more from Third World

countries. If they _____imported_____ more, the United States
                     (**import**)

_____would be able to cut_____ back its imports without hurting the
   (**be able, cut**)

economies of developing countries.

8. In 1988, foreign investments in U.S. property and businesses totaled $250 billion. (The United States had a total of $298 billion in overseas investments that year.) The Japanese own almost all of Waikiki Beach in Hawaii and over one-quarter of the best buildings in downtown Los Angeles. In 1988, Great Britain was in first place, with investments in the United States worth $70 billion. Some Americans worry that people from foreign countries are buying too much of the most valuable real estate and property in the United States. The reason foreign investors are able to do this is that their countries have excess U.S. dollars from selling exports to the United States. If the United States

_____didn't have_____ a trade deficit, foreign investors
   (negative, **have**)

_____wouldn't be able to buy_____ so much U.S. property.
   (negative, **be able, buy**)

9. People like Arnold's father, who worry about the number of foreign investments in U.S. property, say that the United States is like a rich aristocratic family with a lot of land. This family has a very expensive life-style that it can't afford, but it doesn't want to tighten its belt and live with less luxury. Each year the family sells off a piece of land so that it can go on living in luxury. Arnold's father thinks that if the

United States _____*were*_____ more careful with its money and
            (be)

_____*lived*_____ less luxuriously, it _____*would be*_____
   (live)   **(negative, be)**

necessary to sell so much of its valuable real estate.

10. There are other Americans who see foreign investment in U.S. property and business as an important benefit. In 1988, foreign investors in U.S. companies signed paychecks for 3 million Americans. Many

Americans _____*were*_____ unemployed if this country
              (be)

_____*would be able to depend*_____ on foreign investment.
   (negative, be able to depend)

11. Also, countries like Japan share their valuable business know-how—such as management skills, worker training techniques, and technology—when they invest in U.S. businesses. The United States

_____*weren't benefit*_____ from this knowledge if it
   (negative, benefit)

_____*wouldn't allow*_____ foreign investment.
   (negative, allow)

12. Another benefit of foreign investment is competition. Perhaps

U.S. companies _____*would become*_____ a little lazy and
              (become)

_____*wouldn't work*_____ so hard to maintain their position
   (negative, work)

in the world if they _____*weren't have*_____ this competition
                      (negative, have)

from foreign investors.

◼ ACTIVITY 22C

☐ In the following sentences, the *if* clause of an unreal conditional sentence is given. Finish each sentence by writing your own main clause.

1. If a new car weren't so expensive, *I'd buy one right away.*

2. If I had $1 million to invest, *I would buy a house*

_____

3. *I would to sell synthetic gasoline* _____

if we could find a way to produce synthetic gasoline.

4. *I would be a president* _____

if I could find a cure for inflation.

5. If I could live any place in the world, *I would have lot of money*

_____

❑ In the following sentences, the main clause of an unreal conditional sentence is given. Finish each sentence by writing your own *if* clause.

1. Molly would buy an apartment in the city instead of renting if *she could afford to.*

2. My country's economy would be in (good/bad) shape if *the economic minister would change some things*

3. If *I won a lottery* _____,

I'd be a millionaire.

4. If *I could stopp the production of bombs*,

there would be no war.

5. I would be much happier if *I could stay in my country*

❏ ACTIVITY 22D

❑ Ask a classmate questions using the words or phrases in parentheses. Your classmate will answer each question and explain his or her answer.

1. (a famous actress or actor) (what kind of movies) *If you were a famous actress or actor, what kind of movies would you act in?*

2. (a mad scientist) (what kind of crazy inventions) *If you were a mad scientist, what kind of crazy invention would you like to do?*

3. (marry anyone in the world) (who/whom) *If you could marry with anyone in the word with whom would you like to marry?*

4. (meet a famous person in the world) (who/whom) *If you could meet a famous person in the word, who would you like to be?*

5. (travel back in time) (which historic period) *If I could travel back in time, which historic period would you like to live?*

☐ Ask questions that can be answered with yes or no.

1. (marry someone) (rich but very boring) *Would you marry someone if he or she were rich but very boring?*

2. (skydive) (someone/you, $10,000) *Would you skydive if someone gave you $10,000* ?

3. (make a bargain with the devil) (eternal life) *Would you make a bargain with the devil if he promised you eternal life* ?

4. (tell the teacher) (a friend, cheat) *Would you tell the teacher if a friend were cheat you* ?

5. (have a beautiful sailboat) (sail around the world alone) *Would you sail around the word alone if you would had a beautiful sailboat* ?

6. (find $1,000 on the street with no wallet and name and address)

   (police) *Would you call the police if you found $1,000 on the street with no wallet and name and address* ?

7. (find $1,000 on the street in a wallet with a name and address)

   (the owner) *Would you return the owner the money if you found* ?

8. (change your appearance)   (much more beautiful or handsome than you are now) *Would you change your appearance, if you were much more beautiful or handsome than you're now*?

9. (a pill to make you a genius)   (take) *Would you take a pill to make you a genius if you could*?

10. (a crystal ball to tell you the exact date of your death)   (want to know)
Would you have a crystal ball to tell you the exact date of your date if you wanted to know?

11. Ask a male student this question.
(marry a woman)   (much smarter than you) *Would you like to marry a woman if she were more smarter than you -*?

12. Ask a female student this question.
(marry a man)   (less intelligent than you) *Would you like to marry a man if he were less intelligent than you*?

WISH CLAUSES—FUTURE TENSE

When we know that something is impossible or unlikely to happen in the future, we use this pattern.

subject + **wish** + **(that)** + subject + **would** + base form

Arnold wishes that his father would calm down.

Examples

The average price of a car has risen dramatically in recent years. Young married couples say it is more difficult for them to buy a car than it was for their parents. They **wish** the price of a car **would drop** dramatically, but they know that prices will probably continue to rise.

We often use *would* after a *wish* clause when we don't like someone's behavior. This pattern often has a critical tone to it. We use this pattern to express annoyance.

Example

MOLLY and YOLANDA are sitting in a movie theater. The couple in front of them is talking and laughing very loudly.

YOLANDA: Please, I'm trying to watch the movie. I wish you **would stop** talking.

■ ACTIVITY 22E

❑ Finish the following sentences. Tell what someone wishes about the future.

1. It's unlikely that Yolanda's boss will be able to give her a big raise next year.

   Yolanda wishes *he would give everyone a raise.*

2. Yolanda loves flowers, but Arnold never thinks of buying them for her. Next week is Yolanda's birthday.

   Yolanda wishes _____,
   but she knows he probably won't remember.

3. Jack and Arnold took their car to a mechanic. He can't have the car ready before next week. They want to go to the country this weekend.

   They wish _____

4. Arnold, Yolanda, Jack, and Molly want to take a trip around the United States this summer. The price of gas is very high, and it probably won't go down.

   They wish _____

5. Construction workers are working on a building next to where Jack lives. Jack can't sleep because of the noise.

   Jack wishes _____

   ❑ In the following situations, someone is irritated at another person's behavior. Write sentences with *wish,* expressing the first person's irritation.

1. A student is scraping his fingernail on the chalkboard. Another student says, "I wish *you wouldn't do that.* It hurts my ears."

2. Yolanda's mother is concerned because her husband isn't spending much time with the children nowadays. She says, "I wish _____

   _____."

3. Someone is smoking a cigar at the table next to Molly's in a restaurant. The smoke from his cigar is blowing over to her table. Molly says, "I wish _____."

4. A mother is talking to her child, who never puts his clothes away. The mother says, "I wish _____."

5. A boss is irritated because one of his employees is always thirty minutes late to work. The boss says, "I wish _____."

■ ACTIVITY 22F

Tell what these people wish about present and future situations in the world today.

   1. the pope
   2. the president of the United States
   3. the military leaders in my country
   4. the leaders of developing nations
   5. astronauts
   6. psychiatrists
   7. labor leaders

8. teachers

9. parents

10. children

CONTRAST OF *HOPE* AND *WISH* AND OF REAL AND UNREAL CONDITIONALS

Contrast of *Hope* and *Wish*

When we use *hope* followed by a clause, we mean that something is possible in the future. We can see either the future tense or the simple present tense in the second clause. When we use *wish* followed by a clause, we mean that something is impossible or unlikely in the present or future.

Example

Yolanda's sister, Sandra, and her fiancé will probably get married in a year or so. They **hope** that they (**have/will have**) enough money to buy a house. They are saving money to buy one now, but the interest rate on their savings account isn't very high. In a period of inflation, interest rates go up some, but they usually don't keep up with inflation. Sandra and Jeff **wish** the interest rate on their savings **would go** up faster. They also **wish** someone **would give** them $1 million.

 ## Contrast of Real and Unreal Conditionals

When we think that something is possible or likely to happen, we use the real conditional. (See Chapter 7.) However, when we think that something is impossible or unlikely, we use the unreal conditional.

REAL CONDITIONAL

> **If** + subject + simple present . . . , subject + **will** + base form
>
> *If the U.S. government doesn't do something about the huge trade deficit, the U.S. economy will be in trouble.*

UNREAL CONDITIONAL

> If + subject + past tense . . . , subject + { **could** / **would** / **might** } + base form
>
> *If Arnold's father were president, he'd balance the budget.*

Examples

There are no easy answers to the problems of the budget deficit and the trade deficit. These problems will probably continue for a good number of years. **If they continue, perhaps the position of the United States in the world economy will weaken, and countries such as Japan and Korea will probably play a very important role. If economists found a sure cure for the budget and trade deficit tomorrow, we'd all be very surprised.**

■ ACTIVITY 22G

Complete the following sentences with the correct forms of the present real conditional or the present unreal conditional

1. It's very difficult for a person to get into engineering school, so Molly

   has applied to ten schools for next September. She hopes that at least

   one of the schools _*will accept*_ her. Engineering school is also
         (accept)

   very expensive. If she ____*goes*____ to school in the fall, she
           (go)

   *will probably have to* take out a student loan. It takes years
    (probably, have to)

   of hard work and study to become an engineer. If engineering school

   ____*weren't*____ so difficult, we ____*wouldn't have*____ too
       (negative, be)   **(have)**

   many engineers.

2. Yolanda's parents want to buy a house in New Jersey, but they can't afford to pay the interest on a bank loan because interest rates are so high. They wish interest rates ___weren't___ so high. If they
   (negative, be)
   ___could afford___ to buy a new home, they ___would buy___ one near
   (can, afford)   **(buy)**
   the ocean because they love the water.

3. Molly, Jack, Yolanda, and Arnold are planning to go out for dinner, but there's a problem. They are trying to decide whether to go to a Chinese restaurant or a Mexican restaurant. If they ___go___ to a
   (go)
   Chinese restaurant, Jack ___will not be___ very happy because he ate
   (negative, be)
   Chinese food last night. However, if they ___choose___ a Mexican
   (choose)
   restaurant, Arnold ___will no go___ because he doesn't like spicy food.
   (negative, **go**)
   One thing is certain. They aren't going to a French restaurant. If they
   ___went___ to a fancy French restaurant, they ___couldn't have___
   (go)   _(negative, **have**)_
   any money left for the rest of the month.

4. Molly is going to run in another marathon next week. She hopes it
   ___woun't be___ very hot. If it ___is___ hot, she
   (negative, be)   **(be)**
   ___will have___ a much harder time finishing the last mile.
   (have)
   She wants to run faster than she did in the last marathon. If the
   temperature ___is___ above 90°F, she knows she
   (be)
   ___can not make___ very good time.
   (negative, **can, make**)

5.   JACK: Hey, Arnold. Can you lend me about fifty dollars until the end of the week? I have to pay a lab fee for my astronomy course.

ARNOLD: Gee, I wish I ___could___ . I only have twenty-five dollars
          (can)

myself. You know that I ___could lend___ you the money if I
          (lend)

___had___ it. If I ___were___ you, I
  (have)   **(be)**

___asked___ the university to wait one more week.
  (ask)

JACK: Well, I could. I don't know. Maybe I'll ask my parents to lend me

the money. If I ___call___ them, I'm sure they
        (call)

___will ask___ to come home for a visit, and they
  (ask)

___will probably asked___ about Molly. My mother liked Molly when she
  (probably, ask)

visited her. If we ___start___ talking about Molly, my
        (start)

parents ___will suggest___ that I get married soon and settle
      (suggest)

down. I hope I ___can make___ the conversation short.
       (can, make)

ARNOLD: I wish my father ___would ask___ me about Yolanda when I
         (ask)

speak to him. All we ever talk about is my "future career plans."

JACK: Yeah, parents are strange! Why can't they let us make our own

decisions? If I ___were___ a parent, I ___wouldn't try___
      (be)   **(negative, try)**

to control my children's lives so much.

■ ACTIVITY 22H

☐ Arnold's father, a very conservative businessman, is having an argument about the American economy with a radical young lawyer. With a classmate, act out the dialog that takes place between Arnold's father and the radical young lawyer.

☐ Name some of the economic problems in your country. Then discuss how life would be different if these problems didn't exist. How would you change things if you were the leader of your country? What are some things that you wish were true now in your country or that you wish would happen in the future?

☐ Write a letter to the mayor of the city or town you are now living in (in your own country or in the United States) and tell how and why you would change things if you were the mayor.

❑ Suppose you had the money and opportunity right now to build your "dream" house. What would this house be like if money were of no importance? Imagine its location. How many people could live in the house? Who would they be?

❑ If you were a citizen of the United States, how do you think you would feel about foreign investments in U.S. property and companies? Does the United States have a lot of investments in your country? Do some people feel angry or resentful about this or do they appreciate it?

EXPRESSING YOUR IDEAS

1. Is inflation a serious problem in your country? If so, what are some possible ways to deal with inflation?

2. Do you think government should control or regulate the economy of a country, or should it follow a hands-off policy?[6]

3. Who owns the major industries in your country? Are any industries owned and run by the government? Are labor unions strong? Do all unions have the right to strike? Are unions successful in gaining rights and wage increases for their workers?

4. Who are some famous economists in your country? What are their theories?

5. Do people save a lot of money in your country? Why or why not?

[6]*A hands-off policy* means "the government does not control business, industry, or the economy in any way."

WISH CLAUSES AND PAST UNREAL CONDITIONAL

First Virginia regiment in the U.S. Civil War.

Dialog

YOLANDA: I just saw *Gone with the Wind* for the fifth time last night.

ARNOLD: **I wish you'd told me about it.** It's one of my favorite movies.

MOLLY: Me, too. **If I'd known it was playing, I would have gone with you.**

YOLANDA: I called you, but you weren't home.

MOLLY: I really love that movie. It always makes me cry.

ARNOLD: It's a brilliant movie, but it isn't an accurate portrayal of slavery or the Civil War.

JACK: What do you mean?

ARNOLD: To begin with, it romanticizes[1] slavery. It only shows the slaves as happy and loyal to their masters.

YOLANDA: That's true. It doesn't show anything about how miserable the slaves were.

MOLLY: One thing that I've never understood is why slavery lasted as long as it did. I know there were a few slave revolts, but why weren't there more?

ARNOLD: **There probably would have been more revolts if the slave owners hadn't done a number of things to prevent them.**

MOLLY: Like what?

ARNOLD: They systematically separated families and slaves who spoke the same language. Also, it was against the law for slaves to learn how to read and write.

MOLLY: Why was it against the law? **What would have happened if they'd been able to read and write?**

ARNOLD: **If they'd been able to read, they could have read about blacks in the North who were free, and they might have written an underground newspaper.[2]**

YOLANDA: Then **they might have started a revolution.**

ARNOLD: **They might have,** except that the slave owners made it impossible for them to organize.

Listening Comprehension Questions

1. How many times has Yolanda seen *Gone with the Wind*?

---

[1] *Romanticize* means "to make reality seem prettier than it is."

[2] *An underground newspaper* was, at the time of the Civil War, an illegal revolutionary newspaper.

2. Why didn't Arnold and Molly go with Yolanda to see *Gone with the Wind* last night?

3. Why does Arnold feel that the movie isn't an accurate portrayal of slavery?

4. Why weren't there more slave revolts?

5. Why was it against the law for slaves to read and write?

PAST UNREAL CONDITIONAL SENTENCES—*IF* CLAUSES

Statements

When we want to talk about situations in the past that are contrary to what actually happened, we use the past unreal conditional pattern.

If + subject + **had (not)** + past participle, + subject +
$\left\{ \begin{array}{l} \textbf{would} \\ \textbf{could} \\ \textbf{might} \end{array} \right\}$ + **(not) have** + past participle

If Molly had known about the movie, she would have gone with Yolanda.

Examples

The American Civil War was fought from 1861 to 1865 between northern states (the Union) and eleven southern states (the Confederacy). The industrialized Union believed in a strong federal government and the abolition of slavery. The agricultural Confederacy believed in strong state government and wanted to maintain slavery. After Lincoln was elected president in 1860, the South left the Union because Lincoln wanted to stop the spread of slavery. The war began. The war caused more deaths than any other war in American history, cost billions of dollars, ruined the southern economy and land, and increased hatred for seventy to eighty years after the last battle was fought.

Daniel Webster and Henry Clay were two men in Congress who had succeeded in getting the North and South to compromise, but, unfortunately, they died in 1852. No one else was able to take their place.

If the North and South **had solved** more of their difficulties in the Congress, the Civil War **wouldn't have happened.**

If President Lincoln **hadn't won** the election of 1860, the South **wouldn't have left** the Union to form the Confederacy.

Note: We often use a contraction with the subject and *had*.

If *I had* known means "If *I'd* known."

Sometimes we contract the subject with *would*.

I *would have* gone means "*I'd have* gone."

If *I'd* known it was playing, *I'd* have gone with you.

Questions and Short Answers

We can only ask questions in the main clause. In short answers, we use

$$\text{subject} \quad + \quad \left\{ \begin{array}{l} \textbf{would} \\ \textbf{could} \\ \textbf{might} \end{array} \right\} \quad + \quad \textit{have.}$$

Examples

Slavery was an issue in American life as early as 1776, during the American Revolution. Many northerners felt that the Constitution should not have allowed slavery.

Would southerners **have abandoned** slavery if northerners **had been** more insistent at the time of the Revolution?
It's difficult to say, but *they might have.*

What **would have happened** if more blacks **had revolted** against slavery?
Some *would have escaped*, but the rebellions probably *would have failed* because all the weapons were in white hands.

One of the few black rebellions was led by Nat Turner in 1831. He and his followers were captured and killed.

■ ACTIVITY 23A

❑ Fill in the blanks with the correct forms of the past unreal conditional.

The period following the Civil War from 1865 to 1877 is called the Reconstruction Period. It was a time of difficulty and anger between the North and the South. Here is a list of some of the events that happened.

1. Many Confederate soldiers couldn't own land after the war. A great deal of good farmland was left without anyone to farm it, so there was a severe shortage of food after the war. If the North *had permitted*
   (permit)
   the soldiers to own and farm the land, there *wouldn't have been* a
   (negative, **be**)
   shortage of food.

2. Many northerners, called carpetbaggers, went to the South. They often cheated southerners out of their land. The southerners' hatred grew, and bad feelings between the North and South lasted for decades after the war. If these northerners _____ the southern
   (negative, **cheat**)
   landowners, the bad feelings between the North and the South
   _____ so intense.
   (negative, **become**)

3. Northern liberals in the Congress felt that Andrew Johnson, who became president after Lincoln was shot, was too easy on the South. They tried to remove him from office. If Johnson's policies toward the South _____ harsher, northern liberals
   (**be**)
   _____ to remove him from office. A vote was taken in
   (negative, **try**)
   the Senate to remove Johnson. President Johnson won by one vote and remained president. If one more senator _____ against him,
   (**vote**)
   he _____ office.
   (**have to, leave**)

4. Immediately following the war, blacks gained political and economic freedom. However, some conservative southerners began to join the Ku Klux Klan, an organization that terrorized blacks and southern liberals.

It became very powerful, and blacks became afraid to vote. Slowly, conservative southerners gained control of state governments. If the Ku Klux Klan _____ so powerful, blacks _____
_____(negative, be)_____ _____(negative, be)_____
afraid to vote, and conservative southerners _____ so
_____(negative, gain)_____
much power.

5. Because the South never developed industry before the Civil War, it took a long time for the southern states to recover from the war. If the South _____ so dependent on agriculture, it
___(negative, be)___
_____ more quickly.
____(recover)____

6. Many people wonder why the South didn't abandon slavery and industrialize sooner. The invention of the cotton gin is one factor in the South's continued dependence on agriculture and slavery. The institution of slavery was beginning to become unprofitable before the cotton gin was invented. Too many slaves were needed to remove the seeds from the cotton after it was picked. In 1793, Eli Whitney invented a machine that separated the seeds from the cotton. This machine was known as the cotton gin. It made the production of cotton profitable and reinforced the need for slavery, since cheap slave labor was needed to plant the land. If Eli Whitney _____ the cotton
_____(negative, invent)_____
gin, the production of cotton _____ profitable. If
_____(negative, be)_____
the cotton growers _____ able to make a profit,
_____(negative, be)_____
slavery _____ sooner. Eli Whitney tried but was
_____(end)_____
unable to get a patent on his new machine. He never made great profits from his invention. If _____ a patent, he
_____(get)_____
_____ a rich man.
____(become)____

❑ Prepare a brief talk for your class about these subjects.

1. Think of a famous person who was influential in the history of your country. If this person had not lived, how would the history of your country have been different? How would your country be different today? If you had been this person, would you have done things the same way or differently? Why?

2. Think of some of the great mistakes that have been made throughout history. How might the situation have been different if these mistakes hadn't happened? For example, how would history have been different without Napoleon's invasion of Russia? Mark Antony's blind love for Cleopatra? the Watergate scandal?

■ ACTIVITY 23B

Read the first statement. Then write the question, *What would have happened if. . . . ?* Then, using the information given in parentheses, answer the question.

1. Lincoln died soon after the war ended.

   What would have happened if Lincoln hadn't died?

   (*The bitterness between the North and the South*, negative, *be, strong*)

   The bitterness between the North and the South wouldn't have been so strong.

2. England was sympathetic to the South, but England never gave the

   South much financial aid.

   _____if England

   _____the South financial aid?

   (*the South, win the war*)

   If England _____,

   the South _____

3. The South lost many of her finest young men in the war.

   _____if _____

   _____?

(the South, recover, sooner)

If _____

4. Andrew Johnson wasn't a very strong president.

_____ if _____ a stronger president?

(negative, be, so much chaos after the war)

If _____,

there _____

In this part of the exercise, no information is given for the answer. Use your imagination to supply a logical answer.

5. The South didn't win the war.

_____ if the South _____?

_____

6. Slavery was a terrible institution that caused endless problems for the United States. One of the biggest mistakes the United States ever made was to permit slavery.

_____ if _____?

_____

Would _____ if _____?

_____

7. Lincoln was in a theater watching a play on the night of his assassination.

_____ if Lincoln _____

to the theater that night?

_____

8. John Wilkes Booth is the man who shot Lincoln. Booth had made a careful plan with another man, George Atzerodt. Atzerodt was assigned

to assassinate Vice-President Andrew Johnson on that same night.

However, Atzerodt became afraid and lost his nerve at the last minute.

_____if Atzerodt _____?

_____

WISH CLAUSES ABOUT A PAST EVENT

When we talk about something that we wish about an impossible or contrary-to-fact event in the past, we use a *wish* clause followed by a clause in the past perfect tense.

subject + **wish(es)** + **(that)** + subject + **had (not)** + past **(ed)** participle
Arnold wishes that Yolanda had told him that she was going to the movies.

Examples

The South was ruined after the Civil War, because most battles were fought in the South. Homes were destroyed, the land was left in ruins, and cities were burned. Many brave men who could have helped the South rebuild itself were killed in the war. After Lincoln's death in 1865, northern politicians passed laws that harmed the South. The "New South" of today has almost recovered from this destruction but at a terrible cost.

Many southerners *wish* that the North and South **hadn't fought** most of their battles on southern land. They also *wish* northerners **hadn't punished** the South so severely after the Civil War.

After the South surrendered in April 1865, President Lincoln wanted to treat the southern states with mercy, and he wanted them to rejoin the Union quickly. Tragically, he was assassinated soon after. Many people *wished* that Lincoln **had lived** to rebuild the South.

■ ACTIVITY 23C

Read the information given for each item. Then make a sentence using *wish*.

1. Robert E. Lee was the commander of the Confederate troops. He was a brilliant soldier. Lincoln had great respect for him. Lincoln *wished that* Lee *had been* a commander for the Union.
   <u>(be)</u>

2. The Battle of Gettysburg was one of the bloodiest in the Civil War. Almost 50,000 young **American** men lost their lives. After the battle, Lincoln made a speech at Gettysburg. He was terribly saddened at the great loss of human life. He _____ he _____
   (be able)
   to prevent this tragic loss.

3. William Sherman, a Union general, burned Atlanta. Atlanta was a beautiful southern city. When General Sherman burned it, he destroyed some of the most beautiful architecture of the country. Even many northerners _____ Sherman _____
   (negative, burn)
   Atlanta.

4. William Faulkner, a famous American writer, often wrote stories about the relationship between southern whites and blacks. He _____ blacks and whites _____ each
   (understand)
   other better during his lifetime.

5. Martin Luther King, Jr., was a courageous black leader in the 1950s and 1960s. He was assassinated in 1968. Both black and white Americans _____ he _____.
   (negative, die)

PAST-TIME *IF* CLAUSES WITH PRESENT-TIME MAIN CLAUSES

When we talk about an impossible or contrary-to-fact event in the past that we relate to the present, we use this pattern.

If + subject + **had (not)** + past participle,

If the North and South hadn't fought the Civil War,

+ subject + $\begin{Bmatrix} \textbf{would} \\ \textbf{could} \\ \textbf{might} \end{Bmatrix}$ (not) + base form

perhaps the United States would be a very different country today.

Example

In 1863, President Lincoln issued the Emancipation Proclamation. This proclamation abolished slavery. However, for years after the Civil War, many blacks in the South were denied the right to vote, to go to white schools, or to go into white restaurants. After World War II, blacks began to demand their rights vigorously. Today, blacks still insist that there is discrimination against them and that the battle for equal rights continues.

If the southern states **hadn't denied** blacks their rights as citizens after the Civil War, there **might not be** so much racial tension in the United States today.

■ **ACTIVITY 23D**

❑ Read each group of sentences about the United States. Then change the sentences into a sentence with a past unreal *if* clause and a present unreal main clause. Use *would* or *might* in the main clause.

1. Texas was once a part of Mexico, but it fought a revolution and won. It's a state now. If *Texas hadn't won the revolution,* it *might not be a part of the United States today.*

2. The American government bought Alaska from Russia in 1867. It paid $7.2 million. Today the United States has important sources of oil there.

   If _____ ,

   _____

3. England didn't win the war with the American colonies. The United States isn't part of the British Empire anymore.

   _____ ,

   _____

4. America became a separate nation. Pronunciation in American English is very different from pronunciation in British English.

   _____ ,

   _____

5. There was a political scandal known as Watergate in the early 1970s. Many Americans do not have much confidence in their elected leaders.

   _____ ,

   _____

   ☐ Think of a mistake you or someone you know made. How would things be different today if you hadn't made this mistake? Share your story with your classmates.

■ ACTIVITY 23E

   ☐ Fill in the blanks with the correct form of the real conditional, present unreal conditional, past unreal conditional, or clauses with *hope* and *wish*.

   MOLLY: I'm ready for our vacation next month. I wish we

   _____ tomorrow.
   <u>(can, go)</u>

YOLANDA: Why? What's bothering you?

MOLLY: Well, for one thing, New York City is so hot in the summer.

I don't have an air conditioner. I wish I _____.

It's so humid. If it _____ so humid, I
              (negative, **be**)

_____ the heat so much. I hope the rest of the
     (negative, **mind**)

United States _____ as humid as New York.
          (negative, **be**)

YOLANDA: Well, you know you love New York the rest of the year. Any

other problems?

MOLLY: Yes. I took an exam yesterday. I didn't do very well on it.

YOLANDA: Didn't you go to a late-night party the night before last?

MOLLY: Yes, and I didn't study for my test. If I _____
                                           (**study**)

for the test, I _____ better on it.
                  (**do**)

YOLANDA: Well, that's not the only test you're going to have all semester, is

it? There will always be more tests. If I _____ you,
                                     (**be**)

however, I _____ a lot for my next test. Why
              (**study**)

did you stay so late at the party?

MOLLY: Jack and I had a lot of fun dancing and talking to people. We

_____ so long if there _____ so
     (negative, **stay**)   (negative, **be**)

many nice people there. I wish I _____ that test
                         (negative, **take**)

yesterday. My professor is a nice guy. If I _____
                                 (**ask**)

him, he probably _____ me take it at a later
                    (**let**)

date. I hope I _____ an F in the course.
          (negative, **get**)

YOLANDA: Don't worry. You won't fail.

❑ Complete each sentence with the correct form of the conditional clause—real, present unreal, or past unreal.

1. If Cleopatra hadn't fallen in love with Mark Antony, _____

   _____

2. Most Americans wish _____

   _____

3. Most people in my country hope _____

   _____

4. If interest rates on loans go any higher, _____

   _____

5. There wouldn't be so many political refugees in the world today if

   _____

6. American Indians wish _____

   _____

7. If _____,

   Napolean might have won his war with Russia.

8. If we had peace in the world today, _____

   _____

9. My English will improve if _____

   _____

10. After I _____,

    I wished _____

EXPRESSING YOUR IDEAS

1. Has there ever been a civil war or any kind of rebellion in your country? What were the reasons for it? When did it happen? How long did it last? Who won? What are some of its consequences?

2. What other famous civil wars have happened in history? What caused them? Why are civil wars so tragic for a nation?

3. Most Americans feel ashamed that slavery was a part of their country's history. Is there any period or event in your country's history that you or other people feel ashamed about? Explain.

4. How do people in your country feel about the problem of discrimination in the United States? Do you think that Americans are more prejudiced than people from other countries? Explain. Do you think that Americans are honestly trying to do something about racial discrimination? If there were as many racial, religious, or ethnic groups in your country, do you think your country might have the same problems of discrimination as the United States?

Arnold watching TV.

Dialog

(ARNOLD and YOLANDA are watching TV, but the TV set is not working very well, so the picture on the screen is not very clear.)

ARNOLD: This stupid TV! I just **had it fixed** a couple of days ago.

YOLANDA: What **did** you **have done** to it?

ARNOLD: **I had a new picture tube installed.** It cost a lot of money. Not only that, they **made me wait** for two weeks.

YOLANDA: Who **did** you **have fix** it? I won't go to them next time my TV breaks.

ARNOLD: The repair shop around the corner.

YOLANDA: I bet you went crazy without your TV.

ARNOLD: Yeah, I did. I guess I'm a TV addict.[1]

YOLANDA: How can I **get you to turn** this thing **off?** There's nothing but garbage on TV now anyway. Let's go out.

ARNOLD: You're right. Look at that commercial. Stupid commercials like that one **make me want** to throw this set out the window.

YOLANDA: That commercial may be stupid, but it's very persuasive. Even simple-minded commercials **get people to buy** things that they don't really need.

ARNOLD: Yeah, there are too many ads on TV. I think the government should **make the networks reduce** the number of commercials.

YOLANDA: And here's another problem. Most parents **let their kids watch** too much TV. When I was a kid, my parents only **let me watch** one program a night. They **made me turn** it **off** after an hour.

ARNOLD: I know watching TV is really a waste of time. I should **have the garbage collectors come** and **take** this TV **away.**

YOLANDA: Oh, come on, Arnold. You'll never give up watching TV.

Listening Comprehension Questions

1. When did Arnold last have his TV set fixed?
2. What did he have done to it?
3. Is he satisfied with the work that was done?
4. Why is Yolanda trying to get Arnold to turn the TV off?
5. What do commercials get people to do?

---

[1]*Addict* means "someone who cannot stop doing something—in this case, watching television."

6. What does Arnold think the government should do about the number of commercials on TV?

7. Did Yolanda's parents let her watch as much TV as she wanted when she was a child?

THE ACTIVE CAUSATIVE

When one person causes, persuades, or forces another person to do something, we can express this using three different causative patterns.

1. have someone do something

2. get someone to do something

3. make someone do something

The first verb in each of these patterns (*have, get, make*) can be used in any tense, but the second verb does not change. Use the base form after *have* and *make* and the infinitive form after *get*.

Have Someone Do Something

We use *have someone do something* when we ask someone to do something for us, when we hire someone to work for us, or when we have the position, authority, or money to ask others to perform tasks for us. We use this pattern when we want to show that we don't do something ourselves. For example, *Arnold didn't fix his TV himself. He had a TV repairman fix it for him.*

Examples

Many sociologists believe that TV has a negative influence on our society. They are especially worried about the effect of violence in TV programs on children. In one study, sociologists **had children watch** a violent TV program. After the program, they **had researchers observe** these children playing, and they found an increase in aggressive behavior in the children.

■ ACTIVITY 24A

Complete these questions and answer them.

Most people love to imagine being rich and the things that they would have someone do for them if they had enough money.

1. If you were rich, *would you have someone design*
    (have, design)
    the house of your dreams for you?

    Yes, I would _____

    There are many famous architects. Who *would you*

    have design your house _____?
    (have, design)

    _____

2. If you were rich, _____
    (have, entertain)
    _____ at your parties?

    _____

    There are many famous singers and entertainers. Who _____

    _____?
    (have, entertain)

    _____

3. If you were rich, _____
    (have, design)
    _____ your clothes for you?

    _____

    There are many famous designers. Who _____

    _____?
    (have, design)

    _____

4. If you were rich, _____ your relatives
    (have, live)
    _____ with you in your big mansion?

    _____

    Who _____ with you?
    (have, live)

    _____

Get Someone to Do Something

We usually use *get someone to do something* instead of *have someone do something* when it is necessary to use psychological persuasion or to offer a reward to cause someone to do something.

> ### *Examples*
>
> Sociologists complain that commercials **get people to buy** things that they don't need. Commercials have an especially strong influence on young children. After they watch certain commercials, children want sweet junk food and expensive toys. They try to **get their parents to buy** these things for them.
>
> Concerned parent groups are trying to change TV advertising, but they haven't yet **gotten all advertisers to cooperate** with them.

■ ACTIVITY 24B

Complete these questions and answer them. Discuss your answers in class.

In matters of love and relationships between men and women, people often use special persuasive techniques. In most countries, there are superstitions about how to get someone to love you.

1. If a woman is interested in a man, but he doesn't pay attention to her,

   how can she _____ *get him to notice* _____ her?
   (get, notice)

   _____

2. How can she _____ her out for a date?
   (get, ask)

   _____

3. If a man is interested in a woman, but she doesn't pay any attention to

   him, what can he do to _____ him?
   (get, notice)

   _____

4. If a woman refuses a date with a man, how _____
   (get, change)

   _____ her mind?

   _____

5. If a woman thinks the man she loves doesn't love her enough, what

   should she do to _____ her more?

(get, love)

   _____

6. What about a man in this same situation? What should he do to

   _____?

(get, love)

   _____

7. If the person you love isn't interested in marrying you, what can you do

   to _____?

(get, marry)

   A woman can _____

   A man can _____

8. If you don't want to go out with a person, but this person keeps

   bothering you and keeps inviting you out, how can you _____

(get, leave)

   _____you alone?

   _____

Make Someone Do Something

We generally use *make someone do something* when we mean that it is necessary to use some force to cause someone to do something.

Examples

The Federal Communications Commission (FCC) is an agency of the federal government that regulates television and radio programs. It **makes television networks follow** certain rules. For example, it **makes the stations show** programs with sex or violence after 9:00 P.M., when children are in bed. Also, when a movie contains vulgar language, the FCC can **make the networks take** obscene words out before they show it.

Note: Sometimes the causative pattern with *make* does not carry the meaning of force. In the following examples, *make* simply means "to cause something to happen."

1. Sad movies make me cry.

2. A host should make a guest feel comfortable in his or her home.

3. Good music makes people want to dance.

Let Someone Do Something

Let has a different meaning from the preceding three causative verbs. *Let* means "permit." It follows the same grammatical structure as *have someone do something* or *make someone do something*.

Examples

Concerned parents control the amount of TV that their children watch. They usually **let their children watch** one or two hours of TV a day, but they **don't let them watch** it all day long.

■ ACTIVITY 24C

Work with a partner. Ask questions using the active form of the causative. Your partner will answer them. After you practice this orally, write the questions and answers for homework.

1. Make Someone Do Something.
   All parents make their children do certain things that the children don't want to do.

   a. What ____*did*____ your parents ____*make you*____
      (make, do)
      ____*do*____ that you didn't want to do? _____

      _____

   b. _____ they _____
      (make, eat)
      certain food that you didn't like?

      _____

   c. _____ to bed early?
      (make, go)

      _____

d. _____chores to help around
               (make, do)

the house?_____

What _____?

e. _____?

_____

f. _____?

_____

2. Let Someone Do Something.
   Most parents do not let their children do whatever they want to do.

   a. When you were seven years old, ___*did*_____

   your parents ___*let you stay up*_____until midnight?
                   (let, stay)

   _____

   b. When you were six, _____ your mother

   _____ to school alone, or did she take you to school?
      (let, walk)

   _____

   c. _____as much candy as you wanted
              (let, eat)
   when you were a child?

   _____

   d. _____when you were about
              (let, date)
   fourteen or fifteen years old?

   _____

   When _____for the first time?

   _____

e. If you had children, what are some things that you would or would not let your children do?

_____

_____

_____

■ ACTIVITY 24D

❑ Fill in the blanks in the article below. Choose the correct tense for the causative verb (*have, make, get, let*) and choose the base form or the infinitive form for the second verb.

There have been more than 2,300 studies and reports on the effects of watching TV on American society. Most of them show that these effects are mainly negative. Researchers have been especially concerned about children. In the past decade, researchers *have had* children _____(have)_____

participate in numerous studies. A few years ago, a University of ___(participate)___

California research team _____ a group of elementary-school ____(have)____

children _____ a test. From this group, the researchers selected 250 ____(take)____

children who were especially intelligent and creative. They _____ ____(have)____

these children _____ TV intensively for three weeks. Then they ____(watch)____

_____ them _____ a similar test a second time. The results ___(have)___ ___(take)___

showed a drop in the children's creativity. The researchers concluded that watching TV _____ the children _____ some of their ____(make)____ ____(lose)____

creativity.

Many elementary-school teachers agree with the findings of this study. They believe that watching TV _____ children _____ the ____(make)____ ____(lose)____ ability to concentrate in school. Teachers can't _____ children

_____ attention for any length of time because today's children
(pay)

want everything to be as fast and entertaining as TV. Dr. Benjamin Spock,

an expert in child raising, once complained that he couldn't _____
(get)

his grandchildren _____ the TV set when he wanted to take them
(leave)

to the zoo. Some of today's children are so addicted to TV that nothing

else interests them. Parents have to _____ them _____ off
(make)   (turn)

the TV and _____ out to play or read a book. They can't
(go)

_____ them _____ these traditional childhood activities
(get)   (do)

without having an argument over the TV.

Although most of these studies have shown the negative effects of

watching TV, some sociologists argue that it has become a part of our lives.

They do not think that parents should _____ their children
(make)

_____ the amount of TV that they watch to one or two hours a
(limit)

day. They believe that parents should _____ their children
(let)

_____ for themselves what and how much they want to watch.
(decide)

❑ Fill in the first blank in each sentence with the correct active causative
form—*have, make,* or *get.* Fill in the second blank with the verb given
below the blank. Use each causative twice.

1. Most children do not like vegetables, but parents _____

   them _____ vegetables because they are full of vitamins.
   (eat)

2. Arnold's father bought some gas the other day, and he

   _____ the gas station attendant _____ the oil.
   (check)

3. When Yolanda lived at home, her younger brother always used to bother

   her when she was studying. She _____ him

_____ her alone by giving him some money to go to the
     (leave)
candy store.

4. Arnold's father is the president of a bank. He never answers his own

phone. He always _____ his secretary _____ it.
                                                     (answer)

5. Last week there was a robbery at the bank. A man pointed a gun at the

bank teller and _____ her _____ him all the
                                        (give)

money.

6. In the past, a woman could _____ a man _____
                                              (notice)

her by dropping her handkerchief.

> ☐ Fill in the blanks with the correct active causative forms and the correct
> tenses of the verbs given below the blanks. Choose from *have, make,* and
> *get.* For some blanks, you may feel that more than one of these causative
> forms is correct.

Although most studies show the negative effects of watching TV, there

are also some important positive influences. There are many excellent

educational programs, especially for children. Some schools _____

children _____ certain programs in the classroom. They often
         (watch)

_____ them _____ worthwhile programs at home by
                  (watch)

encouraging them to discuss what they have seen the next day in class.

"Sesame Street" is a program that is watched by millions of children

around the world. It uses bright colors, fast timing, and humor in order to

_____ children _____ attention. It _____ children
                         (pay)

_____ learning about the alphabet, reading, and numbers. Some
  (enjoy)

teachers have even found ways to use television to improve reading ability.

Several years ago, teachers in a Philadelphia school _____ children

_____ scripts for TV programs at home, and the next day their
  (read)

teachers _____ them _____ what they had read. By the
(discuss)

end of the semester, some students' reading scores had gone up three grade

levels.

   Television also exposes children to different people and places. A little

girl who had never seen a ballet before watched a famous ballerina on TV.

This program _____ her _____ to become a ballerina
(decide)

herself. TV also increases young people's understanding of other people's

views of life. Many people feel that "Roots," a program on the history of

black people in the United States, is an example of this. Because viewers of

this program became emotionally involved with the characters, "Roots"

_____ some people _____ more compassionately about the
(think)

difficulties of black people in the United States.

THE PASSIVE CAUSATIVE

We use the passive causative for the same reasons that we use any other passive
voice. *Have* is used in the following passive causative pattern.

have   something   done

> ### Examples
> Advertising is very important to TV. Companies **have** careful studies
> **done** by marketing analysts to determine what kind of commercials
> people respond to. Sometimes they **have** special pilot commercials **made**
> and **shown** in one or two test areas in the country. Based on the success of
> these pilot commercials, the companies decide whether or not to **have**
> them **shown** on a national network.

Note:

1. *Have* can be used in any tense, but the second verb is always the past
   participle.

2. *Get* can also be used in the passive causative. When we use *get*, there is
   no *to* before the second verb. (She *gets her hair done* at Richard's.)

SUMMARY OF ACTIVE AND PASSIVE CAUSATIVE FORMATION WITH *HAVE*

Look at the following sentences and notice the difference in form between the active and passive causative.

Arnold's TV set broke a couple of days ago.

1. A repairman **fixed** it.

2. Arnold **had** a repairman **fix** it.

3. Arnold's TV set **was fixed** a couple of days ago.

4. Arnold **had** his TV set **fixed** a couple of days ago.

Sentence 1 is in the active voice. In the active causative (sentence 2), the verb following the causative verb (*have*) is always the base form. Sentence 3 is in the passive voice. In the passive causative (sentence 4), the verb after the causative verb (*have*) is always the past participle.

When you ask a question about the object and use the active causative, you will see *have* + the base form next to each other:

Who did Arnold **have fix** his TV set?
  He **had** a repairman **fix** it.

When you ask a question about the object and use the passive causative, you will see *have* + the past participle next to each other:

What did Arnold **have done** to his TV set?
  He **had** a new picture tube **installed.**

■ ACTIVITY 24E

❑ Fill in the blanks, using *have* and the verb in parentheses.

ARNOLD: I saw a great program on TV last night.

YOLANDA: What was it about?

ARNOLD: It was about a rock star who became a multimillionaire. His

life-style is incredible. He has so many servants that he never

lifts a finger. He never has to do anything. He bought an island,

and he _____ a mansion _____ on it. The
                              (build)

gardens are spectacular. He _____ rare trees and

flowers _____ in from exotic places. In the mansion, he
          (bring)

_____ a huge bathtub _____ into the natural
                                  (carve)

rock, and he _____ gold faucets _____. He
                                              (install)

_____ a stereo system _____ for every room in
                                  (design)

the mansion. His parties are fantastic! He always serves the best

food. He _____ his meals _____ by the finest
                                      (prepare)

chefs of Europe, and _____ caviar _____ in
                                                (fly)

anytime he wants.

YOLANDA: How do his guests get to the island? Does he _____

them _____ in?
         (fly)

ARNOLD: Yes, he _____ them _____ to the island in his
                                        (fly)

private helicopters. And you should see his yacht!

YOLANDA: Did he _____ it specially _____?
                                              (build)

ARNOLD: Oh, yes. There's no other one like it in the world. And his clothes!

YOLANDA: Does he _____ them all _____ to order?
                                            (make)

ARNOLD: Yes.

YOLANDA: Honestly, Arnold, would you really like to live like that?

ARNOLD: I don't know, but I'd like to try it.

❑ Imagine what else this millionaire has done for him by other people.
Write several more examples.

■ ACTIVITY 24F

❑ Use the passive form *have something done* to form questions.

1. *(clothes, dry-clean)*

Do you *have your clothes dry-cleaned,* _____

or do you wash them yourself?

2. *(apartment, clean)*

    How do you keep your home or apartment clean?

    Do you _____

    by a professional cleaner, or do you clean it yourself?

3. *(your hair, cut)*

    When did you last _____?

    How often _____?

    Where _____?

4. *(your watch, repair)*

    When did you last _____

    _____?

5. *(your fortune, tell)*

    Have you ever _____

    _____by a gypsy?

6. *(your picture, take)*

    When was the last time that you _____

    _____?

7. *(your back, scratch)*

    Do you like to _____

    _____?

8. *(your back, rub)*

    Do you like to _____

    _____?

❑ In the next five questions, try to give several sentences to answer each question.

1. *(dry-clean)*

   What should you ___*have dry-cleaned ?*_____

   A silk shirt? A cotton shirt? A wool sweater? Wool pants?

   _____

   _____

2. *(do)*

   Most people have their hair cut in a beauty parlor or a barbershop.

   What else can you _____ in a beauty parlor or

   barbershop?

   _____

   _____

3. *(check)*

   When people take their cars to a garage, what _____

   _____?

   _____

   _____

4. *(make)*

   When you have your photo taken for a passport, how many copies do

   you _____?

   _____

   _____

5. *(do)*

    The president or leader of a country does not have time to do everything

    for himself or herself. What does he or she _____

    by other people?

    _____

    _____

6. *(send)*

    Many students miss things from their home country when they go

    abroad to study. What do students _____

    from home by friends and family?

    _____

    _____

■ **ACTIVITY 24G**

   ❑ Choose between the passive and the active form of the causative. Also
   choose the correct tense for each causative verb given. In the active
   form, choose *have, get, make,* or *let.* In the passive form, use only *have.*

   Many people think that the government should pass stronger laws to

   _____ companies _____ more truthfully and responsibly.
   (advertise)
   Some companies have used deceptive advertising to _____ people

   _____ their products. In the 1960s, for example, some companies
   (buy)
   experimented in movie theaters with a new and unusual form of

   commercial. They _____ an image _____ on the movie
   (flash)
   screen faster than the eye could see. The viewer did not even know that he

   had seen a commercial. All he knew was that something _____ him

_____ a particular kind of soda or candy. This subliminal
      (want)

advertising _____ people _____ certain products without
                                    (buy)

their knowing that they had been influenced by a commercial. Some people

thought that the government shouldn't _____ companies

_____ this form of advertising, and they fought to _____ it
      (use)

_____.
   (ban)

Many people complain about the number of commercials that interrupt

programs. Most TV networks are supported by advertisers who want to sell

their products. The success of a TV program depends on the number of

viewers. Research companies _____ surveys _____ to
                                              (make)

determine the number of viewers that a particular program has. A program

may be very good, but if it cannot attract viewers, it cannot attract

advertisers, and the network _____ it _____ off the air.
                                              (take)

Public TV has no commercials. It is supported by the government and

by contributions from private citizens and corporations. Corporations are

motivated to support public TV because doing so improves their image with

the public. They can also _____ these contributions _____
                                                            (deduct)

from their taxes.

■ ACTIVITY 24H

Imagine that you have just been crowned king or queen of the island kingdom
of Watanango. You have complete power. You can make your people do
anything, and you can have anything done for you. What are your plans? How
are you going to make your people obey you? Will you make everyone bow to
you? Are you going to make people display your picture in stores and public
areas? Will you have your statue erected in public areas? Will you let
newspapers criticize your policies? Will you try to get other countries to give
you economic aid?

Continue with other examples. Use the causative patterns.

EXPRESSING YOUR IDEAS

1. What is your opinion about watching TV? Does watching TV allow people to use their minds? Is it only a waste of time? Which programs do you think are good? Which are bad? Which do you like? Why? Do people read less or talk to each other less when they have TV in their homes?

2. Does watching TV have a negative or bad influence on children? If you think it does, tell how. What good or positive influences does watching TV have on children? Should parents let children watch as much TV as they want, or should they limit the amount of TV that their children watch? Why?

3. What do you think of TV commercials? Do they ever get you to buy things that you don't need? Are there too many commercials? Should the government make the networks show fewer commercials? Should the government regulate commercials that are directed at children? How should the government regulate commercials?

4. Are TV programs better in your country or in the United States? How?

5. Does your country broadcast a lot of American TV programs? Does this affect your culture? How?

6. Do American TV programs realistically reflect American life? What kind of image do American TV programs give you about life in the United States?

7. American TV stations are not owned by the government. Are TV stations privately or publicly owned in your country? What dangers or disadvantages are there when the government owns TV stations? What are the dangers or disadvantages when private companies own TV stations?

8. Should TV programs be censored? By whom? What should be censored? Should sex be censored? What about violence? What about the news?

25 NOUN CLAUSES IN OBJECT POSITION— INDIRECT QUESTIONS

Albert Einstein.

Dialog

(JACK is talking to MOLLY on the telephone.)

JACK: Hi, Molly. What's new?

MOLLY: Hi, Jack. Oh, nothing much.

JACK: What are you doing?

MOLLY: I'm reading an article about Albert Einstein. His life was really fascinating.

JACK: Does the article talk about his childhood? **Does it say if there were any early signs** that he was a genius?

MOLLY: It talks about his childhood, but it says he didn't even begin to talk until he was three.

JACK: I understand that he failed math in school. **I wonder if that story is true.**

MOLLY: This article doesn't mention that, but it says he didn't like school very much. He was rebellious, and he cut classes.[1] One of his teachers once called him a lazy dog and said, "You'll never amount to anything."[2]

JACK: **Can you imagine how that teacher felt** when he heard about Einstein's winning the Nobel prize for physics?

MOLLY: He probably felt like a fool. Here's something interesting. Can you believe that he made his major discoveries when he was working in an office and earning only $675 a year?

JACK: That's amazing. **Do you know how old he was** when he got the Nobel prize?

MOLLY: That was quite a bit later, in 1922, when he was about forty-three.

JACK: I know Einstein became an American citizen, but he was quite old when he came here, I think. **Does it say when he came here?**

MOLLY: In 1933. He left Germany after Hitler came into power. You know, it's interesting to think that Einstein's Theory of Relativity changed the whole way scientists look at the universe, but **I wonder how many people really understand his theory.**

JACK: Do you?

MOLLY: No, not at all. All I know is $E = mc^2$. But you must understand it, since you're an astronomer.

JACK: Well, I'm going to be working in the observatory tonight. Come on over, and I'll explain it to you.

[1]*To cut class* means "to be absent from class without a good reason."
[2]*To amount to something* means "to achieve something worthwhile or important."

Listening Comprehension Questions

1. According to the article Molly is reading, were there any early signs that Albert Einstein was a genius?
2. What kind of student was Einstein?
3. How much was he earning at the time that he made his major discoveries?
4. In which area of science did he receive the Nobel Prize?
5. When and why did he immigrate to the United States?
6. Does Molly think many people really understand Einstein's Theory of Relativity?

NOUN CLAUSES

The normal word order for a sentence in English is subject + verb + object.

Molly is reading an article.

subject + verb + direct object (noun)

Sometimes the object is a clause that has its own subject and verb.

Jack wants to know what she is reading.

subject + verb + direct object (noun clause)

We often use noun clauses in object position when we ask or answer questions. Many of these noun clauses begin with question words *(where, what, when)*. *Do not use the question word order in noun clauses.* In the simple present and simple past tenses, we need the words *do, does,* and *did* for direct questions, but we do not use them in noun clauses.

INDIRECT QUESTIONS

Wh- Questions

Examples

Muhammad Ali is one of the most famous names in the history of boxing. People all over the world are fascinated by his life. Here is an imaginary interview between Muhammad Ali and a reporter.

REPORTER: Ali, I think our audience would like to know **why you decided** to become a boxer.
(Direct Question: Why did you decide to become a boxer?)

ALI: When I was a kid, some bigger kids stole my bicycle, and I couldn't do anything about it. I decided then to learn how to defend myself.

REPORTER: Most people probably don't know **how old you were** when you began to fight.
(Direct Question: How old were you when you began to fight?)

ALI: I fought my first match when I was fifteen.

REPORTER: You started fighting under the name of Cassius Clay. Then you changed your name to Muhammad Ali when you became a Black Muslim in 1964. Many people don't really understand **why you changed your name.**
(Direct Question: Why did you change your name?)

ALI: Do you know **where the names of black people in this country come from?** They are slave names. The slaves often took the last name of their white masters. My religion says we should denounce our slave names and take new names.
(Direct Question: Where do the names of black people in this country come from?)

Yes/No Questions

We use *if* or *whether* to introduce noun clauses that we use in place of questions that we can answer with *yes* or *no*.

Examples

(The interview continues.)

REPORTER: Ali, in 1964, you won the world heavyweight title. Because you refused to go into the army, the boxing commission took that title away from you. I wonder **if you still think** that you were right to refuse to join the army.
(Direct Question: Do you still think you were right to . . .?)

ALI: Yes, I still think so. As a minister in the Black Muslim church, I didn't think I should fight in the Vietnam War. And, in 1971, the U.S. Supreme Court upheld my right to make that decision.

REPORTER: Ali, your first defeat was in your fight against Joe Frazier in 1971. That was a close fight. I wonder **whether or not you agreed**[3] with the judges' decision on that fight.
(Direct Question: Did you agree with the judges' decision?)

ALI: No, I think I won that fight. I was knocked down in the fifteenth round, but I was ahead on points all the way. I didn't have a mark on me after the fight, but Frazier had to go to the hospital.

REPORTER: Ali, to conclude this interview, would you please tell people how you defeat your opponents. Tell us what your secret is.

ALI: It's simple. I'm the greatest. I float like a butterfly and sting like a bee.

Expressions with Noun Clauses

Here is a list of some expressions that we frequently use before noun clauses in indirect questions.

I know . . .	I don't know . . .	Do you know . . . ?
I remember . . .	I don't remember . . .	Do you remember . . . ?
I'd like to know . . .	I wonder . . .	I don't care . . .
I'd like to find out . . .	I'm not sure . . .	
I want to ask . . .	Are you sure . . . ?	
Can you tell me . . . ?	I won't tell you . . .	Can you imagine . . . ?

[3]Notice that we can also say, *"I wonder whether you agreed with the judges' decision or not."*

> Could anyone
>   explain . . . ?   I can't explain . . .   I can imagine . . .
> Would someone please   I can't imagine . . .
>   ask . . . ?
>
> Ask him . . .   Does the sign say . . . ?
> Tell me . . .   Does the article
> Explain . . .   say . . . ?
>   It doesn't say . . .
>
> Try to guess . . .
> Try to understand . . .
> Try to find out . . .

We often use indirect questions to ask for information from people we don't know—for example, in stores, restaurants, and train stations—because such questions are generally more polite. In these situations, we use expressions such as these.

I'd like to know . . .   or   Can }
                                 Could } you tell me . . . ?
                                 Would }

Example

Could you tell me when the next train leaves?

Punctuation

Be careful with the punctuation of sentences with noun clauses. If the main clause is a question (*Could you tell me . . .? Do you know . . .?* and so on), use a question mark. If the main clause is not a question (*I'd like to know . . .*, *I wonder. . . .*), use a period.

Examples

I wonder if that story is true.

Do you know how old he was when he got the Nobel prize?

■ **ACTIVITY 25A**

☐ Here is information about another famous American. Look at the information in the answer first. Use a noun clause to ask for the information.

JACK: What are you reading now, Molly?

MOLLY: The biography of Susan B. Anthony.

JACK: I don't know very much about her. Can you tell me what

_____Susan B. Anthony did_____ ?

MOLLY: She did many things. First she fought against slavery. Then, later, she fought for women's right to vote.

JACK: I guess that was a really hard fight in those days. I know that a lot of women were thrown in jail. Do you know if

_____she was ever arrested?_____ ?

MOLLY: Yes. She was arrested when she tried to vote in 1872.

JACK: In those days, it was unusual for a woman to take part in political protests, speak in public, and be arrested. I wonder how

_____the family felt?_____ .

MOLLY: Oh, I think her family felt that she was doing the right thing. Her father had taught her to be very independent and strong when she was a child. He taught her to read and write when she was only three years old.

JACK: Do you know if _____women got the right of vote_____ before she died?

MOLLY: Well, women got the right to vote in four states before she died.

JACK: Do you remember when _____she died_____ ?

MOLLY: She died in 1906.

☐ Martin Luther King, Jr., is another famous name in American history. In this dialog, imagine that the host of a TV talk show is interviewing the author of a biography about Dr. King. Ask for information, using noun clauses.

HOST: Today we are celebrating Martin Luther King, Jr.'s, birthday, and

I would like to review a few important events from his life.

Martin Luther King, Jr., received the Nobel Peace prize in 1964.

Would you tell us ___what he did_____

_____?

AUTHOR: He was the most important leader in the nonviolent fight for

racial equality.

HOST: And would you tell us ____where he was born_____?

AUTHOR: He was born in Georgia on January 15, 1929.

HOST: Our audience would probably like to know ___what he did____

before he became involved in the fight for racial equality.

AUTHOR: He was a minister.

HOST: Do you know ___if he come from a family of ministers__?

AUTHOR: Yes, he came from a family of ministers. Both his father and

grandfather were ministers.

HOST: I'm not sure exactly ___when he first come to national attention___

AUTHOR: He first came to national attention in 1956. In that year, a black

woman named Rosa Parks got on a bus in Montgomery, Alabama.

In the southern part of the country at that time, all black people

had to sit in the black section at the back of the bus. Rosa Parks

was tired from working all day, and the black section of the bus

was full, so she sat in the white section. The driver stopped the bus, and she was arrested. Dr. King was the leader of a boycott of

the buses. Black people refused to ride the buses for many months.

HOST: Do you know ~~when the US Supreme Court ruled that~~ ? ~~racial~~

~~segregation was illegal in transportation.~~

AUTHOR: Yes, one year later the U.S. Supreme Court ruled that racial

segregation was illegal in transportation.

HOST: Would you please tell us ~~when he led a civil rights~~ .

AUTHOR: He led a civil rights march on Washington in 1963. At that time

in the South, blacks couldn't vote. He led the fight to give his

people the right to vote.

HOST: I don't remember exactly ~~when the federal government~~ .

~~passed the civil rights Act.~~

AUTHOR: The federal government passed the Civil Rights Act in 1964 and

the Voting Rights Act in 1965.

HOST: Please tell us how many times ~~he was arrested~~ .

AUTHOR: I don't remember exactly, but he was arrested and put in jail

several times for his part in protest marches and demonstrations.

HOST: Would you tell us ~~how he died~~ ?

AUTHOR: He was shot in Memphis, Tennessee, by James Earl Ray.

HOST: That was a tragic moment in the history of the United States.

■ ACTIVITY 25B

☐ In normal conversation, we generally mix direct and indirect questions.
In the dialog below, there are both kinds of questions. If a question is
direct, change it to the indirect form. If a question is indirect, change it
to the direct form.

Walt Disney is another American whose name is famous all over the
world. Even people who have never heard his name know his cartoon
characters, Mickey Mouse and Donald Duck. Here is an imaginary
dialog between a magazine writer and the author of a biography of Walt
Disney.

WRITER: I suppose Walt Disney is a name that people all over the world know. I wonder how popular Disney's movies are around the world.

How popular are Disney's movies around the world?

AUTHOR: Well, in 1966, Walt Disney Productions estimated that around the world 240 million people had seen a Disney movie, 100 million people had watched a Disney TV show every week, and 6.7 million people had made the trip to Disneyland.

WRITER: When was Walt Disney born?

Do you know _when he was born?_ ?

AUTHOR: He was born in Chicago on December 5, 1901.

WRITER: I wonder how he got his start in the cartoon business.

How did he get his start in cartoon business

Did he go to art school?

Do you know _if he went to school?_ ?

AUTHOR: When he was a child, he loved to draw, so he took a course in cartoon art through the mail.

WRITER: Could you tell us if his parents encouraged his interest in art?

Did his parents encouraged his interest in art

AUTHOR: His father let him attend an art class on Saturday mornings, but they didn't really give him any other encouragement.

WRITER: What was his first job?

Tell us _what his first job was_

AUTHOR: He worked in a commercial art studio for fifty dollars a month. Of course, he didn't have much money. When he needed a haircut, he gave the barber some of his cartoons instead of money.

WRITER: When did he make his first cartoon with Mickey Mouse? Can you tell us _when he made his first cartoon_? *with mickey mouse*

AUTHOR: In 1927, but the first name he gave his character was Mortimer Mouse.

WRITER: Do you know if those first cartoons made him rich?
Did those first cartoons make him rich?

AUTHOR: Not really. He used all the money to make more cartoons.

WRITER: And do you know what his first movie-length cartoon was?
What was his first movie-length cartoon?

AUTHOR: It was *Snow White*. It came out in 1938. Later he made others—*Cinderella, Pinocchio, Bambi, Dumbo*.

WRITER: When did he open Disneyland?
I can't remember _when he opened Disneyland_

AUTHOR: That was in 1955.

WRITER: Do you know how old Disney was when he died?
How old was Disney when he died?

AUTHOR: He died in 1966 at the age of sixty-five.

WRITER: Why do people all over the world love Mickey Mouse and Donald Duck?
I'd like to know _why people all over the word love mickey mouse & Donald Duck_

AUTHOR: I suppose it's because there is a little bit of all of us in those characters. Mickey is good and sweet and happy. Donald gets angry and insults people. I don't know the reason exactly, but

people all over the world love Walt Disney's movies.

■ **ACTIVITY 25C**

Here are some typical questions that travelers ask in a train station or an airport. Rewrite the questions, using noun clauses.

1. What's the price of a ticket to Washington?

   Could you please tell me what _the price of a ticket to Washington is?_

2. How long is the flight from New York to Washington?

   Do you know _____

3. Do they serve dinner on that flight?

   I'd like to know _____

4. What's the platform number for the train to Boston?

   Can you tell me what _____

5. What's the arrival time for this flight?

   Please tell me what _____

6. What's the difference in price between economy class and first class?

   I'd like to know what _____

7. Is Flight 109 on time?

   Do you know _____

8. What time is it now?

   Can you tell me _____

9. Which gate does the flight depart from?

   I'd like to know which gate _____

10. Is the flight to Washington full tomorrow?

I'd like to know _____

11. Is there any other flight to California on this date?

Can you tell me _____

◼ ACTIVITY 25D

Choose a famous person from your country or choose any famous person that you know a lot about. Imagine that you have written a biography of this person. Your classmate will pretend to be a reporter or talk-show host who is interviewing you about this famous person. The interviewer will ask for information by using both direct and indirect questions.

◼ ACTIVITY 25E

Write a dialog for each of the following situations. Use direct questions and questions with noun clauses.

1. You and a friend are looking at a menu in a foreign restaurant. The menu is in a language that you don't understand very well. You are asking your friend and the waiter for help because you don't know what to order.

2. You are asking for information in a train station or airport.

3. You are in a store, and you see a sweater that you want to buy, but you can't find your size or the color that you want. You are speaking to the salesperson.

4. You and a friend are talking about another friend whom you haven't seen for several years.

5. You are a witness to a car accident or a crime, and the police are asking you questions about what you saw.

EXPRESSING YOUR IDEAS

1. What other facts do you know about Einstein's life? Why were his discoveries so important? Describe some of his ideas or theories. Do you agree that he was a genius? Some people question the importance of his contributions to physics. Why?

2. Name some other major discoveries in physics and mathematics. Why are they significant?

3. Einstein's theories opened the door to the atomic age. If you were Einstein, how would you feel about this now? Why? Name the ways atomic power has changed our lives. What are some of the problems atomic power has created?

4. Many people say Einstein's theories changed our world, but many of us don't understand or can't explain his ideas. Name some other scientific theories and laws that have a major effect on our lives but that you don't understand.

5. Germany lost a great scientist when Einstein left. Why do scientists and other scholars sometimes choose to leave their native countries? Does this happen in your country? Do many professionals or highly educated people go to other countries to work and live?

26 ADJECTIVE CLAUSES

Profile Rock, Echo Canyon, Utah.

NATIONAL PARKS

Dialog

(ARNOLD, YOLANDA, JACK, and MOLLY are planning a trip together.)

ARNOLD: How are we ever going to make up our minds? There are hundreds of parks and monuments **that we can choose from.**

MOLLY: We can't visit every one of them. We have to agree on the ones **which we all really want to visit.**

JACK: Well, I'd like to visit parks **that have a lot of wildlife.** Yellowstone is the park **that is famous for its grizzly bears.** I'd love to see one.

YOLANDA: Grizzlies? I think I'll take a nature walk while you stalk a grizzly. Yellowstone itself sounds wonderful. According to the book **I took out of the library,** Yellowstone is the oldest park in the country and one of the most beautiful.

MOLLY: Yes, I've heard that, and I want to visit Yosemite too. I read that it has sequoias **which are 2,000** years old.

ARNOLD: Sequoias? Are they the same as redwoods?

MOLLY: I think so. I've just been reading about them. They are evergreens. It says here that sequoias are trees **whose height can reach 400 feet** and **whose diameters are sometimes 30 feet.** Isn't that amazing?

ARNOLD: Didn't I see a picture once of a tree **that you could drive through?**

MOLLY: That was a giant sequoia. It's in Yosemite National Park.

ARNOLD: Wasn't it Yosemite **that Ansel Adams photographed?**

MOLLY: Who is Ansel Adams?

YOLANDA: He's an American photographer **who's been taking pictures of Yosemite and the surrounding area all his life**—since the 1920s, I think.

JACK: A book of his photographs was published not too many years ago. His landscape pictures are fantastic.

YOLANDA: Molly, he's the photographer **whose book I showed you last week.**

MOLLY: Oh, yeah. Let's take the book with us and try to find the same landscapes when we get there.

JACK: That's a great idea. We could see the Grand Canyon, Yellowstone, and Yosemite.

ARNOLD: What about visiting the Petrified Forest and maybe the Navajo National Monument after that?

YOLANDA: That sounds so exciting. The Navajo are Indians **I've always been interested in.**

MOLLY: Me too. Let's make some definite plans.

JACK: Who knows a good travel agent? I'll make reservations.

ARNOLD: I do. Go to the travel agency around the corner and ask for George. He's the agent **that I used for my trip to Mexico.**

Listening Comprehension Questions

1. Arnold, Jack, Yolanda, and Molly are planning a trip to some national parks. How does Molly suggest they decide which parks to visit?
2. Why does Jack want to visit Yellowstone Park?
3. What are sequoias?
4. Which park has a giant sequoia that you can drive through?
5. Who is Ansel Adams?
6. Why does Molly want to take Ansel Adams's book along with them on their trip?
7. How does Arnold know that George is a good travel agent?

RESTRICTIVE ADJECTIVE CLAUSES

We use adjective clauses when we want to describe or define more fully a noun in a sentence. The adjective clause must contain its own subject and verb. The first word of an adjective clause is usually a relative pronoun: *who, whom, which, that, whose, where,* or *when.* This relative pronoun always refers to a specific noun in the sentence. This noun is called an antecedent. It should come as close to the adjective clause as possible.

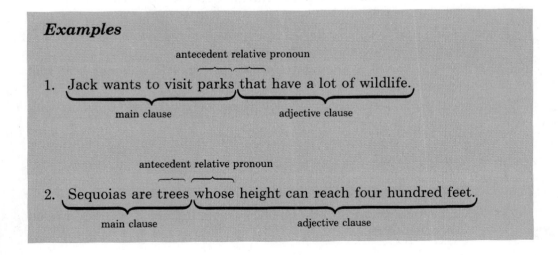

Examples

antecedent relative pronoun

1. Jack wants to visit parks that have a lot of wildlife.

main clause   adjective clause

antecedent relative pronoun

2. Sequoias are trees whose height can reach four hundred feet.

main clause   adjective clause

The Relative Pronoun in Subject Position

Examples

Yellowstone National Park was established in 1872 by the Congress of the United States. It is a park **that has many natural wonders.** For example, there are 200 geysers **that erupt and shoot hot water many feet into the air.** The most famous geyser is called Old Faithful. Most of the park is covered by vast evergreen forests. Yellowstone has many park rangers **who are in charge of protecting the park and helping the visitors.** A tourist **that visits the park in the summer** can go on guided hikes or can go backpacking, boating, and fishing. If the tourist goes in the winter, he or she can take snowmobile trips into the forests.

When the relative pronoun is the subject of the adjective clause, we use *who, which,* or *that* to refer to a noun in the main clause. *Who* or *that* can be used when the antecedent is a person.

A tourist **who** visits the park in the summer can go on guided hikes.

A tourist **that** visits the park in the winter can take snowmobile trips into the forests.

Which or *that* can be used when the antecedent is a thing.

It is a park **which** has many natural wonders.

It is a park **that** has many natural wonders.

Notice that the verb in the adjective clause must agree in number with the antecedent. If the antecedent is plural, the verb in the adjective clause is plural. If the antecedent is singular, the verb in the adjective clause is singular.

It is a **park which has** many natural wonders.

It has **geysers that erupt.**

Note: A common mistake that students make is to add an additional subject after the relative pronoun.

It is a park which ~~it~~ has many natural wonders.

The Relative Pronoun in Object Position

Examples

Mount Rushmore, a famous national monument, is located in the Black Hills of South Dakota. A sculptor named Gutzon Borglum carved the faces of famous presidents here. The cliff **which he chose for this project** is made of granite and is 6,000 feet high. The presidents **whom he selected to be sculpted** were George Washington, Thomas Jefferson, Abraham Lincoln, and Theodore Roosevelt. Of these four, Theodore Roosevelt is the one **we associate with parks and conservation.**

Each face is about 60 feet in length. The models **that Borglum made first** were only 5 feet high. So he had to multiply the measurements by twelve when he worked on the actual faces on the cliff. Of course, he had to have help on the project. The miners **that he hired** used dynamite and drills to carve out the features on each face. The entire project took fourteen years to finish. The money **Borglum used to pay for the project** came from the federal government for the most part. The total cost was about $1 million.

When the relative pronoun is the object of the relative clause, we use *whom, which,* or *that* to refer to a noun in the main clause. Notice that we can omit the relative pronoun.

We use *whom* or *that* if the antecedent is a person.

The miners **whom he hired** used dynamite.

The miners **that he hired** used dynamite.

The miners **he hired** used dynamite.

We use *which* or *that* if the antecedent is a thing.

The cliff **which he chose** is made of granite.

The cliff **that he chose** is made of granite.

The cliff **he chose** is made of granite.

Note:

1. In spoken English, many Americans don't use *whom*. Many use *who* even though it is not technically correct. In written English, *whom* is the correct form.

2. Be careful not to repeat the direct object in the adjective clause, since the relative pronoun has replaced the direct object.

The models that Borglum made ~~them~~ first were only five feet high.

The Relative Pronoun as the Object of a Preposition

Examples

Casa Grande, a national monument in Arizona, is an archeological site. Around A.D. 700, Indians were able to farm this desert area by using irrigation canals. Here are a few facts about these early Indians and their life-style.

The canals **from which water was taken** were sometimes fifteen miles long.

The crops **which the Indians depended on for food** were corn, beans, and pumpkins.

The plant **that they made cloth from** was cotton.

The houses **they lived in** were made of baked mud and dried plants.

    Later, around A.D. 1150, other Indians came to this area and mixed with the first inhabitants. They are called the Pueblo. The Pueblo built Casa Grande, a large four-story building, which served as a watchtower and place of residence. The Pueblo were Indians **for whom agriculture was a way of life.** The people **that this tower was built for** were probably the leaders of the tribe and their families. This area ceased to be inhabited around 1450, probably because the land became waterlogged as a result of too much irrigation.

    Notice that adjective clauses can be written in several different ways when the relative pronoun is the object of a preposition. Look at these sentences, in which the antecedent is a person.

The people **for whom** this tower was built were the leaders.

The people **whom** this tower was built **for** were the leaders.

The people **that** this tower was built **for** were the leaders.

The people this tower was built **for** were the leaders.

Now look at these sentences, in which the antecedent is a thing.

The houses **in which** they lived were made of mud and dried plants.

The houses **which** they lived **in** were made of mud and dried plants.

The houses **that** they lived **in** were made of mud and dried plants.

The houses they lived **in** were made of mud and dried plants.

In spoken English, we usually begin the adjective clause with the relative pronoun and place the preposition at the end of the clause. If the preposition comes at the end of the clause, we can omit the relative pronoun. In written English and in more formal usage, we use *whom* or *which* after the preposition at the beginning of the adjective clause. *That* cannot be used after a preposition.

Whose in Adjective Clauses

For people and for things, the relative pronoun which designates the possessive is *whose*.

Examples

The Grand Canyon is one of the most famous sites in the United States. This is a canyon **whose walls were created by 8 million years of erosion and geological change.** The rock formations are of many different and beautiful colors. In addition, Indians lived there for many centuries. They were an ancient people **whose houses were built into the stone walls of the canyon.** These dwellings can still be seen today.

Where and *When* in Adjective Clauses

Where and *when* can also be used to introduce adjective clauses. Since *where* or *when* cannot be the subject, the adjective clause must have a subject and a verb.

Examples

The year **when the National Park Act was passed** was 1872. Since then, a large number of parks have been added to the park system. There is a great deal of variety in these parks. There are parks **where volcanoes still erupt;** there are parks **where you can still see cliff dwellings of primitive people;** there are parks **where you can go for miles and miles without seeing another living person.**

■ ACTIVITY 26A

Answer each of these questions with a definition. Write an adjective clause, using *which*, *who*, or *that* in your sentence.

1. What's a geyser? *A geyser is a fountain of hot water which shoots high into the air.*

2. What's a snowmobile? _____

3. What's a park ranger? _____

4. What's a travel agent? _____

5. What are evergreens? _____

6. What are backpackers? _____

7. What are conservationists? _____

8. What's a volcano? _____

9. What are grizzly bears? _____

10. What is a desert? _____

11. What is a bird-watcher? _____

■ **ACTIVITY 26B**

Finish these sentences by using adjective clauses.

1. I like to visit places which *I've never been to before.*

2. I like to visit places where _____

3. I like to eat food that _____

4. I like to stay in hotels whose prices _____

5. I like to travel with people who _____

6. I like to meet people with whom _____

7. I don't like tourists whose attitudes _____

8. I don't like tourists whose behavior _____

9. I don't like tourists whose manners _____

10. I detest tourists that _____

■ **ACTIVITY 26C**

Ask a classmate the following questions and discuss the answers.

1. What kind of person makes a good friend?

   A person who is honest and loyal makes a good friend.

2. What kind of person is impolite?
3. What kind of person annoys you?
4. What kind of person bores you?
5. What kind of person makes a good teacher?
6. What kind of person makes a good language learner?
7. What kind of person succeeds in business?
8. What kind of person succeeds as a politician? An artist? A doctor?
9. What kind of person would you like to marry?
10. What kind of country do you like to travel to?
11. What kind of town or city would you like to live in?
12. What kind of school would you want to send your child to?
13. What kind of car would you like to own?
14. What kind of restaurant do you like to eat in?
15. What kinds of clothes do you like to wear?

■ ACTIVITY 26D

❑ Make sentences in which you define certain things that are true about your country, for example, *"The United States is a country that is composed of many different ethnic groups."* Then choose several of your sentences and give examples or specific information to explain and expand on your ideas. Discuss your ideas in class.

❑ Make sentences in which you define the national character of the people of your country, for example, *"Americans are people who are always on the move."* Then choose several of your sentences and give examples or specific information to explain and expand on your ideas. Discuss your ideas in class.

■ ACTIVITY 26E

This exercise is based on the information in the first part of the chapter. Each numbered phrase is the first part of a sentence. Choose the correct ending of each sentence from the lettered items that follow the sentences. Put the sentences together by using adjective clauses. You will have to change some of the sentences slightly. This activity can be done in groups.

A. Use *which* or *that.*

1. Yosemite is the national park *which is located in central California*.

2. The Grand Canyon is the park _____

   _____

3. Yellowstone and Yosemite are parks _____

   _____

4. The Grand Canyon is the park _____

   _____

5. Yellowstone is the park _____

   _____

6. Mount Rushmore is the name of the cliff _____

   _____

7. Mount Rushmore is the monument _____

_____

8. Casa Grande is the monument _____

_____

9. Yellowstone is the park _____

_____

    a. It is located in central California.
    b. They are covered by forests of evergreens.
    c. There are many geysers there.
    d. The government paid almost $1 million for this monument.
    e. It was formed by centuries of erosion.
    f. Its history dates back to A.D. 700.
    g. Its grizzlies have been known to be dangerous.
    h. Borglum chose to sculpt the faces of four presidents on this cliff.
    i. People visit it to see beautiful rock formations of many colors.

B. Use *who, whom,* or *that.*

1. Ulysses S. Grant was the president *who dedicated the first national park.*

2. A forest ranger is a person _____

_____

3. The Pueblo were Native Americans _____

_____

4. Washington, Jefferson, Lincoln, and Roosevelt were the presidents

_____

5. Borglum was the sculptor _____

_____

6. Ansel Adams is the photographer _____

_____

7. The Navajo are Indians _____

_____

8. The Pueblo were people _____

_____

    a. He dedicated the first national park.
    b. Borglum sculpted them at Mount Rushmore.
    c. He watches out for forest fires.
    d. Their houses were several stories high and were built of mud and clay.
    e. They were able to farm the desert of Arizona.
    f. Yolanda has always been interested in them.
    g. Yosemite has always been important to him.
    h. The federal government paid him to sculpt the faces on Mount Rushmore.

C.   Use *when* or *where*.

1. Summer is the season _____

_____

2. Winter is the season _____

_____

3. Yellowstone is the park _____

_____

4. Yosemite is the park _____

_____

    a. Visitors can see Old Faithful.
    b. Visitors can go camping then.
    c. Visitors can see giant sequoias.
    d. Visitors can take snowmobile trips.

■ ACTIVITY 26F

Combine the following groups of sentences by using adjective clauses. Some of the sentences are incomplete without the adjective clause.

A. The Everglades.

1. The Everglades is a national park . . . it is the third largest park in the country.

    The Everglades is the national park which is the third largest in the country.

2. The Everglades is a national park . . . it is located in southern Florida.

    _____

    _____

3. It is unique because it is the only park . . . it is mostly covered by water.

    _____

    _____

4. It is a vast area . . . its fresh water supply comes from lakes and rivers farther north.

    _____

    _____

    Hunters came to this area around the turn of the century.

5. Some birds almost became extinct at this time . . . the feathers of these birds were used to decorate women's hats.

    _____

    _____

6. The Everglades is a park . . . many rare birds and animals are protected here.

    _____

    _____

7. There are also Indians . . . they live in the Everglades.

_____

_____

8. Before Europeans came to this area, there were Indians here . . . the rich resources of the Everglades had attracted them.

_____

_____

9. In the nineteenth century, other Indians arrived . . . white settlers and the army had pushed them south to the Everglades.

_____

_____

Later white settlers came to this area.

10. They were hunters and traders . . . the Indians sold them beautiful bird feathers and alligator hides.

_____

_____

Many people were concerned about protecting these animals.

11. Theodore Roosevelt was one . . . he was concerned about the preservation of these rare and beautiful birds.

_____

_____

12. The Audubon Society[1] sent a warden . . . his duty was to protect the wildlife.

_____

_____

[1]*The Audubon Society* is an organization interested in protecting and studying wild birds.

13. In a tragic incident, the person ... was shot ... the Society had sent him.

_____

_____

Not long after this incident, the Everglades was made into a national park.

B.   The Navajo

1. The Navajo are Indians ... they live at the Navajo National Reservation in Arizona.

_____

_____

2. Basically, the Navajo have been a tribe ... this tribe has depended on ranching and farming for their livelihood.

_____

_____

3. They live on a reservation ... oil and gas reserves were found here.

_____

_____

4. They are Indians ... their tribal income has been steadily increasing because of the oil deposits on their land.

_____

_____

5. They are people ... their religion is highly complex with many ceremonies.

_____

_____

6. They settled in the same area . . . the Pueblo had lived here.

   _____

   _____

7. The Navajo are Indians . . . the Pueblo taught them to weave.

   _____

   _____

8. The Navajo are Indians . . . the Mexicans showed them how to work with metal, especially in jewelry making.

   _____

   _____

9. The Navajo are Indians . . . their silver and turquoise jewelry has always been popular.

   _____

   _____

NONRESTRICTIVE ADJECTIVE CLAUSES

Nonrestrictive (or nonessential) adjective clauses have a different function in the sentence from that of restrictive adjective clauses. Restrictive adjective clauses supply information essential to the meaning of the whole sentence; a nonrestrictive clause gives extra or additional information about the noun it modifies. This information is not essential to the meaning of the main clause.

Look at the following examples.

Trees that are used to make paper are fast growing.

The main clause in this sentence is *Trees are fast growing.* This sentence is not true. It means that all trees grow fast. However, some trees grow very slowly. The adjective clause is essential to make the sentence accurate; it identifies particular trees. This adjective clause is restrictive (or essential).

Sequoias, which originated in China, are found in great abundance in
California.

The main clause of this sentence is *Sequoias are found in great abundance in California.* This sentence is a statement about sequoias in general. The adjective clause is not essential to the meaning of the sentence. It only gives extra information.

Nonrestrictive adjective clauses are formed in the same way as restrictive adjective clauses except for these three differences:

1. *That* is never used in nonrestrictive clauses.

2. The relative pronoun can never be omitted in nonrestrictive adjective clauses.

3. Commas are always placed at the beginning and end of the nonrestrictive adjective clause.

Examples

Theodore Roosevelt, **who was an active conservationist,** established five new parks and set aside about 150 million acres of forest reserves during his presidency. He also expanded Yosemite, **which he visited in 1903.** While he was there, he had his photograph taken in front of the Wawona Tunnel Tree. This tree, **whose tunnel was carved out in 1881,** finally fell in a storm in 1969. It was calculated to be 2,200 years old.

In this paragraph, the main clause of each sentence with an adjective clause can stand alone as a meaningful sentence. In the first sentence, we learn that Theodore Roosevelt established five new parks. This is a true statement. The fact that he was also an active conservationist does not change the meaning of the sentence.

Now look at the following sentences that have restrictive adjective clauses.

One president **who was very famous as a conservationist** was Theodore Roosevelt.

The famous sequoia **which fell in 1969** was called the Wawona Tunnel Tree.

Roosevelt disliked people **who had no appreciation of nature and wildlife.**

In these sentences, the adjective clauses are necessary (restrictive) because they define or tell *which* president, *which* tree, or *which* people.

Note: It is often difficult to decide whether an adjective clause should be restrictive or nonrestrictive. However, there is one rule which will always hold true. If the adjective clause modifies a proper noun (the name of a person, place, or thing), the adjective clause must be nonrestrictive. These clauses are generally more common in writing than in speaking.

■ ACTIVITY 26G

Read the following paragraphs. Decide which relative pronoun is correct and fill in each blank. Then decide which clauses are restrictive and which are nonrestrictive. Add commas where necessary. If there are two blanks, add the necessary preposition.

Hawaii is a state _____ is composed of many islands in the middle of the Pacific Ocean. Some of these islands still have volcanoes _____ erupt from time to time. A spectacular eruption began in November 1961. Lava _____ is liquid or molten rock began to flow from Kilauea volcano. At one point, lava _____ was forced up by pressure and steam reached a height of 1,800 feet above the top of Kilauea. This period of activity lasted for five years, until July 1966.

In 1977, there were more eruptions. The inhabitants _____ the authorities had warned of the danger refused to leave their villages. They believed that the fire goddess Pele _____ they worshiped would not harm them. The lava flow didn't reach their villages, and no one was hurt.

Kilauea and Mauna Loa _____ are both active volcanoes are located within the boundaries of a national park. In this park is the Hawaiian Volcano Observatory _____ was established in 1911. This agency studies volcanoes and tries to predict eruptions. Whenever an eruption occurs, many sightseers rush to see it. Some even fly in small planes in order to get a closer view of the eruption.

Another unusual park is Hot Springs National Park _____ is located in the state of Arkansas. The park has forty-seven hot springs _____ _____ water emerges from a break in the earth's crust. The water _____ is 143°F is channeled into reservoirs _____ bathers can go swimming. Generally, only people _____ _____ doctors have prescribed these waters come to bathe. However, a doctor's recommendation is not necessary. A person _____ obtains a permit at the park may use the facilities.

Hot springs have long been popular all over the world. The water _____ contains different minerals is thought to help cure certain illnesses. Bath, England _____ the Romans built an elaborate system of baths has long been famous for its hot springs. All the baths _____ the Romans built had a cooling system. In the eighteenth century, wealthy people again came to "take the waters" and relax in Bath _____ the facilities had been rebuilt. Until recently in this country, also, hot springs were for the wealthy _____ visited them for their healing qualities.

EXPRESSING YOUR IDEAS

1. What is the most famous park you have ever visited? Describe it.
2. Does your country have a system of national parks? What is the concept of a park in your country? What activities are provided for visitors to parks?
3. In your opinion, what function should parks serve? What do you expect from a park when you visit one?
4. How would you compare the parks in your country with those in the United States? Do thousands of people travel to these parks to camp, hike, backpack, and see the wonders of nature?

5. There are many different kinds of gardens around the world. France is famous for its very formal gardens, while English gardens appear to be more natural. The Japanese have their own style of garden; one well-known type of Japanese garden is the rock garden. Ask different members of your class if they can describe any of these gardens or a typical garden from their country.

6. What are some of the natural wonders that a tourist might visit in your country? Are these places protected by the government?

7. In the United States, about two percent of the land area is set aside as national parks. Do you think the government should set aside a certain percentage of land for use as parks? Should wildlife also be protected in parks?

Fill in each blank with the verb in parentheses, using one of the tenses that you have studied in this book. Choose between active and passive voice. When you see *modal + verb,* choose the correct modal auxiliary verb, tense, and voice. When you see two verbs next to each other below the blank, put the second verb in the infinitive or gerund form.

(YOLANDA, ARNOLD, JACK, and MOLLY are still on vacation. They are sitting around a campfire in Yellowstone Park. It is midnight.)

YOLANDA: This _____ has been _____ a really super trip so far. I
(be)
_____ have never enjoyed _____ anything so much in my life.
(never, enjoy)

ARNOLD: Yeah. We _____ have been traveling _____ for three weeks. We
(travel)
only _____ have _____ one week left. I wish we
(have)
_____ were not _____ so near the end.
(negative, be)

MOLLY: You know what my favorite part of the trip

_____ has been _____ so far? Remember the
(be)
beach in Florida? We _____ were swimming _____ in the Gulf
(swim)
of Mexico at night, when all of a sudden the moon

_____ came _____ out from behind a cloud and
(come)
_____ made _____ our bodies _____ shine _____
(make) **(shine)**
like silver.

JACK: That's because there are tiny phosphorescent organisms that

_____ *live* _____ in the ocean. Every once in a while
(live)

the tide _____ *brings* _____ them in to shore.
(bring)

MOLLY: Oh, Jack. You always _____ *think* _____ like a scientist.
(think)

You __ *are not* __ very romantic.
(negative, be)

YOLANDA: It's too bad that we _____ *did not take* _____ any pictures that
(negative, take)

night. I wish we _____ *had taken* _____ our cameras to the beach.
(take)

YOLANDA: That was probably the most beautiful moment of the trip. We

have had _____ some really funny moments on this
(have)

trip too.

ARNOLD: I think the funniest thing that *has happened* so far
(happen)

was when I _____ *forgot* _____ _____ *to tie* _____
(forget)   (tie)

the suitcases on top of the car after we _____ *checked* _____
(check)

out of the motel one morning. We _____ *had already driven* _____
(already, drive)

about ten miles down the road by the time Molly

_____ *noticed* _____ that the rope *was dangling*
(notice)   (dangle)

down from the roof and that the suitcases weren't there. We

_____ *have to drive* _____ all the way back to the motel to get
(modal + drive)

them. Luckily, by the time we _____ *got* _____ there,
(get)

the motel owner _____ *had found* _____ our suitcases all over
(find)

the parking lot and _____ *had already picked* _____ them up.
(already, pick)

YOLANDA: Arnold, look at the fire. It *was blazing* a few
(blaze)

minutes ago, but now it's _____ *getting* _____ low. We
(get)

_____ *need* _____ _____ *to put* _____ some
(need)   (put)

more wood on.

PAST possibility → modal + have + P.P.
could have taken.

ARNOLD: Okay. I'll **GET** _____ some.
(get)

JACK: Speaking of the most beautiful moment and the funniest

moment of the trip, what about the most frightening moment? I

think we all **AGree** _____ that the most frightening
(agree)

moment was when our canoe **capsized** _____ on the
(capsize)

Colorado River.

ARNOLD: We *shouldn't have taken* _____ a canoe on that river. It's much
(negative, modal + **take**)

too dangerous.

Natalia

JACK: Yes, we *could have been killed.* _____. Luckily we're all good
(modal + **kill**)

swimmers, and we **had** _____ our life jackets
(have)

on at the time.

YOLANDA: At first I thought I was drowning, but finally I

_____ **was able to swim** to shore. That water was
(be able, swim)

really cold. It *must have been* _____ about 45°.
(modal + **be**)

ARNOLD: It *was* cold. It's too bad that some of our equipment

_____ **had lost** when the canoe capsized.
(lose)

JACK: Yes, but fortunately our canoe **was saved** _____ by that
(save)

fisherman who was down the river.

MOLLY: Yolanda and I will never forget how we **were rescued** _____
(rescue)

by that cute forest ranger.

YOLANDA: He certainly was attractive. If I **weren't** _____ with
(negative, be)

you, Arnold, I **would enjoy** **getting** _____
(enjoy)   (get)

to know him better.

ARNOLD: _____ **Are** you **TRY** _____
(try)

to make _____ me jealous?
(make)

YOLANDA: I ____*we joue do*____ .
(joke)

MOLLY: You know Yolanda always ____*enjoys*____
(enjoy)

____*teasing*____ you, Arnold. You know she
(tease)

____*loves*____ you. It ____*is getting*____ late.
(love)   (get)

Let's talk about what we ____*will see*____ next week.
(see)

We ____*don't have*____ much time left. I'm concerned
(negative, **have**)

that we ____*will not able to see*____ everything that's on our itinerary.
(negative, **be able, see**)

JACK: I just hope that the rest of the trip ____*will be*____ as
(be)

beautiful as what we ____*have seen*____ so far.
(see)

ARNOLD: Nothing could be as beautiful as the Painted Desert and the

Grand Canyon.

JACK: Or the Everglades, in my opinion. I (wish) everyone in the United

States ____*have had*____ the opportunity to travel across
(have)

our country. It's breathtakingly beautiful.

YOLANDA: What ____*will*____ we ____*see*____ next?
(see)

ARNOLD: Because we ____*have run*____ out of time,
(run)

we ____*can drive*____ straight to Yosemite.
(modal + **drive**)

JACK: I agree. We ____*haven't to try*____ ____*seeing*____
(negative, modal + **try**)   (see)

everything else on the way. We really don't have time.

YOLANDA: How long ____*will*____ it ____*take*____
(take)

us to get to Yosemite from here? I ____*do not look*____
(negative, **look**)

forward to ____*ride*____ in the car again. I
(ride)

____*am getting*____ a little tired of ____*sitting*____ .
(get)   (sit)

I wish we ____*have*____ a van instead of a car.
(have)

JACK: Yeah. If we _____have_____ a van, we

(have)

_____will lie_____ down in the back when we

(lie)

got tired.

MOLLY: After we ____I'll visit____ Yosemite, how much

(visit)

time _____DO_____ we _____have_____

(have)

left to spend in San Francisco?

ARNOLD: Just a few days. And don't forget that we

____have to sell____ the car before we

(modal + **sell**)

_____fly_____ home.

(fly)

YOLANDA: Where _____will_____ we _____STAY_____ in

(stay)

San Francisco?

ARNOLD: Our hotel reservations __have already made__ at the Hilton by

(already, make)

our travel agent in New York.

YOLANDA: Oh, yeah. Now I ____Remember____.

(remember)

MOLLY: What time is it?

JACK: It's almost 1:00 A.M. We ____must go____ to sleep, or

(modal + **go**)

we ____will be____ exhausted tomorrow.

(be)

ARNOLD: Wait a minute. Before we _____GO_____ to sleep,

(go)

Yolanda and I have something we ____want____

(want)

____to tell____ you. We ____have DECIDED____

(tell)   (decide)

____to get____ married.

(get)

MOLLY: Congratulations! That's wonderful! I'm so happy for you two.

JACK: That's great news. When _____will_____ you

____get____ married?

(get)

YOLANDA: As soon as we ____'ll get____ back to New York.

(get)

JACK: We _____will celebrate_____ when we _____'ll arrive_____ in
                (celebrate)   (arrive)

San Francisco. Molly and I _____will take_____ you out to
                                   (take)

one of the best restaurants there. If we _____have_____
                                     (have)

a bottle of champagne, we _____can celebrate_____ right now.
                             (celebrate)

Do you think Yolanda and Arnold's decision to get married is realistic? Is it a good decision? Do you think they are well matched? Do you think they will be happy? What do you think will happen?

APPENDIX: IRREGULAR VERBS IN ENGLISH

Here is an alphabetical list of most of the irregular verbs in English. Some of the less common verbs are not included in this list.

Base Form	Past	Past Participle
be (am, is, are)	was, were	been
bear	bore	born
beat	beat	beat
become	became	become
begin	began	begun
bend	bent	bent
bet	bet	bet
bite	bit	bitten
bleed	bled	bled
blow	blew	blown
break	broke	broken
bring	brought	brought
build	built	built
burst	burst	burst
buy	bought	bought
catch	caught	caught
choose	chose	chosen
come	came	come
cost	cost	cost
cut	cut	cut
deal	dealt	dealt
do	did	done
dig	dug	dug

draw	drew	drawn
drink	drank	drunk
drive	drove	driven
eat	ate	eaten
fall	fell	fallen
feed	fed	fed
feel	felt	felt
fight	fought	fought
find	found	found
fit	fit	fit
fly	flew	flown
forbid	forbade	forbidden
forget	forgot	forgotten
forgive	forgave	forgiven
freeze	froze	frozen
get	got	got (or) gotten
give	gave	given
go	went	gone
grow	grew	grown
hang	hung	hung
have	had	had
hear	heard	heard
hide	hid	hidden
hit	hit	hit
hold	held	held
hurt	hurt	hurt
keep	kept	kept
kneel	knelt	knelt
know	knew	known
lay	laid	laid
lead	led	led

leave	left	left
lend	lent	lent
let	let	let
light	lit	lit
lose	lost	lost
lie	lay	lain
make	made	made
mean	meant	meant
meet	met	met
pay	paid	paid
put	put	put
quit	quit	quit
read	read[1]	read
ride	rode	ridden
ring	rang	rung
rise	rose	risen
run	ran	run
say	said	said
see	saw	seen
sell	sold	sold
send	sent	sent
set	set	set
shake	shook	shaken
shine	shone	shone
shoot	shot	shot
shut	shut	shut
sing	sang	sung
sink	sank	sunk
sit	sat	sat

[1]Pronunciation change.

sleep	slept	slept
speak	spoke	spoken
speed	sped	sped
spend	spent	spent
split	split	split
spread	spread	spread
stand	stood	stood
steal	stole	stolen
stick	stuck	stuck
sting	stung	stung
strike	struck	struck
swear	swore	sworn
sweep	swept	swept
swim	swam	swum
swing	swung	swung
take	took	taken
teach	taught	taught
tear	tore	torn
tell	told	told
think	thought	thought
throw	threw	thrown
understand	understood	understood
wake	woke	woken
wear	wore	worn
win	won	won
wind	wound	wound
write	wrote	written

In the following section, the verbs from the alphabetical list of irregular verbs are grouped into different categories. Some of the verbs in the alphabetical list do not fall into a special category and therefore do not appear in this section.

begin	began	begun	bleed	bled	bled
run	ran	run	feed	fed	fed
sing	sang	sung	lead	led	led
ring	rang	rung	speed	sped	sped
sink	sank	sunk	read	read[1]	read[1]
swim	swam	swum	feel	felt	felt
drink	drank	drunk	keep	kept	kept
			leave	left	left
bring	brought	brought	mean	meant	meant
buy	bought	bought	sleep	slept	slept
catch	caught	caught	sweep	swept	swept
fight	fought	fought	meet	met	met
teach	taught	taught	deal	dealt	dealt
think	thought	thought	kneel	knelt	knelt
grow	grew	grown	break	broke	broken
know	knew	known	choose	chose	chosen
throw	threw	thrown	freeze	froze	frozen
blow	blew	blown	speak	spoke	spoken
draw	drew	drawn	steal	stole	stolen
fly	flew	flown	wake	woke	woken
			bear	bore	born
drive	drove	driven	swear	swore	sworn
rise	rose	risen	tear	tore	torn
ride	rode	ridden	wear	wore	worn
write	wrote	written			
			pay	paid	paid

[1]Pronunication change.

| shake | shook | shaken | say | said | said |
| take | took | taken | lay | laid | laid |

| hide | hid | hidden | sell | sold | sold |
| bite | bit | bitten | tell | told | told |

sting	stung	stung	find	found	found
swing	swung	swung	wind	wound	wound
hang	hung	hung			
stick	stuck	stuck			
strike	struck	struck (or) stricken			
dig	dug	dug			

INDEX